LEARNING DISABILITIES EXPLAINED

LEARNING DISABILITIES EXPLAINED

The Lamm Institute's guide to diagnosis, remediation, and help for your learning-disabled child

STANLEY S. LAMM, M.D.
and
MARTIN L. FISCH, Ph.D.
with
DON McDONAGH

Doubleday & Company, Inc., Garden City, New York, 1982

Photographs courtesy of Bob West and Herb Newlin.

Library of Congress Cataloging in Publication Data

Lamm, Stanley S.

Learning disabilities explained.

Bibliography: p.

Includes index.

1. Learning disabilities. I. Fisch, Martin L. II. McDonagh, Don. III. Title.

LC4704.L34 1982 371.92 AACR2

ISBN: 0-385-15781-9

Library of Congress Catalog Card Number 82-45232

First Edition

Printed in the United States of America

To the children, their parents and the staff of the Stanley S. Lamm Institute who provided the inspiration for this book, and whose tireless efforts offer the best hope for the future.

For discussion in specific areas of diagnosis and treatment, and for the identification of illustrative case histories, we are indebted to a number of our colleagues and associates at the Institute, including Clifford Fisch, Dr. Rhandy PeBenito, Steve Phelps, Gita Porway, Irene Preiss, Laura Reisler, Dr. George Wing, Arlene Wisan and Chong-In Yuin. We thank Dr. Arthur Rose for his thoughtful review of the manuscript and for his constructive criticism.

We also wish to thank Richard Boehm for his sustaining encouragement, Nan Grubbs for her most valuable editorial assistance, and Santa Lausell for her able secretarial work.

CONTENTS

PREFACE

It is estimated that up to 15 percent of grade school and nursery school children have some form of learning disability that prevents them from achieving their full academic and social potential. It is this group of children that we, as a society, have really only recently begun to help in a systematic manner.

When I started in private practice, over fifty years ago, the emphasis in childcare was placed almost completely on growth and proper infant feeding. Physicians in the nineteen-thirties and perhaps through the forties sought to insure a child's physical well-being through good nutrition, regular exercise and proper amounts of sleep. In general, the treatment of learning disabilities was considered the responsibility of the schools rather than of the physician, and for good or ill, that was the end of it.

Then in the fifties, the medical establishment, reflecting the growing interest in psychiatry and psychology, began to focus attention on the emotional health and development of the child. Later, in the sixties and seventies, we saw an increasing, and increasingly productive interest in the learning process itself, coupled with great advances in diagnostic equipment and, of even more importance, growing awareness on the part of schools and public health officials of their responsibilities toward the learning-disabled child.

The most concrete example of this concern, on a national scale, was passage of Public Law 94-142 amended "Education for All Handicapped Children Act" in 1975, that sharply increased the federal commitment to insure that all handicapped children receive "full and appropriate educational services." And children with subtle brain dysfunctions *are* handicapped, as any parent of an intelligent but chronically failing child knows.

My own experience has convinced me that the most productive and efficient way to approach any sort of learning disability is to bring together in one place all of the medical and allied specialists—the practitioners of remedial-care disciplines, the social counselors and educational evaluators—as a team to formulate a complete diagnostic profile for each child in need of assistance.

A pediatrician in private practice can certainly perform a good general medical examination, but must then refer the child to outside specialists in reading, speech and language training, physical therapy or occupational therapy, psychiatric care and so forth. This is a time-consuming process which may stretch over many months, with the various specialists submitting their individual reports without ever having had the opportunity to exchange findings and observations with one another. In our Institute, interaction between the various professionals is facilitated, and this ease of communication and exchange of ideas gives substance to the concept of the "team" approach in both diagnostic and treatment activities.

The team approach condenses this process and facilitates the direct exchange of information, with the result that the child is seen as a whole and not in isolated segments. It is also decidedly easier on the parents who know that all of the diagnostic and much of the therapeutic care they need for their child can be found under one roof. I believe strongly in establishing a good working relationship with parents and being perfectly frank with them about our findings and our plans for therapy.

Just as I believe the basis for a good education starts in the home, so also do I feel that the successful course of treatment of learning difficulties depends on the understanding and cooperation of the parents. My associates have heard me say many times that the mother is our best informant. And, indeed, she often is the most valued member of our team.

STANLEY S. LAMM M.D.
Medical Director, The Stanley S. Lamm
Institute for Developmental Disabilities
The Long Island College Hospital

INTRODUCTION

From the beginning of his practice Dr. Lamm has concerned himself with the identification of the special needs of children with developmental disabilities. In 1951 he was awarded a grant by the United Cerebral Palsy Association of New York City for the purpose of establishing an out-patient diagnostic-and-treatment service for children with cerebral palsy. This work was carried out in the Department of Pediatrics of The Long Island College Hospital, in Brooklyn, New York.

It soon became apparent to Dr. Lamm and his staff that there were considerable demands for a greater range of services than those offered in order to assist the growing numbers of children suffering from a wide variety of neurological impairments and related disorders. In 1967 the Children's Center for Development Disabilities was created to unify these services.

In 1971 the New York City Department of Health and Mental Retardation entered into a major contract with the center, and in 1974 it was renamed the Stanley S. Lamm Institute for Developmental Disabilities.

At present, more than half of all children seen at the Institute come with problems related to learning disabilities.

The working methods of the Institute can briefly be outlined in six steps:

1. Evaluations are conducted in each of the specialist areas.
2. A presentation of test findings by the specialists is made in a diagnostic conference.
3. The diagnosis is formulated after the presentation of these findings.
4. A recommendation for a system of care, is proposed.
5. An individualized treatment plan, specifying both short-term and longer-range goals, is prepared for each child. This becomes the

comprehensive program of care, against which progress may be measured at specified times (quarterly, semiannually, etc.).

6. The diagnosis and the proposed system of management are discussed with the parents immediately after the diagnostic conference by the specialists involved. An appointment is made for another meeting, approximately one month later, to afford the parents the opportunity to clarify any uncertainties that may have arisen out of or subsequent to the initial discussion.

By bringing together school reports (either from a guidance counselor or a teacher), family histories obtained through interviews with the parents, and our own evaluations, we are able to address the whole child. Collectively, the tests, reports and histories are called a "work-up" and include a complete physical examination with whatever laboratory tests are deemed necessary.

The reader will find areas of overlap which may, at times, seem repetitive and unnecessary. We should like to stress the value of having different specialists—each with his own professional expertise and experience—look at similar test data in order to arrive at the most comprehensive understanding of each child's strengths and weaknesses. In our discussions we have used the vocabulary of our professions, and we have tried to be as clear and uncomplicated as possible without sacrificing precision. You may find the Glossary helpful in explaining any unfamiliar terms.

When all of the tests have been completed, the child is scheduled for a diagnostic conference. Ordinarily, these are held once a week and may include as many as ten specialists. Guidance counselors, teachers, social workers or any other concerned professionals are encouraged to participate in these conferences, along with the various medical and remedial care specialists.

After the individual findings have been presented, the parents and child are invited into the conference, at which time they may be asked further questions by any of the specialists, or the child may be given a brief additional examination to sharpen the focus of the diagnosis. The parents and the child are encouraged to ask any questions that they may have at this time.

The diagnosis is formulated and entered into the child's record along with written reports from each of the specialists. Then a program of care is set up, based on the diagnosis. Following the conference, the parents are met by representatives of the staff who have worked with the child and diagnosis and treatment are fully discussed. Here again, questions are encouraged.

The Board of Education of the City of New York works closely with us to establish the Individual Education Plan (IEP) and to find the most appropriate public school class in which to place the child while the course of remedial treatment is being carried out.

These classes may be available within the actual school the child is attending or they may be available only at another school, in which case a transfer is recommended. If no appropriate class is available within the public school system, a special class in an appropriate private school may be recommended. If the child's difficulties are noticed before school age, we can recommend a suitable preschool program.

It has been our experience, however, that for the most part these disabilities are initially noticed after the child starts school, except in cases of severe mental retardation. It is in the competitive atmosphere of school, in a social situation outside the protective environment of the home, that learning difficulties manifest themselves most clearly. It is also true that the earlier we are able to work with the child, the more successful the course of treatment will be.

We maintain an active interchange with the Board of Education so that we are able to move quickly and efficiently to provide the most suitable educational setting for the child. It has also been our policy to encourage school guidance counselors to visit our facilities and to schedule meetings with them in groups, to tell them of our work and the services we provide that may be of help to them. The diagnosis of a learning disability is only the first part of the Institute's work. All our efforts are then directed toward placing the child in the most appropriate learning situation and providing the therapeutic services necessary to help the child achieve his full potential.

MARTIN L. FISCH PH.D.
Executive Director, The Stanley S. Lamm
Institute for Developmental Disabilities
The Long Island College Hospital

LEARNING DISABILITIES EXPLAINED

I. PINPOINTING THE PROBLEM:

The Essential First Step

Broadly speaking, the term *learning disability* describes a condition or a series of specific conditions that interfere with the normal learning process in a child who is of average or above average intelligence. There is much yet to be learned about the exact mechanisms that cause the disability, but in recent years, we have been able to distinguish the learning-disabled child from other handicapped children to a far greater degree than has been possible in the past.

In our practice we routinely see children suffering from a wide variety of disorders such as cerebral palsy, mental retardation, epilepsy, schizophrenia, trauma to the brain, deafness, autism and communication disorders, as well as those with true learning disabilities. It is with the latter that we shall concern ourselves primarily in this book.

These children are caught in a maelstrom of confused and confusing information that inhibits their ability to make sense out of the world around them. They find themselves struggling valiantly to keep up with the other children in their class but find that they experience repeated failure. They begin to doubt themselves and their abilities. They may develop serious emotional problems, but at the very least they are frustrated. Learning ordinary school subjects is a stormy experience. Their inner state is turbulent as they expend a great deal of effort to achieve success but end up with little that is positive to show for it.

The children we are discussing are those who are sometimes thought to be backward or otherwise not achieving as well as they should at their age level in school. They are children with average to above average intelligence, who experience extreme difficulty in learning how to read or to manipulate mathematical concepts, or who have difficulty in handling a pencil, buttons or shoe laces.

They can be cruelly teased by their classmates for clumsiness or "stupidity," and are frequently labeled as "disciplinary" problems by their teachers because they may cut up in class to camouflage their lack of preparation. Parents frequently warn them to "settle down" and put some real effort into their work. The children themselves are frequently unaware that they are working with a handicap, that their experiences are not "normal." The difficulties they experience appear to them to be the rule rather than the exception since they have never experienced anything else. Frequently in the past, and to a certain extent today as well, such children have matured and gone through life, still impaired, still making adjustments, never having been helped because the nature of their disability had not been recognized.

We will not be talking about children who have substantial, readily apparent brain injury, such as cerebral palsy, severe sensory impairment or severe mental retardation. These conditions are usually quite obvious and are classified as gross injuries to the brain as opposed to the minimal injury or dysfunction which is the focus of this book and which, because of its subtlety, is difficult to diagnose through standard examinations.

The magnitude of the injury in the cerebral palsied child, for instance, is manifested in a variety of ways, such as severely impaired speech, paralysis or a poor gait, or disturbed coordination. A number of children with this type of injury may also be retarded and have periodic seizures; the latter are caused by unusual excitation of the brain cells which can be charted by electroencephalography or EEG. Characteristic "spikes" clearly indicate a malfunction either generalized or localized. The EEG pattern for a child with a minimal injury ordinarily does not offer any such clues. For all intents and purposes such an EEG reading appears to be within normal limits,* or there may be a slight and diffuse dysrhythmia. That is, some unevenness in pattern but not enough to qualify as meaningful.

The book does not deal with the severely mentally retarded in-

* In this examination, as in all others we conduct, we speak of normal limits, since there are small variations between individuals that fall within a fairly tight cluster and are considered normal. There is no such thing as the single "correct" pattern, any more than there is any single IQ score that marks the retarded, the average or the superior individual. There are normal ranges of scores, patterns and reflexes that are expected in the general population of individuals who are able to function and be self-sustaining in the everyday world.

dividual who would not be able to cope independently with the demands of ordinary day-to-day living, nor does it deal with the schizophrenic child whose behavior is marked by seclusiveness and a generalized withdrawal of interest in his surroundings. Also outside the scope of this book is epilepsy, a condition in which seizures of greater or lesser intensity periodically disturb the functioning of the individual. During these episodes, disorientation, impaired balance and coordination or loss of consciousness may occur, depending on the severity of the seizure. Epilepsy presents a clear clinical picture, for which drug therapy can offer a means of controlling the number and severity of the attacks. With such control, learning can continue in a more normal fashion.

The conditions described above are all severe and may be associated with "hard" neurological signs, contrasted with the more minimal deficits, "soft signs," that characterize the learning-disabled child. The latter may show some attention lags, some temper tantrums prompted by frustration and anger, some lack of coordination, some slurring of words and a certain incapacity to deal with the day-to-day conditions that children of their own age are handling. The very fact that learning-disabled children share certain traits with the more severely damaged children makes the diagnosis of their true condition more difficult.

It is for this reason that we do not prejudge the nature of the difficulty that any child has until we have made evaluations in each of the medical and remedial-care areas. Many children who have been categorized as learning disabled have been sent to us because they were deemed to be hyperactive by a school guidance counselor. An examination of one such child showed that he had a verbal deficiency, stemming from a bilingual home environment. He displayed the fidgety, excessive physical activity only in school, where he was uncomfortable because of the difficulty he was having in trying to keep up in a language that he understood only imperfectly.

At times we have even found that a child, referred to us because he is having learning problems, is actually doing poorly in school because he has a minor hearing impairment. The child is failing because he does not hear the teachers' instructions clearly. In such a case, a hearing aid can help restore a child to his grade level without any further care needed. Perhaps simply moving the child to a seat in the front of the room, closer to the teacher, will be enormously helpful.

It seems all too simple, and yet the condition might be overlooked in any examination that did not routinely examine all of the social, psychological and physical factors affecting the child's performance.

Once a child is referred to us he is scheduled for a series of examinations and evaluations, which we call the work-up. The primary purpose of each of these tests is to identify any dysfunction in the central nervous system and to determine its exact nature, so that we might design a course of remedial treatment.

These evaluations fall into three broad groupings; the first comprises those concerned with the child's general, innate physical and mental capacity. The second group of tests looks for specific deficits, and the third, emotional complications. The first consists of the *pediatric neurological* examination from which we expect to receive a report of any discernible physical impairment to the nervous system. It also includes the *psychological evaluation,* which is important to us not only for its assessment of the child's intellectual capacity, his IQ, but also for insight into his thinking processes and problem-solving strategies. We need to know whether we are dealing with an average, below-average, or above-average child and this sets the limits on the types of remediation that can be successfully employed. The psychologist, in addition to providing us with this invaluable information, also offers appropriate counseling and psychotherapeutic services, depending on the individual's needs.

The second large grouping consists of specific evaluations in each of the remedial disciplines. An educational evaluator conducts a comprehensive educational assessment to determine the child's level of accomplishment in the traditional academic subjects of reading, writing and arithmetic and makes recommendations for specific remediation. The *occupational therapist* examines the child's motor functions minutely to see precisely where, in the complex chain of stimulus and response behavior, the dysfunction exists. Once this has been determined, a course of treatment is devised to develop an alternative pathway around the blockage, always based on the individual child's specific strengths.

If a childs motor function is grossly impaired, the *physical therapist* would help him devise muscle strategies to overcome the deficit insofar as it is possible. This, however, is not generally a major problem with the learning disabled child. Since language and communication skills are essential to everyday functioning they occupy a very important area of concern in the individual's work-up. The *speech pathologist/language therapist* assesses the level of the child's expressive and receptive skills; that is, his ability to process and respond to language stimuli. Again the examiner attempts to specify the exact point in the chain of information handling where the difficulty is experienced and then proposes a program of remedial help designed to strengthen the deficit area.

The third grouping of assessments concerns itself not with physical dysfunction but with emotional difficulties. These may range from the severe mental states of schizophrenia to the milder forms of anxiety. In each case, however, these must be distinguished so that the appropriate support might be given. If an emotional problem is identified during the course of the *psychiatric evaluation,* regular therapeutic sessions are scheduled in which the child is helped to understand and cope with his difficulties. The *social worker* may, during the course of the evaluation, uncover a difficult home situation that is interfering with the child's ability to learn. Like the other specialists he prepares an evaluation of the child and makes specific recommendations at the diagnostic conference that is scheduled after all of the assessments have been made.

It is at this time that all of the specialists who have been working individually are able to bring together all of their information and, with the moderator of the conference, arrive at a diagnosis and then a recommendation for treatment. This conference is the heart and soul of the case-management process. This multidisciplinary approach insures the broadest possible base upon which to make the diagnosis and avoids the pitfall of treating real, though ancilliary problems, while neglecting the core difficulty. Any specialist, as well as the moderator, is able to ask for further information from fellow specialists to clarify the diagnosis and to prescribe the optimum course of treatment. Each of the disciplines has that opportunity to exchange information as well as present individual findings.

In the following pages each of the special examination areas are explained in some depth to show precisely what the individual tests are designed to uncover. This information is offered with the hope that it will help parents and others to recognize and to place into perspective any difficulties they have encountered with their learning-disabled or potentially troubled children. It is by no means a do-it-yourself diagnostic kit, since the value of these tests lies in their expert interpretation. It is rather a sharing of information with all who are concerned.

The story that follows shows how easily the symptoms of a learning disability can be mistaken for something entirely remote from the true difficulty. The youngster—let us call him Patrick—was fortunate in that he had a supportive family that helped him through his trying experience before he was referred to us for assistance. It was a difficult period for him and for them, but his mother never stopped trying to find the proper educational setting for him despite numerous setbacks.

❧

Math was the only thing that I was good at. I wasn't good at reading. I was failing, but I was also one of the biggest kids in the class so no one called me stupid or dummy. I wasn't a bully, but they left me alone. I became a kind of teacher's pet. They knew I couldn't do the work so they would send me on errands in the school. Pat, get this! Pat, get that! I felt dumb. I thought that I must have been absent the day they taught us how to read. I used to hate it. I didn't want to go to school but my mother said, "You have to go!" I'd say, "I'm sick," and I came close to staying out.

The worst part was when I'd fail, and I'd have to bring a paper home to have my mother sign it. I didn't mind it so much when the teachers would yell at me. Yeah, it would bother me because I'd say to myself, "Why can't I do this?" but when my mother would yell at me, that really hurt. My brothers who were in high school and my sisters would yell at me and say, "What's wrong with you?" They had all gone to the same parochial school, and I was the only one having this trouble. My mother just couldn't take the school calling up all the time, and so she finally just left my sisters there and took me out and put me into public school. I had been in parochial school through the third grade. They said that "I would just get over it."

My mother thought that I could relax in public school. She had heard about this new program where the kids could do different things on an informal basis and there was less emphasis on "sit-up-straight" discipline. It was a school in which we did everything verbally at first. I felt good that I was finally coming home with good marks and my mother was happy. For a month or two I was really doing well.

The classroom was different. There were no desks. You had a spot on the floor with a piece of carpet. It was very relaxed. There were about sixty kids in the class, but there were four teachers. It was more on a one-to-one basis. I liked that class. At first we would go for a lesson and the teacher would read out the lesson, and then she would ask us questions about it and she would grade the responses. Then after a while we sat down and started with the pencil and paper and books again, and that's when I started to fail all over again.

That's when they said that something was the matter. I'd just be sitting in class and they'd say, "Pat, go down to the office!" Well, I was used to that from the other school. I went down, took a test, and came back. The guidance counselor gave me a couple of tests and told my mother that he would continue to test me but said that I was being lazy. I asked my mother why I was being tested and she said, "Maybe you need glasses."

I didn't know what was wrong. I thought that everyone was like me and had trouble reading. I thought that everyone read the way that I did. I could read the words from memory but I couldn't sound them out. If I had to read a whole sentence, sounding out each word, I'd lose the first word by the time I got through the second and finally I couldn't make any sense out of the whole sentence. So what I used to do and still do is to sound out words and memorize them because I have a good memory.

I stayed in that school for the fourth and fifth grade, and then I was going to have to go into a regular junior high school. They decided that junior high school was out and that they were going to have to find another program for me. The fall came around and they didn't find a program for me and they said, "How would you like to repeat the fifth grade?" I asked why, because I didn't want to.

So they put me in another school and there they assigned me to the fifth grade so I had to repeat it anyway. I knew all the work already, but I learned something and I was really good at the math. I ended up doing fifth-grade work for another year and I graduated from that school.

Then around came the fall again and the problem of what to

do with me, so I was put in another school which had a special program. I went to that special school for about half a year, but it was a program for the neurologically impaired. That was the worst. I just sat there. I was in the seventh grade and it was like second-grade work. The math was addition and the reading was words like "cat," sight words that I had memorized years ago when I was a little kid. I never got in trouble. I never talked. They probably wondered why I was so quiet. The other kids in the class made noise; some were retarded, some had emotional problems and some were tough guys—behavior problems. But I was big and so they didn't bother me.

My mother felt bad about that school, and I was absent a lot, but I would go in when they said that I had to pass a test for my report card. I'd do that, but usually I'd stay home one or two days every week. My mother didn't make me go to that school the way she did before; she felt bad for me. It was a short day from ten to two, and we never had a full-period class. I hated that school. I couldn't wait till two o'clock to go. My mother thought that I should see a psychologist because of my problem. What was my problem, anyway? I didn't have an emotional problem. I just didn't want to be there because it was a total waste of time. I didn't belong there. Finally, the guidance counselor sent me to the Lamm Institute where they checked everything and found that I had a reading problem. That I was dyslectic. I wasn't mentally disturbed, and I wasn't mentally retarded.

Finally the school looked at my case again and I complained that I didn't want to be left back and that I had done the fifth grade three times and I wanted to be promoted. Well, since I had been messed around with for three years they promoted me, but to the eighth grade, and that was tough for me. All of the grades were tough, but that was the toughest. But I passed. I made it a point to work extra hard so as not to fail.

School would be out at two-thirty, and I would stay there and work until four. Then I'd go home to work and I would do sixth- and seventh-grade work to catch up. When they would talk about the atom I would have to learn the preceding material, so that I could understand about the atom. One teacher gave me a lot of help; she was there when I needed her to fill in the background information so that I could keep up.

Last year I went to high school as a freshman in a regular class, and now I'm still there, so that this is one of the best years ever. I'm relaxed now, and I'm not shy. When a teacher asks me to stand up and read page 101–103 during the class, I can say to her I have trouble reading and I can't do that. I never used to be able to say that. The teacher then says that she'll talk to me after class, and I explain it to her. I know what is wrong with me, and the people know what is wrong, so I don't have to worry. I know what I have to do to get around it and how to help myself.

When first learning how to write in grade school I would confuse the "b" and the "d" and other things. And the teacher would make me walk backward so that I would learn the difference between frontward and backward. I didn't like getting yelled at, so I started to write in capitals because the "B" and the "D" go in the same direction. Even now when I write in capitals, I still do reversals, but I can recognize that there is something wrong now, and also I type a lot of my work because that is helpful. I've also slowed down a lot—I always wanted to be a speed demon—and I write slowly, because I want to keep my work neat. Also, I read over the work and examine the words.

As a kid I got interested in the telephone because I saw my mother using it. I used to take it apart and put it back together again because it was color coded. There were no word instructions, only colors. Even the screws were colored so that if you knew the difference between a screw and a nut you could do it. I used to fix all sorts of things around the house, and I guess that my mother figured that I wasn't as dumb as my school reports said.

Right now my record says that I'm very bad in vocabulary, back at a fifth-grade level. But in conversation when someone uses a word, I know what the word means and can use it. But when it comes to a written test, I still have problems. If we get a test and I have trouble reading the questions, I can take it to my resource-room teacher, and she can read the questions to me and then I can do the test. Sometimes a teacher doesn't like that and thinks that I am trying to get away with something, so I have to take the test in the room with the rest of the students, and sometimes I don't do so well.

But my close friends know that I have a problem and the teachers really are nice. I joined lots of clubs, and I'm in a play and am part of the stage crew doing lighting and carpentry. It's a lot of fun!

Unfortunately, this experience is not so unusual among children with learning disabilities. Inability to do well in the first few grades is often attributed to laziness or lack of discipline, and the child is frequently berated at home and in school, which only serves to raise his level of anxiety and heighten doubts about himself and his ability. His parents don't understand what the difficulty is, and the complaints from the school mount. A school transfer helps for a time, but then the pattern of failure begins again, and the child is channeled into a program for the mentally retarded. With proper diagnosis and remedial care for the specific reading disability, Patrick is finally beginning to reach his potential, but only after years of mishandling.

Another child displayed similar symptoms, but upon careful physical examination showed marked relaxation of the tendons and joints and hyperelasticity of the skin. This indicated a more basic neuromotor and neurophysiological problem underlying his listlessness and behavioral difficulties. These symptoms were the result of a physical problem that required specific treatment. It is because of such experiences that we make no *a priori* judgments about a child's condition.

The history of learning disabilities is replete with misunderstanding, and it is only within recent years that any large-scale attention has been directed toward remediating the problem. In the past, more likely than not children were punished or publicly shamed in front of classmates for scholastic inability instead of being helped. It is only by establishing a complete clinical picture, with information derived from a series of related disciplines, that we are comfortable with a diagnosis of the real, but difficult to assess, learning disability.

We look at each child as a whole individual and not as a collection of symptoms. Donnie, a three-and-one-half-year-old boy, was referred to us because he had a severe speech and language delay. The most frequent reason for speech delay is mental retardation; the second most frequent is an auditory deficit of significant magnitude. After checking these two basic considerations, if we find no problem we look elsewhere. Are there environmental problems or emotional difficulties, or disturbances in receptive or expressive language (dysphasia)? In Donnie's case, he showed some potential for normal development in non-verbal areas of psychological testing, but he was being overly protected by his mother. She reported that he only played with his brother, and during testing she cuddled him and offered him a bottle to quiet him. Since the child was not retarded and possessed normal hearing, we recommended that he be placed in a group where he would be exposed to other children and have his speech and language enriched in an atmosphere outside that of the home.

The learning-disabled child may be perfectly able to deal with verbal instructions, but find reading an immense trial since he is not able to take the written letters on the page and translate them into words that make any sense. And yet these are the same words that in many cases he can recognize and respond to verbally. However, somewhere in the chain of information processing there is a blockage that impedes the transformation of a visually perceived stimulus into conceptual or cognitive awareness. Since this blockage may not exist aurally, children with such problems have been placed in classes for the visually impaired with some success.

In the context of the average school, these children are at a severe disadvantage and in all likelihood would be classified as slow learners. Without recognition of the problem, the child would experience increasing difficulty as he progressed in school from first to second grade and certainly any grade beyond. Depending on the child's personality, he might become quiet and withdrawn or, conversely, might begin to show disruptive aggressive behavior. Ironically, the child who exhibits aggressive behavior is often better off than his more passive, withdrawn counterpart because the disciplinary problems posed by the former tend to prompt earlier attempts at diagnosis and treatment.

Though not retarded, these children can be mistakenly classified as such because they simply do not do well in certain types of structured tests. Children scoring below 70 on standardized intelligence tests—such as the widely used Wechsler Intelligence Scale for Children-Revised or the older Stanford-Binet Intelligence Scale—are considered to be retarded to a greater or lesser degree. But a child with average or even above average intelligence may perform poorly because of specific deficiencies in reading, mathematical skills and visual-motor coordination.

Time can also be a factor working against a learning disabled child confronted by a standardized test. He may be able to come up with the right answer if given sufficient time to reflect, but many standardized tests have specified time limits on certain items. Quickness in responding is actually not an indication of intelligence but simply a factor of how speedily a child processes information. The ability to produce the correct answer is the primary task. We must, of course, recognize that speed of response is a necessary consideration in the real world; one might say that valid tests with no time limit measure intellectual power, while those with time limits measure intellectual efficiency.

One of the most common forms of learning disability with which we are confronted is dyslexia. Dyslexia comes in many different guises, but its most common manifestation is difficulty in pronouncing unfamiliar words encountered on the printed page. Children have a tendency to take a stab at them, but often the result is a selection of a word that has little relationship to the one that is actually on the page. At other times a letter reversal will make the word "dig," for instance, emerge as "big," or the child may substitute "was" for "saw." In still other cases words may be left out of a phrase or one word repeated several times when it is not called for. In attempting to pronounce a word, a child may leave out a syllable, shortening a word to a more manageable size, or conversely he may add a letter which will change the meaning of the word ("tip" becomes "trip"). The result, however, is the same. The child has extreme difficulty in extracting any sensible meaning from printed material. And although any child can make such mistakes occasionally when learning to deal with the written word, the dyslectic child continuously makes these errors and will persist in making them unless he secures remedial help. The normal classroom instruction which benefits the non-learning-disabled child has little effect in correcting the errors made by the dyslectic child.

For such children, reading, by which we acquire so much of the information that is needed in daily life, becomes a painful, even hateful operation. In a rural, undemanding society such a child could mature and take a responsible place in his community without too many adverse effects. However, in an advanced, technologically oriented society reading increases in importance to the point where the dyslectic child finds himself severely restricted in his ability to function at any but the lowest levels of employment. He might have difficulty securing a driver's license, which requires passing a written examination, and might even encounter difficulty deciphering unfamiliar names and street addresses while attempting to run a series of errands.

The inability to translate the written word into a meaningful concept, the inability to spell, to work with mathematical concepts, or to write down words and phrases in a legible manner—all of these have been grouped together as specific learning disabilities. Two terms commonly associated with learning disabilities are *minimal brain dysfunction,* frequently abbreviated as *MBD,* and *attentional deficit disorder, ADD.* There is no clear agreement in the field as to which term is preferable, but these two are the most commonly employed. Neither is really a diagnosis (like pneumonia). Rather, they are generalized, descriptive terms used to connote or imply certain behavioral characteristics that may adversely affect the learning process.

Minimal brain dysfunction is understood to mean a mixture of learning and behavioral difficulties (hyperactivity, for instance) which may be related to an inborn maldevelopment or malfunction of specific parts of the brain. Less likely, but still possible, is that MBD may be related to a slight insult to a portion of the central nervous system. The "insult" may be an injury that is not apparent in the normal neurological examination but is inferred from the medical and developmental history and behavioral observations. It does not necessarily represent the destruction of neurological pathways, but does indicate some difficulty, perhaps some sort of interference, that blocks the normal functioning of the brain. Awkward and clumsy movement may be present.

An earlier, harsher phrase was *brain damage,* a term that caused an unreasonable and unnecessary amount of anguish to parents. The term dysfunction indicates some lack of normal operation but does not stigmatize the child with the suggestion of irreparable destruction when there is no evidence to support this diagnosis. The deliberate softness in tone of the phrase MBD does, in fact, carry its own difficulties. There are those who say that the term does not tell us much about the condition of a child, but there are others who have devoted most of their working lives to the field who say that it tells us a great deal.

In many cases, it has been used so carelessly or loosely that it has been stretched beyond usefulness. It can mean too many things and lacks real precision though it sounds like an accurate medical description. It is for this reason that we prefer to use a broad, simple descriptive term such as learning disability until scientifically precise terminology is warranted.

Attentional Deficit Disorder, the term currently favored by the American Psychiatric Association, represents an attempt to focus on underlying causes rather than surface manifestations such as hyperactivity. It is believed that the learning-disabled child is unable to sustain attention on a task long enough to complete it satisfactorily. He can focus on it quickly, but just as quickly becomes distracted and involved with something else. Thus he is unable to get the complete instruction or to see a line of reasoning through. As a young child he may betray the shifting focus of his thoughts by visible hyperactivity, though as he grows older, he generally learns to control the obvious physical activity.

One of the most important tools used in arriving at an accurate diagnosis is the taking of an extremely careful history. And here we touch upon communication with the parents, especially the mother. After all, in the traditional family arrangement (and particularly when she does not hold an outside job) she spends more time with the child than anyone else. At times the doctor does not listen carefully enough; often he has too many children to see. And it is true that occasionally the parents may appear to be overly concerned, or at other times the parents may see little things which they consider significant. But if we listen very carefully, we will learn a great deal about the behavior of the child and about what factors ought to be considered in the thorough medical, psychological and remedial work-up.

The following terms or phrases represent a selection of the most frequently heard descriptions we get from parents when they talk about the behavior of a child who has begun to act in a way that suggests difficulties. The parent will use terms like "clumsy," "has two left feet," "slow to catch on," "gives up too easily," "in constant motion," "a bundle of nervous energy," "has a low boiling point," "can't sit still," "has above-average intelligence but is not quite making it," "bull in a china shop," "always into things," "nothing seems to work," "strong willed."

A child may be overactive because he is nervous, and he may be nervous for the same reasons that adults are: a chaotic household situation, feelings of insecurity, a perceived lack of attention, affection and love—a whole host of emotional factors may contribute to overactivity in a child. The common expression that there is very little new under the sun pertains to learning disabilities as well. Going back in the German literature 130 years, we find a childrens' book called *Shock Headed Peter* in which is described all the behavior that we now ascribe to learning-disabled children. But they did not have a name to assign to it at that time.

If we go back thirty to thirty-five years, we find that Alfred A. Strauss and his co-workers in this country were attempting to differentiate between the child who had brain damage, resulting from birth trauma or encephalitis for example, and the mentally retarded with no history of insult or damage to the brain. He began to notice definite differences, and these were important because they gave us a clue as to how these children could best be helped. The retarded children without demonstrable brain injury displayed a kind of even, uniform depression in intellectual ability. In the brain-injured child, there was evidence of a great deal of variability, with high performance in some areas and low performance in others.

It became apparent that the child with brain injury had a great deal of difficulty with visual motor perception and visual motor function. The term *brain damaged* is a frightening one because we are taught that if brain cells are damaged or destroyed there really isn't very much we can do about repairing them. Even in those instances, however, we can tell you with some note of optimism that it is not always necessary to think about repairing them but rather to find ways to use the healthy, intact portions of the brain more effectively. Thus we have the concept of *plasticity* of the immature, developing brain. That is, the ability of one portion to take over control of processes usually associated with some other area. An example would be the development of the primary speech centers on the right side of the brain if the left side were damaged.

But all the same, the term is a frightening one and the terms learning disabilities, MBD and ADD came into being when the experts in the field began to recognize that there were children who showed some of the *same symptoms but with no real evidence of brain damage*. Then the neurologists began talking of "soft" neurological signs, and that is when we began to regard in another light the child who was just a little clumsy, who couldn't copy a circle or a square quite as well as the other children, who couldn't handle a pencil quite as well or whose handwriting was not up to par.

The origins of these slight brain dysfunctions are diverse, but the main causitive factors include prenatal maternal infections, poor prenatal nutrition, effects of alcohol, drugs, or tobacco or other toxic substances used excessively by the mother during pregnancy, and perinatal (birth) injuries resulting from anoxia, hemorrhage or both. There are other factors of an organic nature as well, and these are related to the chromosomal makeup the child inherits from his parents, and the unexplained but real vulnerability of male children as opposed to female children. The actual ratio is six males to one female who suffer from learning disabilities.

In addition to these physical conditions, there are general factors that may seriously hamper a child's school performance without actually causing a learning disability. These factors include deficient nutrition, lack of stimulation in the home, poor living conditions, overly crowded school rooms or teachers who have low expectations for their pupils' performances. These factors are more likely to aggravate rather than cause a learning disability.

Ironically, deprivation in the home can occur among the wealthiest as well as the poorest of families. In poor households there may be a lack of intellectual stimulation because the parents themselves are overwhelmed by the demands of sheer economic survival. In the higher economic population, two working parents may be too busy with their own concerns to give sufficient attention to their child's development. While these children would display the same types of problems as the children of the lower socioeconomic group, their parents may be more likely to seek help earlier from a physician or other professionals.

In discussing environmental factors, we must keep in mind that these conditions are imposed on growing infants and children who are born with temperamental differences. These differences are, in large part, determined by genetic inheritance. Hence, the same environmental stimuli may produce different responses. While the term *personality* may be difficult to define in a precise manner, we understand what is generally meant by it. It has now been put on a more scientific basis, in the sense that behaviors that have been demonstrated in infancy and childhood have been catalogued and built into a system of classification. This classification enables us to talk about different temperaments that are already demonstrable in infancy and childhood.

The current furor over testing is, in a small way, based on the factor of personality. It is recognized that testing to establish levels of competence is a necessary process for admission to a school or professional academy. The furor stems from the fact that while we can test the knowledge the individual has acquired, there are certain traits in the individual, which we refer to as personality, that are more difficult to measure. So, while the schools recognize that an "A" average is excellent, it does not tell them whether the student with such an average will make a good doctor or lawyer. A psychological examination may give them more insight into the student's temperament, and help them to judge whether or not he would be likely to adjust satisfactorily to various stress situations that may arise in his chosen career. To repeat, over and above an individual's physical and intellectual attributes, there are certain factors that we refer to as temperament or personality that enter into in the child's ability to cope successfully.

At another level, we ask ourselves why a certain person may become depressed or exhibit schizophrenic reactions in a given situation when others may not. We are beginning to feel that the answer lies in that part of the makeup of the individual that determines his response to noxious stimuli. Whether that makeup includes a deficiency or an excess of certain enzymes or biochemicals or a response pattern determined largely by prior experience remains a challenge to our current knowledge.

Concordant (same ovum) twin studies in Nordic countries, where they have kept records on the subject for hundreds of years, have shown situations in which identical twins who have been separated for one reason or another and have been brought up in different environments, have developed personality disorders, autistic behavior or schizophrenia to a much greater degree than discordant (separate ovum) twins, who do not possess an identical genetic makeup. Such findings underline the significant role of genetic factors and the constancy of their manifestation in a variety of environments.

As we have discussed, there are a variety of factors that may cause learning disabilities. Some of these have been clearly documented and others are only dimly understood. The record of confusion and misdiagnosis has made us realize that all aspects of the child's physical condition, behavior, background and environment have to be assessed in order to draw a clear profile of the learning disabled child.

It is for this reason that every child who is referred to the Stanley S. Lamm Institute (hereafter referred to as the Institute) is given a complete evaluation by a pediatric neurologist, a psychiatrist, a psychologist, specialists in occupational therapy, physical therapy, speech and language disorders, an educational evaluator and a social worker. These reports, together with those of the ophthalmologist and audiologist and any related laboratory studies, comprise the work-up. When the work-up has been completed, the child is scheduled for a diagnostic evaluation and treatment-planning conference.

It is at this time, with the *entire team present,* that we have the best opportunity to assess a child's strengths and weaknesses and make sound recommendations. It takes a great deal of time and effort, but we don't believe that there is any reliable shortcut.

The care of a child with a learning disability is a long-term process involving many months and often years of work. During this period of time the child, the parents and the professionals work collaboratively in helping to reach a maximum level of functional achievement on the part of the child and his or her family. The diagnostic and treatment services offered by the Institute involve several professional disciplines each of which is concerned with helping the child achieve optimal physical, social and intellectual growth.

The Institute has always endeavored to monitor each child's progress as closely as possible. In this way, feedback can be provided to the parents along with timely suggestions for additions to or modifications of the child's treatment program. In recent years, this process has become formalized by government regulations requiring the quarterly preparation of an Individual Program Plan for each child under active care. As the number of children participating in our program has grown larger, it has become increasingly difficult to perform effective monitoring utilizing conventional methods. Therefore, to help us maintain continuity and quality of care, we have chosen to utilize data processing technology. The installation of a minicomputer has allowed us to create a data base or "bank of information" that is used to keep track of all recommended services and insure that they are being carried out.

The process begins with a neurological examination by a child neurologist. All of the examiner's recommendations are stored in the data base. As services are scheduled, the computer creates a letter notifying the family. When the family arrives at the Institute for a scheduled visit, the receptionist has a computer-printed listing that assists her in directing them to the appropriate department and specific staff member. Occasionally, a conflict arises between appointments that have been scheduled and the family's ability to come at those specific times. The computer identifies such situations so that appropriate assistance can be offered.

We have always attempted to complete the diagnostic evaluation of a child as rapidly as possible. In addition, government regulations are forthcoming that will require that this process be completed in no more than sixty days. The computer helps us keep track of children according to the date on which they first come to us for help, so that those evaluations that are taking longer than average to complete can be offered priority scheduling.

A child's program often involves periodic revisits for neurologic, psychologic or laboratory examination. The computer reminds us of when such services are due. When appointments have been arranged, the computer sends a notification letter to the family, and a copy is placed in the child's folder.

A summary of every child's program status is printed for each staff meeting and each physician visit. In this way, outstanding needs can be quickly identified.

It is sometimes desirable to utilize medication as an adjunct to treatment. Patients receiving medication require careful monitoring so that prescriptions can be provided as needed with dosages adjusted in accord with the degree of improvement that has been attained. The computer maintains a list of all patients receiving medication to assist us in providing careful supervision of that program aspect.

Many children are seen on a weekly basis for specific functional therapies. The computer maintains a treatment schedule for each staff therapist to assist in program planning. The therapist is provided with information concerning the number of children awaiting service, their diagnostic indication of need and length of time since the particular service was recommended. This facilitates long-term planning and schedule adjustment with a view toward program initiation for each child under care as rapidly as possible.

For those children on an active treatment program, our system provides the therapist with a list indicating when quarterly program reviews are due.

Our interest and responsibility in caring for every child brought to us for help extends beyond the services provided entirely within the Institute. Appropriate educational placement is an integral part of the treatment plan. The Institute participates in making recommendations to the local educational authority and in providing advocacy services for families where we feel that the educational services being offered are inadequate with respect to the child's needs.

The computer maintains indices that remind staff when placement reviews are due. Follow-up lists are also maintained for children who require initiation of a placement recommendation, require follow-up of a previous placement recommendation or require short-term feedback regarding an interim placement.

When not engaged in helping us provide direct services, the computer is used to facilitate research aimed at increasing scientific understanding of the complex interaction of many factors involved in learning disabilities, and enhancing program planning for the future. For example, we are currently attempting to correlate medical diagnoses with causative factors as they become known.

The data base is also being used to measure the contribution of new diagnostic procedures, such as the CAT Scan, to our understanding of specific brain abnormalities or more subtle differences from the normal, which may result in a learning disability. Our goal here is to facilitate early identification and early intervention using the most appropriate treatment techniques.

Our data base is constructed in such a way that unanticipated questions can be posed easily with rapid response obtained. In this way, new ideas can be tested with a minimum of effort and expense.

In sum, our effort is to apply computer and information technology to help keep the humanity in our human service and to keep costs at a manageable level. Should *you* ever have occasion to receive a computer-generated letter from the Institute, please remember that it was a caring professional staff member, with knowledge of your child's needs, who instructed the machine to send it.

II. FREQUENTLY ASKED QUESTIONS

Who Is Considered a Learning-Disabled Child?

With the hope that it will bring some comfort to parents and teachers who have been struggling with the concept for years, we should like to acknowledge that the professionals in this field had difficulty agreeing upon a generally accepted definition of a learning disability until 1978. We now have the definition contained in the federal legislation (Public Law 94-142 amended "Education for All Handicapped Children Act"), which defines a learning disability as performance in an academic area—reading, arithmetic, etc.—that is two years or more below the child's over-all intellectual level.

The critical point here is not performance below that which is expected for the child's *chronological* age but below that which is expected for the individual child's *mental ability*. Therefore, we would say that if an eight-year-old child had an IQ of 100 (average), his chronological age would be the same as his mental age, and he would be defined as learning disabled only if he were reading at a level two years below that.

The value of this type of analysis is that it allows us to say that a child who is ten years old and who is reading at an eleven-year-old level might still be classified as learning disabled in reading. The reason for this is that if, in fact, the child had an overall IQ of let's say 140, that would lead us to expect him to be functioning at a fourteen-year-old level, regardless of his chronological age. Thus, he is still reading two grades or more below that which might be expected for his mental-age ability.

A child functioning at a borderline level would not be classified as learning disabled, unless in a specific area—say reading—he was two years below the already lower level that would be anticipated on the basis of his borderline score. This formulation really allows us to look at all children from the same perspective, whether they fall above, below or at the average intellectual level.

What Does IQ Really Mean?

IQ (Intelligence Quotient) is a mathematical measurement assigned to a constellation of mental abilities primarily related to abstract reasoning ability.

Let us begin by stating that measures of IQ do not have the same precision as that of a blood test, for example, in establishing a sugar level. Over the years there have been many attempts to develop IQ tests that are culture free; that is, tests that will be accurate over a broad range of socioeconomic, socioethnic and sociocultural populations. Devising such a test, however, is easier said than done.

Many of the early so-called *culture*-free tests were actually *language*-free tests, the assumption being that by eliminating the verbal component of a test, its cultural biases would also be eliminated. That assumption becomes rather important because actually among the best-known tests of intellectual development for use with children, and the one with the longest history, is the Stanford-Binet.

To a great extent it has been forgotten that the Stanford-Binet originally had a verbal and a non-verbal form. During World War I, the army alpha and beta tests, modeled on the Stanford-Binet, were used as selection techniques by the U. S. Military Forces in order to establish some base line by which to judge an individual's ability to acquire the basic knowledge required in military training. Minimum acceptable scores were set, and that was one of the very first large-scale standardization efforts for a paper-and-pencil test of intelligence. At that time a significant portion of the population of the United States was illiterate and the examiners developed an alternate form that required no verbal responses. It consisted of visual-motor-and-perception material that would be familiar to most people.

It is true that the alternate test gave a more accurate and representative assessment of intellectual capacity for an illiterate subject than one based on language (which he was not capable of taking), but it was a far cry from being culture free. To press the point a bit further, let us consider the test that is today the most widely used in assessing children's intellectual capacity—the Wechsler Intelligence Scale for Children-Revised. It has both verbal and non-verbal sub-tests. Some of the latter are based on the perception of the relationships among geometric forms. There are other cultures where geometric form does not have the same relevance or meaning that it has in our culture. Therefore, resulting scores would not have the same significance.

This discussion regarding the validity and reliability of IQ testing may appear to be somewhat esoteric or academic. It is particularly important, however, because within the past ten years tests have been developed in an attempt to reach the street savvyness of some of the population groups that are commonly referred to as socioeconomically deprived, disadvantaged, minority and so forth. In the United States this refers primarily to three groups: Blacks, Hispanics and Chicanos. Whereas it used to be thought that vocabulary is a part of school performance that correlated very highly with intelligence, tests specifically designed for minority groups demonstrate that vocabulary may correlate even more highly with cultural attributes.

However, the fact is that members of minority or disadvantaged groups ultimately must function in a society that is dominated by the majority, so that it becomes intellectually challenging to determine what the long-term meaningfulness of that kind of differentiation is. We feel that the comparative data offer valuable information, but nonetheless if a child grows up with a very extensive vocabulary that is all his own—that is in effect a foreign language—he may still have difficulty integrating into the dominant group.

A prime point of discussion currently is the value of bilingual education, and unfortunately the pedagogic considerations often get submerged beneath the very emotional cultural heritage aspect. We absolutely believe that every vital aspect of every cultural heritage, of every group, minority or majority, should be part of each individual's fullness as a person. However, this doesn't have anything to do with the fact that if a child is attending a school in an English-speaking country that the primary language of instruction should be English.

Does the IQ Score Change Over Time or with Education?

This is a question that has been debated by clinical and educational psychologists for half a century or more. The subject is generally referred to in the professional literature under the heading of *con-*

stancy of the IQ. The early research purported to prove that the IQ was highly constant. Since the IQ expresses a ratio relationship between mental development and chronological age, it was thought to remain relatively constant from childhood to adult life, barring either physical or emotional trauma.

Generally, this is a defensible statement, but it does not mean that there may not be changes in IQ resulting from enriched educational experiences in life. Our best evidence suggests that the greatest opportunity for environmental enhancement of IQ comes during the preschool years, while the infant brain is still in a period of rapid growth.

The changes that result from increased exposure to academically stimulating environments, whether in school, home, or life experiences, are, in fact, measured by tests of achievement, rather than tests of intellectual capacity. There are many in the field who question whether or not those two concepts can be so clearly and sharply differentiated. In most psychoeducational and psychosocial measures, we are speaking of group data, but certainly there are major individual differences. In an attempt to conceptualize, we might say that 90 percent of what we describe as intellectual behavior is innate and the remaining 10 percent is susceptible to variation, depending on subsequent experience.

The description above applies to the "normal" population. In our work, where we are dealing with developmentally disabled and learning-disabled children, we have a very different kind of experience. Where we find specific deficiencies, they are very much reflected in the IQ scores. And where we are successful in remediating or correcting some of those deficiencies, we will see corresponding improvement in the IQ scores. Score changes are even more significant where there is an associated severe neurological disability that we have been able to remediate or correct. Thus it is particularly important to note any indication of higher potential in the psychological report.

I've Heard the Terms "Reliability" and "Validity" Used in Reference to Tests. What Do They Mean?

These are probably the two most important terms in the description of any test, not just intelligence or academic tests. *Validity* deals with the extent to which the test accurately measures the variable that it is purported to measure. Therefore, we ask of an intelligence test, "How do we know that it is measuring intelligence and not something else?" The way that the validity of a test is measured is based on the predictive value that a given test score may have.

Validity testing is a very complex issue dealing with a question that is difficult to define. For example, it was not so very long ago that intelligence was defined in a truly circular manner as "that which is measured by tests of intelligence"—which tells us absolutely nothing. If we were to measure or attempt to measure a vocational aptitude by designing a test to see whether or not a child has the aptitude to become an effective carpenter or cabinetmaker, that can be measured pretty objectively. The test scores are correlated with a later evaluation of the individual's success in the tasks that are indentified with carpentry and cabinetmaking. If the child scored highly in the test and then turned out to be an excellent carpenter, then one might conclude that the test has good predictive value and therefore it is valid. If the child scored very low yet still turned out to be an excellent carpenter, one might come to the conclusion that the test is totally invalid, or that it may have an inverse predictive value.

Reliability is simply a measure of how consistently a test measures a specific trait. Therefore, if we compensate for the practice effect of any given test, and we find that a child scores consistently at an IQ level of 115 and that score doesn't vary more than two or three points above or below on three, four or five successive administrations, then the test is highly reliable. And therefore, a higher order of predictive value can be attributed to that test. If, on the other hand, we find widely scattered test and retest correlations, it is less predictive and less reliable as a measure of a given trait.

When the Teacher Tells Me that My Child Is Below Grade Level, What Does That Mean?

It means that on standardized tests of achievement (arithmetic and reading, for example), as opposed to tests that purport to measure intellectual development in a more generic way (the ability to abstract principles from specific examples), the child falls below the median score for children in the same grade. These are always in terms of standardization data; that is, norms that have been established. Some tests are better standardized than others, meaning that they use a broader sampling technique and have a larger data base for comparison.

Some tests are considered by many to be less predictive than others because it is alleged that their standardization population is non-representative. A classic example is the raging controversy found in the professional literature and the popular press on whether the most widely used tests of intellectual development thoroughly measure the intellectual development of minority populations, specifically Blacks, Chicanos and Hispanics. (See: What Does IQ Really Mean? [page 000].

Who Do I Turn to for Help When the School Tells Me My Child Can't Keep Up?

We would assume when the school tells you that your child "can't keep up," it has already asked for your permission to have a child study team evaluate your child's strengths and weaknesses. If that has not been done, then the first thing to do is to ask the school whether it has a child study team available to make that assessment, so that you will not be dealing with a vague, global statement such as "can't keep up." After such an assessment you will then be able to focus in on what the particular areas of difficulty may be.

The child-study team should make specific recommendations for the kinds of help and remediation that would be most beneficial for your child. The school may also recommend a more detailed evaluation by an outside agency. You may or may not agree with those recommendations, and you have the absolute right to then seek another opinion or additional data to clarify the difficulties that the school tells you your child is experiencing. So, in brief, the first place to turn to is the school itself.

What If the School Does Not Have Such an Evaluation Team?

The next place to look would be in your own community, where you should seek out either a pediatric neurologist or a pediatrician with a strong interest in the area of learning disabilities. This is not to suggest that the pediatrician or the pediatric neurologist alone can offer all of the help that may be needed, but there are two factors that make a pediatric neurologist a good first step. One is that the possibility of a neurological problem must be ruled out before there is any further extensive investigation into possible causes. The second factor is that the pediatric neurologist will probably be well aware of the other assessment resources that can be marshaled in your community. He will have a history of experience with educational specialists, clinical psychologists or psychiatrists, and with social workers who make a specialty of working with problems in this area. He is also qualified to organize the data submitted to him and go over the findings with you.

There are some communities in which you are not going to be able to find a pediatric neurologist, and this is the occasion to look for a local chapter of the Association for Children with Learning Disabilities or the Association for Children with Retarded Mental Development. Both organizations have experience in this area and will be able to offer assistance. The Special Education Department of your local university is another excellent resource.

Do Teachers Take Courses to Help Them Identify Learning-Disabled Children?

Absolutely! As a matter of fact, there is a title within the educational system for a Learning Disabilities Specialist. This is a professional category that is not more than five to seven years old. However, one has to say that the record is spotty. There are tremendous variations among states, among cities within states, school districts within cities and among schools within the same districts. Ultimately, much responsibility rests with the teacher. A dedicated, charismatic teacher who can develop a motivational level in a child is probably the single most important contributing factor to the child's development.

What Is Mainstreaming?

Mainstreaming is an attempt to keep a learning-disabled child with a peer group in the appropriate grade. The intent is to avoid stigmatizing the child. Mainstreaming is usually accomplished by withdrawing the child from regular class only on a limited basis for remedial work in a resource room, rather than placing him in a specific special-education class. This means that if a child has a problem reading, he may be given the opportunity to go to the resource room for reading remediation during some portion of his regular day, and continue to take other subjects with his peers.

What Is a Resource Room and What Does It Do?

A resource room provides the special remedial help that a child requires after the child has been evaluated as being learning disabled or in need of special help. This permits the child to remain in the mainstream of educational life. And this too represents an issue where we have come full circle. When children with special needs were first identified, it was decided to give them all the help that was possible, and a proliferation of special classes resulted. It soon became apparent that there was no way in which the system could have a special class for each specific educational handicap or need that had been identified. That would lead to such a huge number of special classes that there would be no way of organizing them effectively. Nor do we have the resources or trained personnel to staff them. At that point the idea of grouping—putting together children with handicapping conditions that required similar types of intervention—came to the fore. And that brings us to the current "resource room" thinking, to which we can subscribe if the resources are adequate to the need. This type of thinking allows us to look at the child first—not as a series of handicapping conditions, but as a whole child. We look at the physical, physiological, psychological, social and educational needs. If we say the task is to educate the whole child and to provide him with such special remediation as an analysis of his strengths and weaknesses may require, then we get to the concept of mainstreaming.

Do Schools Ordinarily Ask Parents to Participate in the Decision as to the Type of Program to Be Recommended?

Committees on the Handicapped (COH) are the prevailing organizations within the educational systems that are concerned with special educational programming involving parental participation. Every locality and school district provides some organizational structure or similar form, but not necessarily designated as such. *The involvement of parents is required by law* in the acceptance of the special educational program as recommended by the Committee on the Handicapped.

The parents may, after a discussion and explanation, agree to the recommendation. If they disagree, they are entitled to a hearing. Here, expert testimony can be brought forward to question the appropriateness of any given special-class placement that has been offered.

In terms of available resources for parents, we find a scarcity of trained personnel. We are talking here primarily about counseling, psychotherapeutically oriented work with parents to both help them accept their child's limitations and to contribute in a positive manner to improve the child's functioning through appropriate school placement or through reduction of stress in the home. Whatever the reasons may be, whether a parent may be overly demanding or overly protective, the child and parents would benefit if such counseling were available. We can find sketchy programs in some public school systems where funding for a continuing program has been restricted. In some of the wealthier school districts there are more effective programs. But in general the focus has been on the child, and it has been a strain to get necessary funding to develop the other equally essential parts of the intervention model—the parents. Very often a program will be limited to an assessment process and a recommendation to the parents that they get outside help to cope with some of the problems.

What Is the Present Commitment of Schools to Aid Learning-Disabled Children?

There is generally a growing recognition of the needs of these special children, and an increase in commitment within the limits of budgetary capability to provide special services. In general, more densely populated states and those areas with universities having strong special education departments have led the way in this area. (See Sources of Help.)

What Would Be the Educational Prescription for the Learning-Disabled Child vs. the Retarded Child?

To design an educational program for the mentally retarded child, there must be a careful evaluation of the child's assets and deficits. Then the instructional material has to be scaled to his level of capacity, or preferably a little above, so that the child doesn't just sit in the classroom, but has something to aspire to.

For the child with either a specific learning disability, minimal brain dysfunction or attentional deficit disorder, we want a careful analysis of his visual-motor functions; does he see things as others do and is he able to reproduce what he sees in the same way? The prescription then would be designed to include the specific materials best suited to correct the exact types of deficits the child has. Thus, we have areas of sensory-motor training that can be particularly useful for the child with a perceptual-motor problem, but that might be less useful for the mentally retarded child without a perceptual-motor problem. The individual program materials require the services of a highly skilled and specially trained teacher or reading therapist to utilize them fully.

What Is Hyperactivity?

What may be called a hyperactive child in one family may be seen only as a very active child in another. It is critical, therefore, to differentiate between the truly hyperactive child and the child who is very active and has a normal, healthy curiosity about the world he lives in and learns about that world by getting into things, although he may be a pain in the neck to us sometimes. We should recognize and appreciate the fact that this is part of the normal, healthy development of the child.

A truly hyperactive child is one who literally cannot sit still for more than a couple of seconds, or a couple of minutes at best. In professional parlance, there is a fine distinction between hyperactivity and hyperkinesis, the latter term referring to the quality of the movement (agitated, fidgety or twitchy). The hyperkinetic child, when seated, shuffles his feet, plays with his fingers and squirms most of the time, not just occasionally.

Hyperactivity is a more involved locomotor activity, with a child running around and getting into many things. Hyperactive behavior is not directed at a specific goal as ordinary activity is. The amount of activity may be no more than normal but is misdirected and purposeless. There is a difference between hyperactivity and MBD, yet the two terms are often confused in the popular press. MBD may include hyperactivity but is not the same thing. There are some children who are less active than most children and yet they have MBD.

To be described as having an MBD pattern, a child must show an accumulation of signs, some of which are: normal or potentially normal IQ, learning difficulties, clumsy motor patterns, and behavior difficulties such as hyperactivity or a very short attention span. Literally, the child is unable to concentrate on a task for more than a few moments. The child will usually be very impulsive and his responses reflect more than just not thinking too carefully before he acts, but take on an almost driven quality. He must pursue whatever stimulus catches his eye or ear at a given moment.

An example of hyperactive behavior would be the child sitting in a classroom who hears a fire engine in the street. This would be a little bit distracting to most children, but some children might be so deeply engrossed in a task that they would not attend to it at all. The hyperactive child, however, literally cannot prevent himself from jumping out of his chair and running to the window to see what's going on. After that he may return noisily to his seat, thereby distracting every other child in the class.

While we don't want rigid regimentation in the classroom, we do need a certain amount of structure in order for the educational process to take place. The youngster has to be able to attend to what is going on.

My Child Is Hyperactive What Is the Likelihood of His Being Helped?

The answer to that depends on a number of factors. The first is how early in the child's development a confirmed diagnosis of hyperactivity is made. During the course of our work, it has become pretty clear that the earlier such an identification is made, the greater the likelihood of a helpful therapeutic program, the outlook for which can be quite good.

In some cases, providing the child with a structured environment—one that is as free from needless distraction as possible—is helpful. In the most severe cases, we would prescribe drug therapy. Some of the most frequently used drugs are methylphenidate hydrochloride (Ritalin), dextroamphetamine sulphate (Dexedrine), and pemoline (Cylert). The exact workings of these drugs, and others that affect the central nervous system, are not fully understood at this time, but they do seem to help the hyperactive child screen out distractions and attend to the task at hand. As is the case with any course of drug therapy, we monitor the child's reactions on a regular basis.

Is Medication a Recognized Way to Treat Hyperactivity?

There is controversy among the various experts and professionals in the field about the use of medication to treat hyperactive children. During many years of treating hundreds of children with hyperactivity, we have found that the use of medications, generally known as central nervous system stimulants, has proven to be of some value. Though they do not, by any means, cure the condition, they do make the child less subject to the disorienting effects of extreme distractibility and a short attention span. The medication permits the child to participate more readily in classroom and any other activities that require him to focus his energies and attention.

Medication is used only in selected cases and for a specific period of time. Results are carefully monitored and when necessary the dosage is modified, up or down. Many parents are understandably wary about the use of medication of any kind. Among the most commonly expressed concerns is the fear of drug addiction.

We know of no instance in which a child treated with central-nervous system stimulants for the control of hyperactivity has developed into a drug addict. Despite the fact that the drugs are in many ways similar to those that are commonly referred to as "uppers" or "pep" pills, the drugs have exactly the opposite effect in these children. Instead of stimulating them, they tend in most cases to have a calming effect.

As yet we do not know the precise mode of action of these drugs, but they appear to alter the way in which nerve impulses are transmitted. Generally, individuals function in an environment that constantly presents them with a flood of visual and auditory stimuli. There is one part of the central nervous system (the reticular system) that alerts the individual to changing stimuli and identifies the important ones, so that he doesn't respond to all of them but selects those that are relevant to the task at hand. It is thought that these medications help this selection mechanism.

Are There Any Side Effects to These Medications?

In a very small number of cases side effects may occur. These may include loss of appetite and changes in sleep patterns. It is critical for the pediatrician or pediatric neurologist to follow the child very carefully on a continuing basis to observe any undesired side effects, and to determine when medication is no longer needed. Careful monitoring is necessary so that the most effective dosage may be achieved.

If side effects should occur, the medication dosage can be readily modified and the side effects will generally disappear. Too often, however, out of fear or apprehension, the medication may be discontinued before there has been an opportunity to properly evaluate its effectiveness. This is another reason that careful monitoring is necessary.

If the Drug Is Discontinued During Summer Vacation and the Child Functions Normally, Should He Be Reevaluated?

We often recommend drug "holidays" or "vacations" in the summer so that the child does not have to be on medication all of the time. Frequently, a change of environment, a change in the type of situation in which the child is functioning, may produce a marked improvement, which may or may not be long lasting. When such a marked change is noted, the parents should talk to their pediatrician about a reevaluation.

My Son Can Do Arithmetic as Well as Anyone in His Class and Yet He Can't Read. What Does This Mean?

Since your child can do arithmetic as well as anyone in his class, we can rule out the possibilities of limited intellectual ability or mental retardation. This leaves us with three further avenues to explore: Your child may have a specific reading disability that will respond favorably to traditional remedial reading instruction; he may have a more deep-seated disability generally known as dyslexia; or he may be experiencing an emotional block unrelated to any fundamental inability or impairment.

This last instance is a possibility because effective functioning in math does not require as much interaction with other people who may be threatening or who may represent an authority figure conflict. Reading and a demonstration of comprehension can put a child on the spot a little bit more. There are many nuances. Testing reading is not a simple "Yes I know!" or "No, I don't know!" proposition, as it is with mathematical exercises.

The other reason that might cause emotional difficulty is that a child who is an accomplished reader by age three is praised and made to feel that he has accomplished a great deal. If the child can count from one to ten, that is fine. But if he *reads,* that is special, and it gives rise to all types of expectations for future achievement, which, in turn, places a lot of pressure on the child. In fact, there is no real evidence to suggest that early skill acquisition is necessarily in the best interests of the child's long-term development.

What Is Dyslexia?

Dyslexia is simply a term that means dysfunctional or impaired reading ability. In and of itself that doesn't explain anything about the cause or the specific form it takes, such as reversals, rotations, blockages or problems in gestalt perception. The dyslectic child cannot derive meaning from words unless he hears the word. Seeing them does not set off the smooth innate process of encoding and decoding that ordinarily allows us to scan printed symbols and perceive them meaningfully.

When Was Dyslexia First Recognized?

A German physician, Adolph Kussmaul, is credited with being the first researcher to isolate the condition, which he referred to in 1877 as "word blindness." About ten years later the term dyslexia was proposed by W. P. Morgan as a broader description of the wide variety of reading, writing and spelling disorders that began to be recognized and classified. James Hinshelwood, a Scottish eye surgeon writing in 1902, made an observation that has remained essentially true to the present day, despite continuing controversy as to the cause and preferred treatment of dyslexia. "I have little doubt that these cases of congenital word blindness are by no means so rare as the absence of recorded cases would lead us to infer. Their rarity is, I think, accounted for by the fact that when they do occur, they are not recognized. It is a matter of the highest importance to recognize the cause and the true nature of this difficulty in learning to read which is experienced by these children, otherwise they may be harshly treated as imbeciles or incorrigibles, and either neglected or punished for a defect for which they are in no wise responsible."

The majority of Hinshelwood's contemporaries concerned with these disabilities tended to share the opinion that their cause was to be found in some type of brain defect. They were not able to describe its nature but assumed logically that it was there. In the 1920s another school of thought emerged in the United States, according to which the difficulty these children experienced arose from a delay in development rather than any injury to the central nervous system.

With the publication of the work of Samuel T. Orton during the 1920s and 1930s, the emphasis was again placed on the structure of the brain itself. During the course of his work with retarded children, he began to make connections between these learning disabilities and certain other physical traits. He found that children who reversed letters or who were ambidextrous also had difficulty in reading. From this, he concluded that there was some type of physiological malfunction that interfered with the establishment of the normal dominance of one half of the brain, and that this was the cause of the difficulty.

Ordinarily, we notice that people are either right- or left-sided in the performance of everyday tasks. If a child is asked to hop on one foot, without instructions as to which one to use, he will choose the one that he ordinarily favors. If asked to pick up an object, he will use the favored hand. Or if given a piece of paper with a small hole in the center and told to look through it, he will place it to the favored eye. Nine times out of ten this will be the right foot, the right hand, and the right eye. In the remaining cases, it will be the left or a combination of right and left. This tendency to select between the right and left is what we mean by *sidedness* or *laterality*. The uncertain or inconsistent selection of one or the other indicates a lack of anticipated dominance found in the normally functioning child.

During the 1940s, there was much interest in the work of Strauss and his co-workers in the related areas of behavior and learning. After his findings were published they proved to be a great stimulus toward bringing together the various disciplines concerned with these functions. Since Macdonald Critchley published his classic work on developmental dyslexia in 1964, the term has been subject to much abuse and misuse. It gives rise to fear, apprehension and confusion on the part of parents genuinely concerned with their child's academic performance. It may be incorrectly used to describe school failures that are related to factors other than a reading disability, or simply to describe generalized problems of the slow learner. In some school districts, the term is literally banned, so it is important to know precisely what dyslexia is and what it is not.

As a result of the cumulative efforts of the past hundred years, the focus of our interest has been shifted more and more onto the basic workings of the brain itself. The development of various instruments to measure the electrical activity of the brain has advanced to the point where we can measure extremely slight electrical shifts, indicating activity of precise areas of the brain that control specific functions.

What Is the Cause of Dyslexia?

While there is considerable disagreement among the experts, our experience and a review of the literature in the field strongly suggest that the predisposition to dyslexia is inborn—that is, present at birth—and also that there is a genetic factor involved, with some suggestion of sex linkage, since far more boys than girls manifest the symptoms. The work of Birch and Belmont suggests that the problem lies in the area of visual-auditory integration and in the area of directional confusion, or confusion between right and left.

There is a general consensus that the camera lens function of the eye is not the likely source of reading difficulties. Stated in another way, it is now believed that problems of eye dominance, strabismus (inability to focus both eyes on the same point), depth perception, ocular imbalance, nystagmus (rapid involuntary movement of the eyeball), and visual perception have relatively little to do with reading ability per se.

This does not mean that deficits in these areas should not be corrected to the greatest extent possible. Quite the contrary. Every effort should be made to promote optimal ocular health as part of the child's total health status. It is for this reason that a complete ophthalmological examination is part of our work-up.

Bruno Bettelheim has written extensively on the role of psychodynamic and emotional factors in reading disabilities. While we agree that these are important considerations, there is increasing evidence pointing to physical differences in the brains of dyslectic individuals. Norman Geschwind and his co-workers have made significant contributions in this area.

How Would You Describe a Typical Dyslectic Child?

Keeping in mind that a description is not a diagnosis, we would observe that such a child is more likely to be male than female, by a ratio of six to one. Generally, he has average or above-average intelligence, as measured on a recognized IQ test. He shows no specific neurological disturbance. He does reasonably well in academic areas other than reading and perhaps spelling, and often comes from a family in which the father, uncle or male cousins have a history of reading problems.

What Is a Reversal?

A reversal is the mirror image of a printed letter. Take the letter "E," for instance. It has one vertical line, and three horizontal lines projected to the right. A reversal occurs when an individual sees the letter with the prongs pointed to the left. Similarly, a child asked to write a lower case *b* might actually produce a *d*. Such difficulties are also encountered with the letters *p* and *q*. Occasionally we find a child confusing the number *9* with the letter *q*, though this is quite rare. Ordinarily, a child who is having difficulty and confusion with letter recognition may have absolutely no confusion at all with numbers.

What Is a Rotation?

A rotation describes any severe diversion from the normal vertical orientation of a printed letter or a combination of letters. In writing we allow for the normal deviations due to personal styles of writing and slanting. Rotations fall clearly outside the range of expected variation.

What Is a Blockage?

An interruption of uncertain nature that occurs somewhere in the chain of information processing is a blockage. It impedes or prevents the transmission of a visually perceived stimulus and its subsequent conversion into cognitive or perceptual awareness.

What Is Gestalt Perception?

The term gestalt is used to describe the total perceptual field. All of the component parts of the visual field are seen as related parts of the whole; it is a global perception rather than the perception of disconnected or unrelated parts. A dyslectic child or adult will have difficulty integrating the parts of the field into a meaningful whole.

How Do You Treat Dyslexia?

To date the best results have been achieved by focusing directly on the problems of reading and spelling. The work of Orton and his students Gillingham and Stillman led to specific treatment programs for the dyslectic child. These methods use intensive phonetic training that includes multisensory reinforcement involving sight, sound and touch.

There is increasing evidence that suggests a multiple, rather than a unitary, concept of dyslexia. This is an important consideration because it leads to a specific remedial approach for each type. Thus we see some dyslexias with the primary problem in the area of visual recognition (word gestalt) and others in which the problem is in the area of sound transmission. The most severe problems are seen in children who have both types.

It is our belief that in most cases, particularly those with developmental dyslexia, the brain learns to compensate for these faulty intrasensory connections, usually by the age of ten or eleven. In some children, the brain compensates earlier, before the child's reading is obviously affected. In most cases, however, reading problems do occur and emotional scars may result from repeated failures and loss of self-esteem.

A recent study by Frank and Levinson found that 97 percent of the poor readers showed evidence of cerebellar-vestibular dysfunction. They believe that the defect lies in the brain circuitry between the cerebellum and the inner ear, producing a mild form of motion sickness, which may be responsible for the difficulty in sequential scanning of letters and words.

One treatment approach following this hypothesis involves the use of antimotion sickness medication. The value of this treatment is still under assessment. Indeed, many experienced researchers seriously question the reliability of any conclusions based upon vestibular testing in children.

Other studies, currently in progress, are evaluating the effectiveness of certain drugs in improving short-term memory. We shall follow this work with interest.

What Courses of Treatment Have Had Less Success with Dyslectic Children?

Various treatment methodologies have been employed as one theoretical approach or another has gained dominance. It is generally agreed at present that indirect attempts to solve the problem—including visual-motor training, eye-hand coordination, establishing dominant laterality, optometric training, and working on emotional conflicts and parent-child relationships—have minimal effect.

What Should a Parent Do if a Dyslectic Condition Is Suspected?

When a reading problem is suspected, the concerned parent ought to proceed in the following manner: First, arrange for a complete pediatric and pediatric-neurological evaluation in order to rule out any medical problems that may account for the difficulty. These might include, but are not limited to, a study of vision, hearing, neurological development and nutritional status.

Second, a psycho-educational evaluation should be made in order to assess the level of intellectual development and to identify the specific strengths and weaknesses. Third, a conference with the teacher and reading specialist should be held in order to determine the need for a remedial program and the extent to which parents should be involved in tutorial work at home. Fourth, join appropriate parents' groups and support efforts to insure that your local board of education or school district, provides the needed classes, resources and trained teachers in accordance with existing federal and local statutes.

What Should a Parent Avoid Doing?

First, do not become preoccupied with your child's reading problem. Some parents may get unnecessarily concerned if their child is not reading at age four or five. The dangers of premature diagnosis or overdiagnosis are very real and may lead to an impaired self-image or a loss of self-esteem, and thus lead to a self-fulfilling prophecy.

Second, do not spend your energy and financial resources pursuing every new cure that you read or hear about. The responsible professionals with whom you've been dealing will be aware of any new developments in the field and will certainly contact you if they think the new technique may be helpful to your child.

Third, don't make your child feel like a failure. There's more to him and to his life than his reading difficulty.

Fourth, don't forget to give appropriate rewards and positive reinforcement for his successes, even small ones.

To summarize, keep a sense of proportion, do what is necessary, but don't overdo it. Of what value is it to improve your child's reading ability, if the cost leads to emotional bankruptcy? Too often, overly concerned parents sharpen the child's awareness of his difference from other children, which may lead to progressive withdrawal from social interaction with them.

The dyslectic child runs the risk of becoming part of a monotonous routine of doctor's visits, special tutors, long hours of study and drill at home, repeated failure experiences and a diminished sense of self-worth. These emotional factors compound the problem and are sometimes mistakenly identified as its cause. Remember that in many cases, children will catch up if they are not turned off by the whole reading experience.

My Son Can't Read. They Say He Has Dyslexia. Will He Ever Grow Out of It?

Everyone has heard or read about the famous figures in history who were dyslectic as children and who went on to major achievements in their respective fields of endeavor. One need only mention a few: Leonardo da Vinci, Albert Einstein and the late Vice-President Nelson Rockefeller. But it doesn't help our understanding of the problem to talk in terms of "growing out of."

We don't believe that a child grows out of dyslexia. The maturing child develops skills that can help compensate for a reading problem. The child can develop strategies that minimize the global effect of the reading problem, but we think that the child retains a reading problem. This does not preclude the possibility that the child can achieve mightily in specific areas of interest and intellectual pursuit.

What Is the Success of Reading Therapy in Helping Dyslectic Children?

This is probably one of the most difficult areas with which we have to cope. We cannot honestly say that the success rate has been terribly high with traditional kinds of reading therapy or remedial reading. There are some who feel that dyslexia can only be treated by teaching reading, and yet, in our own experience, we have found that using traditional techniques very often results in increased anxiety and increased inefficiency on the part of the child in such a situation. It is essential to discover the particular key, the unique individual approach, that will turn a child on. We must find something that the child will relate to best and that will help develop a positive motivation; something that will allow him to sustain the effort.

In a recent book, Bettelheim stresses the importance of *meaning*. Merely teaching the mechanics of reading is not sufficient. We must help the child understand the meaning of the material being read. Thus, the conceptual and cognitive functions of the reading process require equal attention.

At the risk of repetition, we know of no "quick cures." We continue to stress a structured remedial approach, emphasizing vocal-auditory methods of reinforcement. We build on areas of strength that have been identified for each child to develop a highly individualized program to meet his or her needs.

In addition to reading therapy, training in visual recognition and vocal-auditory reinforcement, we believe that psychotherapy oriented toward anxiety reduction and self-concept enhancement is very important. There is continuing interest and research in the areas of the neurophysiological and neuropsychological causes of this puzzling disorder.

What Is a Milestone?

The use of the term had its beginning in the field of pediatric neurology, where an attempt was made to look at what the normal developmental expectations were at any given chronological age in the growth of the infant and child. Actually, the pioneering work in this field was that of Arnold Gesell and his co-workers who compiled records of thousands of children to make his observations and establish the norms. These are given in ranges during which time we would expect to see an average child sit up or begin to say single words, and so on. A developmental or maturational lag is identified when a child fails to achieve these milestones by the expected age.

At What Age Should a Pediatrician Be Able to Determine That There Is Some Developmental Lag?

A well-trained pediatrician can certainly recognize the child with a real developmental problem by the time the child is two months old. As a matter of fact, an examination of infants shortly after birth by a trained team of doctors and other specialists at The Long Island College Hospital has identified some children considered to be at risk, who later showed signs of learning disability.

What Does Maturational Lag Mean?

This term is used to describe (if not to explain) a failure on the part of the child to acquire sensory-motor skills that are identified as being within the normal range for a given age, skills that we call milestones. For example, the examiner is presented with the fact that the child is three years old and is not yet saying "Mama" and "Dada," or that the child is two and one half and not walking independently. If after a very careful and comprehensive assessment is made and no specific neurological, medical or psychological areas of deficit are identified, the examiner is left with the term, for want of a better one, *maturational delay*. It would be inappropriate to use the term to describe such failures if there was evidence of impaired neuromotor function or psychological deficit. It is a term used to describe an existing condition whose origin can only be inferred.

What Is Dysgraphia?

The inability to produce in written form letters, numbers and words has been designated dysgraphia.

What Is Dysmusica?

This is an inability to recognize musical sounds or notes or reproduce them.

What Is Dyscalculia?

This describes an inability to do simple arithmetic functions involving them, such as counting a column of figures. We can make some of the same generalizations about dyscalculia that we have about dyslexia. Visual perception of numbers is impaired, thereby blocking the meaningful interpretation of these numbers in the brain. As is known, we do not actually see with our eyes; the eyes are simply like the lens of a very sophisticated camera. The image that is recognized and acted upon is visualized in the brain.

What Do They Test When They Ask Children to Name Body Parts?

We are essentially testing body concepts that are the result of two major influences. One influence involves the acquisition of information that later becomes the basis for performance on intelligence testing. Whether it's simply a folk pattern or something else, most of us in our own child-rearing experiences have gone through the playful type of game saying "Show me your nose," "Show me your eyes," and so forth. It seems to be a natural part of the child-rearing process. To the extent that this becomes incorporated into standardized tests like the Stanford-Binet, where a child is shown a picture of a small child and asked to indicate the nose and the eyes and so on, it then becomes a measure of how well he has learned those things that are part of the experience of most children.

But it has a broader significance, and this concerns the psychodynamic interpretations of body concept and how comfortable a child feels with his body. This extends beyond "Show me your eyes" and "Show me your nose" and gets into things such as his feeling of comfort in dealing with the sexual areas and excretory functions of the body. And it tells us something about the emphasis and the extent of the taboos still placed on these parts of the body, even by enlightened young parents.

What Is the Relationship Between Food Additives and Diet and the Treatment of Learning-Disabled Children?

As yet, there is no conclusive evidence that there is long-term benefit from changes in diet or the elimination of additives for the majority of learning-disabled children. This certainly does not mean that there may not be some children who show dramatic changes and improvement in behavior and amelioration of symptoms with changes in diet. However, study data indicate that the symptoms of the vast majority of cases of children described as "hyperactive" are not related to additives in their diet. On the other hand, one might say that since food dyes have no nutritive value, why not simply eliminate them from the child's diet?

Unfortunately, we are in a field where despite a growing body of knowledge, there is still much to be learned. When science is in this stage of development we can expect to see new "miracles" every five years. And philosophically, we distrust panaceas; single answers to a whole constellation of problems. Life simply doesn't work that way and it never has.

As an example, about twenty years ago, a study was published that asserted the claim to have found a cure for mental retardation. The "miracle" substance was glutamic acid and the claim was that its inclusion in the diet of a group of institutionalized children significantly raised their IQ levels. Later it was found that particular group of children had been fed a diet that was extremely low in protein, and the glutamic acid merely provided the protein that was needed for good, healthy development. This enabled them to function better. However, this did not prove a relationship between glutamic acid and an increase in IQ, but rather between protein deficiency and IQ.

As concerned professionals we keep open minds to developments in the field, but at this time we are not prepared to suggest that controlled diet—the elimination of additives or food coloring from a child's diet—will bring about a significant improvement in large groups of these children.

What About the Megavitamin Theory?

The use of massive doses of vitamins as a form of treatment has to fall into the same category as that of the food additives, diet control and food coloring. There are reported instances where megadoses of vitamins have helped, but there have been no conclusive large-scale studies that they are of major long-lasting benefit. In addition, large doses of vitamins (particularly fat-soluble ones) over a long period of time may result in harmful side effects.

Is There Any Differentiation in the EEG or Brain-Wave Patterns for Hyperactive Children and Those with MBD?

The use of the electroencephalogram (EEG) is a part of a comprehensive work-up for any child. The data derived from this examination have not, in general, provided any significant new knowledge nor have they yet significantly helped to identify the child with MBD. Their main use has been to identify the child with an epileptic disorder.

Currently, there are a number of programs in which EEG patterns are being analyzed in different ways, with the help of computers. The use of this technology, which can analyze very small differences, may begin to help us derive some additional clues and make better use of the EEG data in helping to diagnose children, who manifest symptoms of MBD or ADD.

What Is the Value of Patterning Programs?

We have had considerable experience with patterning over the years, and we have found it of minimal value at best, and potentially damaging, at worst. Parents are often made to feel responsible for the child's difficulty and are expected to commit themselves to an extremely demanding, intensive program of exercise each day. In addition, siblings are often denied the attention they need to foster healthy growth and development because of the almost total concentration on the handicapped child. We regret that recent articles appearing in pediatric journals are, once again, placing inordinate responsibilities on parents.

What Is the Federal Government Doing to Help Children with Learning Disabilities?

The government has a number of programs, as a result of constant and insistent pressure from parents and concerned professionals, and is beginning to recognize its responsibilities in this area. This is reflected in such legislative acts as Public Law 94-142-Amended "The Education for All Handicapped Children Act." These efforts on the federal level generally channel funds through state educational departments. These departments are required by law to have a comprehensive plan, including the specific ways in which they are making provision, within the various communities and the various school districts, for special education for learning-disabled children. These plans must be approved by the federal government to make local government eligible for matching and revenue sharing funds. The federal mandates have begun to spur states to develop comprehensive planning for learning-disabled children by developing annual and five-year plans.

If There Is a Federal Requirement to Aid Learning-Disabled Children, Why Aren't These Programs in Existence in All States?

There are probably a number of reasons, not the least of which is that there is a prevalent feeling that the federal government imposes very stringent and very costly programs and has been very slow in coming up with the dollars to fund them. Also, the economic climate that has prevailed during the last several years poses a problem. With continuing cutbacks, it has been a matter of shifting priorities. Since special education is a relatively new priority, it has not fared well in relation to other more established priority items.

What Is an Individual Educational Plan?

The IEP is, in fact, part of the mandate in the legislation that we referred to previously. It developed because there were too many instances in which proposed special educational programs were so general in their description that they were not uniquely tailored to the needs of the individual. And as our research has become more sophisticated it has become evident that this kind of individual planning is an absolute requisite.

We might also say that another source that has given impetus to the development of this kind of plan has been recent attention given to the treatment (or lack of treatment) offered to the mentally retarded. That is, the criticism of the huge, depersonalizing institutions that were serving essentially as "warehouses," a term that came into widespread use during the Willowbrook exposé. These children, including those with severely limited intellectual potential, now have the benefit of an individual educational plan, addressed to the specific strengths of the individual, with adequate recognition of the weaknesses and disabilities. It requires formulation of a long-term goal and a series of short-term objectives in order to move toward the long-term goal. And it is required that these goals be stated in behavioral terms, so that progress can be measured and quantified. These efforts begin to address the issue of "accountability" in the administration of programs designed for children with special educational needs.

Is There Any Connection Between Learning Disability and Juvenile Delinquency?

At this time there is not sufficient evidence to pinpoint a cause-and-effect relationship between the two; nor would we want to suggest a physiological connection. However, much experience suggests that there is a relationship in some instances, and in such cases factors in addition to learning disability play a role.

Take the case of a child who was disruptive at home and who begins first grade with the reputation of being a bit wild. School is supposed to "straighten him out," but instead compounds his problem. He doesn't do as well as the other children academically and so substitutes clownish or aggressive behavior to draw attention away from his failures, failures that he has already experienced at home.

This, in turn, is distracting and disturbing to the other children in the class. The child occupies an inordinate amount of the teacher's attention and significantly interferes with the classroom learning process and perhaps the attitude toward learning for all of the children in that setting.

Suspension doesn't help, and as the child becomes older he falls farther and farther behind until he just can't stand the hurts inflicted by repeated failure. He drops out of school, hangs around his neighborhood, perhaps doing menial jobs or perhaps not. In either case, he is unemployable in the mainstream of society. He has no marketable skills there, but he does in the street world, and he may decide to use them.

III. THE CENTRAL NERVOUS SYSTEM

The human brain is infinitely more sophisticated than any computer that now exists or that is even in the planning stages for the foreseeable future. It is unlikely that these wonderful machines will ever rival the brain in its capacity for thought and memory. The most advanced computers today can store approximately 250,000,000 bits of information. The National Archives in Washington, D.C., contains roughly 12,500,000,000 bits of information. The individual human brain has been estimated to contain 100,000,000,000 cells capable of storing information. There is continuing research to assess the brain's ability to store information, and it is our opinion that further research will reveal an even greater capacity than is currently projected.

The brain controls and directs a system of nerves that receives impressions from outside, makes sense of them, and then implements a course of responsive action or reaction. It translates written symbols into thoughts, takes aural impulses and recognizes them as words and extracts their sense. In addition, it interprets the tactile sensations, tastes and odors that surround us every day. It continuously makes decisions about which impulses to pay attention to and which to ignore, unlike the camera which passively records everything within its scope, or the open microphone picking up every stray sound indiscriminately. The brain is not only the most remarkable organ, pound for pound, in the human body; it is the most remarkable organ in the natural realm.

HISTORICAL DEVELOPMENT OF KNOWLEDGE

The exact function of the brain has been one of the most persistently debated questions in all of medical and psychological history. And the knowledge that we now possess has been amassed slowly and painstakingly. That knowledge is far from complete, but it does represent a tremendous advance over that of the earliest researchers. The greatest anatomist of classical antiquity was Galen (A.D. 129–199) whose work led him to designate functional areas of the brain. He postulated that the cerebellum contained motor nerves and that sensory nerves were to be found in the cerebrum.

During the medieval period attention was directed toward the ventricles, the four small cavities within the brain. It was thought that the various mental processes took place in one or another of these cavities. While attention shifted from the mass of the brain to the spaces within it, the notion that specific areas of the brain were responsible for specific functions was still generally accepted. According to the medieval scheme, one of the ventricles (hollow spaces) made images, another manipulated these images and processed the raw information, and the resulting knowledge was then stored in yet another ventricle. It was a neat and tidy theory but bore little relationship to the actual processes of the brain.

During the Renaissance, when philosophical and artistic attention was redirected to the models of classical antiquity, medical researchers rejected the medieval idea of the brain's operations and returned to the classical model. While the classical anatomists had done pioneering work, their methods were somewhat primitive and several misconceptions resulted. One of these was that the nerves were actually fine little hollow tubes, through which passed some type of "animal spirits" which were generated in the brain, stored in the ventricles and sent out as needed. Renaissance scholars also put great store by a mysterious collection of blood vessels called the "rete mirabile," which was uncovered in the dissection of animal brains. No special function could be attributed to it, so it was postulated that it must have something to do with thought processes. The difficulty was that this mass of vessels did not exist in humans but was found in the ox and the pig, the animals on which most of classical anatomical research was based. The force of tradition was so strong that most anatomists of the Renaissance persisted in placing it in their drawings of human anatomy.

André Vesalius (1514–64), the greatest of the Renaissance anatomists, had the courage to break with the classical anatomists when his own research did not confirm their findings. He thus rejected the "rete mirabile" vigorously and established the foundations of subsequent anatomical inquiry. By the end of the sixteenth century, medical schools were teaching that the spinal column contained bundles of nerves that descended from the brain and radiated out to all parts of the body.

The most significant advance made at about this time was the discovery, by the English anatomist William Harvey (1578–1657), of the circulation of the blood through the vascular system, by means of the pumping action of the heart. Harvey substantially challenged the thesis, held by nearly all philosophers and researchers up to that time, that the heart was the seat of the emotions and the soul. Partially in response to Harvey's challenge, more attention was directed to the function of the brain as related to emotions.

Franciscus de la Boe, also called Sylvius (1614–72), after whom the large fissure in the brain, the "Fissure of Sylvius," was named, postulated that the actual places in which the "animal spirits" were manufactured were the cerebral cortex and the cerebellar cortex. Little was added to our knowledge of the operations of the central nervous system during the eighteenth century except that the erroneous concept of "nerve fluid," bearing kinship to the classical Greek "Humors," had replaced the equally erroneous idea of "animal spirits." Both notions were based on a view of nerves as being little, thin, flexible pipes through which these spirits or fluids flowed.

Franz Joseph Gall (1758–1828), a German physician, conceived the pseudoscience of phrenology toward the beginning of the nineteenth century. He was a good anatomist but a poor theoretician. His careful examination of the brain suggested to him that the humps and fissures of the cerebral cortex denoted specific locations for individual mental processes and that the sizes of these humps and fissures indicated the strength of the function located there. In drawing other researchers' attention to the specific locations of functions, he stimulated thinking about this localized approach to function, but his attempt to discern such qualities by the examination of the irregularities of the skull was quickly discredited.

To a great extent the modern concept of the brain's operations emerged by the end of the nineteenth century. (Gall's work, while largely discredited, did stimulate research interest in this area.) The cortex was stimulated with low-voltage electrical current by a number of researchers to produce observable responses, and the great mapping activity of the brain occupied the largest part of brain research activities through the early twentieth century. The motor and perceptual areas were identified, and the hill (gyrus) and gully (sulcus) surface of the brain was recognized as a highly organized entity with specific functions, rather than the somewhat random-looking bundle of "intestinal" coils that had struck previous generations.

There is still a great deal to be learned about the precise operations that transpire within the brain that enable us to think and act as we do, and perhaps some of these operations will always remain tantalizingly out of reach. However, the picture of a purposefully organized and related system of chemical and electrical impulses, directed from specific locales within the cortex and controlling the flow of stimuli and responses, has been drawn.

While we shall be describing specific centers for certain functions, we must remember that the brain operates as a whole.

GENERAL OPERATIONS OF THE BRAIN

The upper portion of the brain is comprised of two hemispheres, the right and the left. Each side is divided into four major lobes; the *frontal,* the *parietal,* the *occipital* and the *temporal.* Each of these lobes is involved in specific functions. Visual stimuli are processed in the occipital lobe. The parietal lobe handles spacial and perceptual stimuli. Now if we look at the medial aspect of the brain, the *corpus callosum* can be seen connecting the two hemispheres, the right and the left. In view also are the limbic lobe and the hippocampal gyrus, which lie on the inner side of the temporal lobe and are considered by many to be the vital areas for the emotions and, less certainly, for memory. The frontal lobe controls motor functions. The temporal lobe is the end station for hearing, and the posterior and lateral section of the superior temporal convolution is where Wernicke's area is located. This is where interpretation of auditory stimuli takes place.

The *medulla* regulates breathing and heartbeat, those functions that are referred to as the vital signs. If the individual sustains an injury to the medulla, such as a vascular hemorrhage, death is almost inevitable. In contrast, if one sustains an injury, such as a stroke, to the upper portions of the brain, there may be a loss of certain sensory or motor functions, or a paralysis, but the individual does not necessarily die. In addition, many descending fibers from the two hemispheres cross over in the medulla en route to the spinal cord.

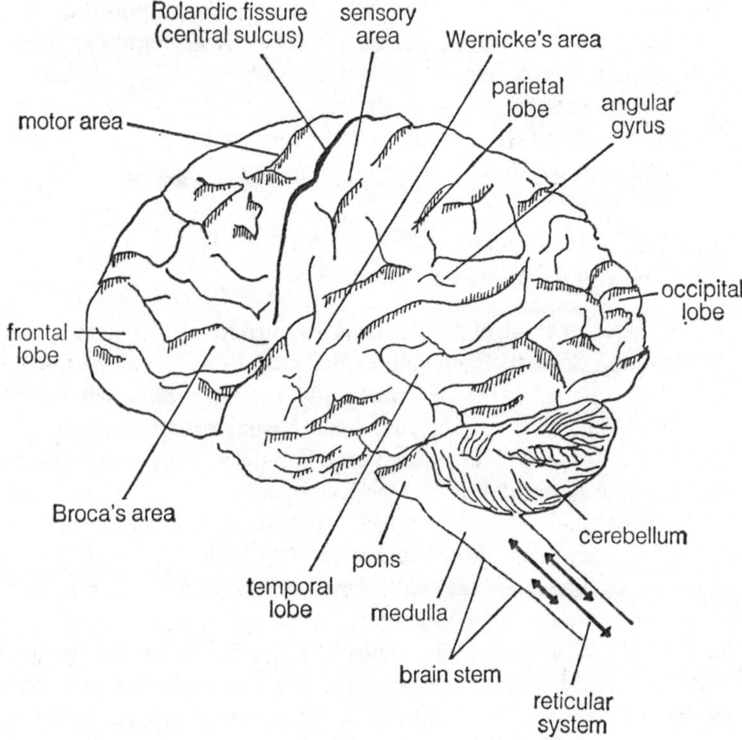

Fig. 1. Lateral view of the brain.

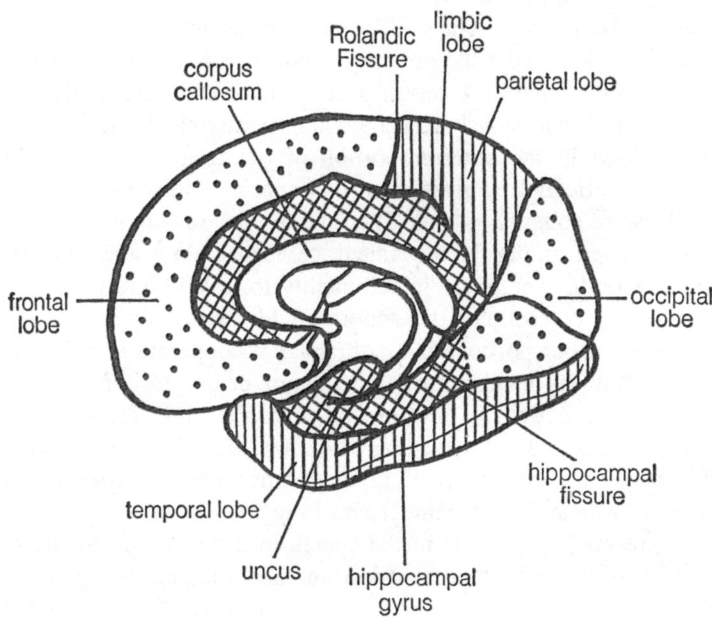

Fig. 2. Medial view of the cerebral hemisphere.

Just above the medulla is the *pons,* the Latin word for bridge. The *pons* contains nuclei of cells associated with the eyes, face and auditory apparatus. Thus, injury in the area of the pons might result in facial paralysis.

The *cerebellum* controls coordination and balance, and enables the individual to walk a straight line without lurching and staggering like someone under the influence of alcohol. It also has some inhibitory effect on portions of the cortex and severing some of these fibers has helped some people suffering from Parkinson's disease. The cerebellum also refines all of our movements.

For example, take the ordinary action of stretching out one's legs while seated. There are several factors involved. First the individual has to think consciously that he wants to stretch the legs, and that takes place in the anterior portion of the frontal lobe. The post-sensory, parietal area gives a sense of spacial distance through which the legs are going to extend. Then the motor area commands the act itself. In performing the movement, cerebellar fibers assist in imparting a smooth, even, coordinated quality to it. Without the participation of the cerebellum, the action would be wobbly and irregular. There are other portions of the brain that cooperate in this refining action, but the cerebellum is the major center for fine and gross coordinating activity. There are other bodies and hollow spaces in the brain that we are not going to discuss, since for the purposes of this book we are interested in the central nervous system and its capacity to learn, to remember and to express ideas.

There are nerve tracts in the spinal cord that go up to the brain and other tracts that go down from the brain to the spinal cord. Areas of the brain are connected by a third set of nerve fibers that are referred to as association tracts. This means, then, that stimuli can proceed in a variety of directions, either directly or by way of these association pathways.

The brain, as we mentioned, is composed of more than 100,000,000,000 nerve cells, or neurons, that give forth electro-chemical signals. Each neuron consists of a body, a large main fiber called an axon, which transmits impulses away from the cell, and many branches of fibers called dendrites, which receive stimuli. The points at which a nerve impulse passes from one neuron to another are called synapses. Transmission of the messages that travel through the nerves is by way of electrical impulses that are modified at the synapses by chemical transmitters (such as dopamine, serotonin and norepinephrine). Without these transmitters, the message could not travel along the nerves, because they could not cross the synapses. These impulses carried by the neurons can be either excitatory or inhibitory; in either case, they determine our physical responses to environmental stimuli.

The cortex of the brain has two sides, the left and the right, and much interest has developed in recent years concerning the functions of either side. It is obvious that there would be no purpose in having the two sides doing the same thing; this would be a waste of a great deal of brain tissue. Consequently, researchers feel that the two sides have different purposes in order to maximize the functions of the brain.

The left side is specialized particularly in relation to speech and language. Tests have established that the area referred to as Broca's area in the left frontal cortex is closely related to the parts of the face that have to do with speech, including the tongue, lips, palate, larynx and facial muscles.

The right brain is felt to be more involved with spacial concepts, music, the recognition of complex visual patterns and perhaps emotional expression. It also seems to control perceptual analysis and non-verbal relationships. The bridge or connecting link between the two cortices of the brain is called the corpus callosum. Much recent experimental work on the brain has involved severing the corpus callosum in animals, then studying the effects of such separation. In a few instances the separation has been performed on humans as a by-product of the surgical removal of a tumor. In general, and particularly in the case of children, such separation does not have too great an effect, although in some instances involving adults, one side of the body fails to recognize what the other is doing.

The skeleton encloses the spinal cord and brain so that they are not subject to outside injury. The brain is not only covered by the bony skull, but between the brain and skull there are three membranes for protection. Between two of these membranes flows the spinal fluid, one of the purposes of which is to serve as a hydraulic cushion in case the skull is struck.

Because of its high consumption of the body's energy supply, the brain is very vulnerable to oxygen and glucose deprivation. We

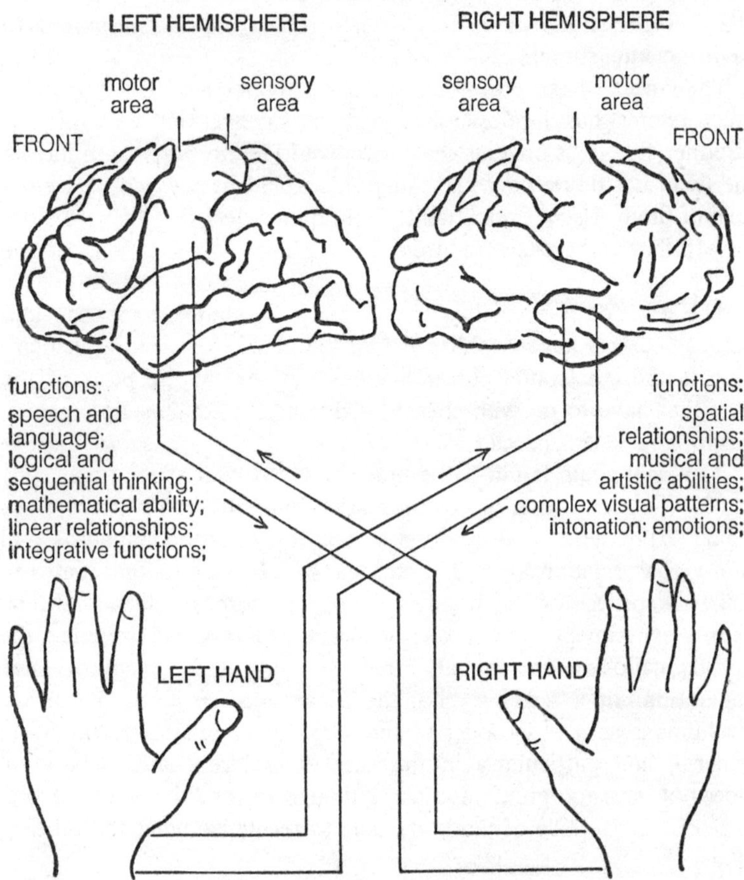

Fig. 3. Motor and sensory pathways to and from the hands are crossed so that each hand is primarily served by the cerebral hemisphere on the opposite side.

believe that hypoxia (diminished oxygen supply) during the birth process is the major cause of brain injury. As a result of a loss of oxygen-bearing blood, the brain's capillaries, the smallest of the blood vessels, begin to contract, the walls weaken, blood flows out and there are hemorrhages. However, in our experience we have occasionally seen babies who did not seem to breathe for quite some time after birth, and yet were perfectly fine ten years later. Others failed to breathe for only a few moments, received a lot of oxygen and survived but were devastated. This is especially true in premature birth. It is exceptionally difficult to predict what the outcome of such birth traumas will be.

THE BRAIN'S ROLE IN LEARNING DISABILITIES

Learning, as it involves the functional use of the brain, encompasses behavior and social responsibilities of society. The English philosopher Bertrand Russell aptly posed the question, "How is it that individuals, whose contact with the world is so short, personal and limited, are able to learn as much as they do?" The concept of the functioning of the brain has been defined as involving three large regions. While we shall describe these regions separately, it is important to emphasize that the entire brain functions as an integrated whole.

The first region is the brain stem and the reticular system. Looking again at a lateral view of the brain (p. 76) we see the brain stem nerve fibers passing down toward the spinal cord. Within this stem we have the reticular system, which is a bundle of fibers that goes up and down the brain stem and spinal cord and receives afferent stimuli from various parts of the cortex, the periphery of the body, the cerebellum and the vestibular apparatus. Normally, the reticular system functions to maintain wakefulness, to tone up and energize the cortex, to keep it responsive to all stimuli and to control the level of attention.

In the ordinary course of events, we are being constantly bombarded with stimuli. Right now while you are reading, perhaps a television set or a radio is playing in another room, and maybe traffic is going past the house in the street outside. It may be hot or cold in the room, and you may be drinking or eating something sweet. Thus we have a number of different stimuli arriving at the same

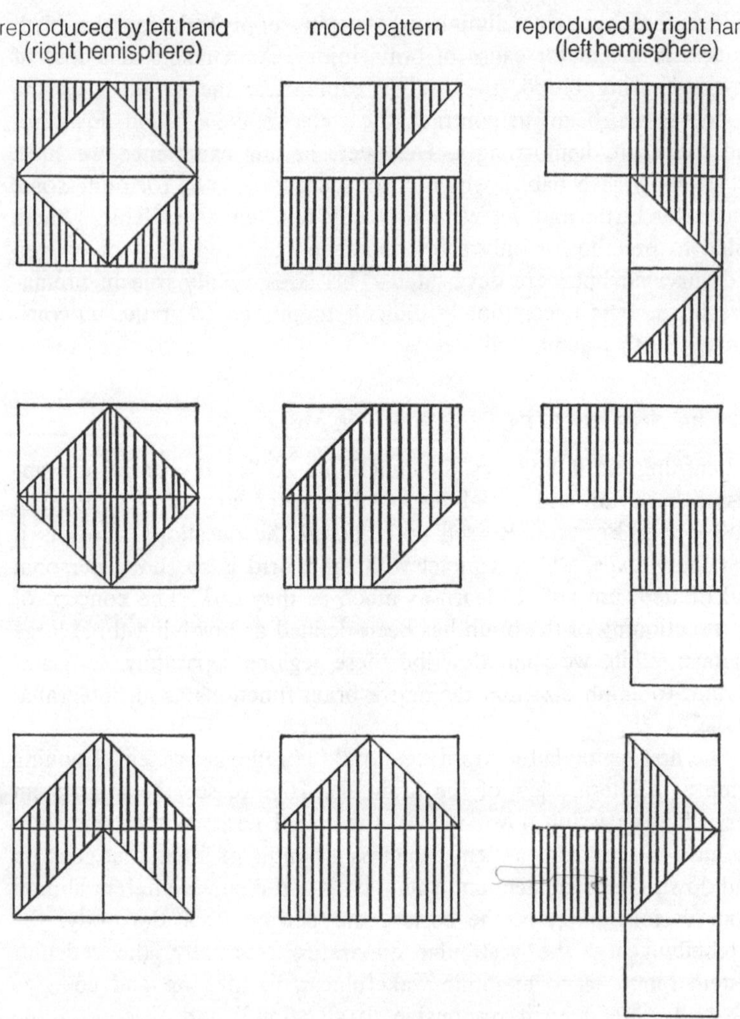

Fig. 4. The capabilities of the two hemispheres of the cerebral cortex were tested in a subject whose hemispheres had been surgically isolated from each other. The surgical procedure consisted of cutting the two main bundles of nerve fibers that connect the hemispheres (the corpus callosum and the anterior commisure). In the test, each of the patterns in the middle column was presented to the subject, who was asked to reproduce it by assembling colored blocks. The assembly was carried out either with the

time, and yet ordinarily you are able to concentrate on the reading of this book regardless of the other stimuli that are in the picture. This ability to concentrate is one of the functions made possible by the reticular system. It permits us to inhibit, and this is the cardinal word, the minor stimuli and to allow the major stimulus to take hold of one's attention.

The next major region is the area posterior to the Rolandic fissure, embracing the largest part of the brain. It includes the somatic or sensory system, the kinesthetic system, the visual system and the auditory system. Anatomically, it includes the parietal, occipital and temporal lobes. Here analysis, coding, storage and perhaps accumulation of information take place, permitting recall or memory. The final region is in the premotor frontal area, and it is here that planning and intention are carried out.

In 1861 Pierre Broca discovered, through autopsy examination, an area that now bears his name. He found that damage to this area resulted in inhibiting certain patients from speaking properly or using language adequately (aphasia). For a long time there was speculation over whether Broca's area was bilateral, but today it is felt that Broca's area in the left hemisphere is the primary speech area involved, even in left-handed individuals.

An interesting point is that in observing children after injury we see much greater recovery in the use of speech and language than one finds in adults. The reason for this is that the developing brain is, in general, more plastic. That is, it is less fixed with respect to function since localization has not yet taken place fully. There is,

---

right hand alone (which communicates mainly with the left hemisphere) or with the left hand alone (which is primarily controlled by the right hemisphere). Errors were equally frequent with both hands, but the kinds of errors typical of each hand were quite different. The results suggest that each side of the brain may bring a separate set of skills to bear on such a task, a finding consistent with other evidence that the hemispheres are specialized for different functions. What is equally apparent, however, is that neither hemisphere alone is competent in the analysis of such patterns; the two hemispheres must cooperate. The test was conducted by Edith Kaplan of the Boston Veterans Administration Hospital.

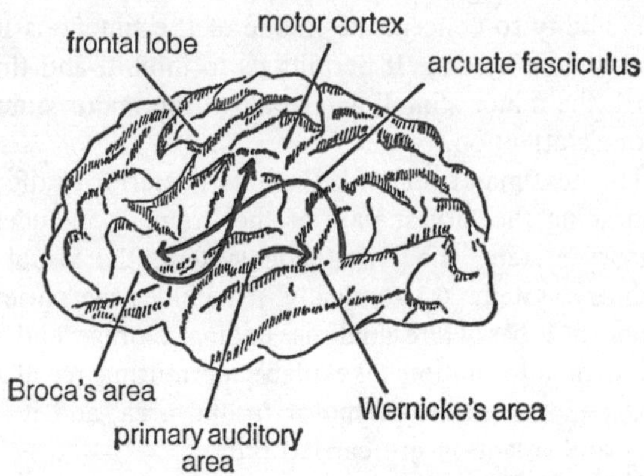

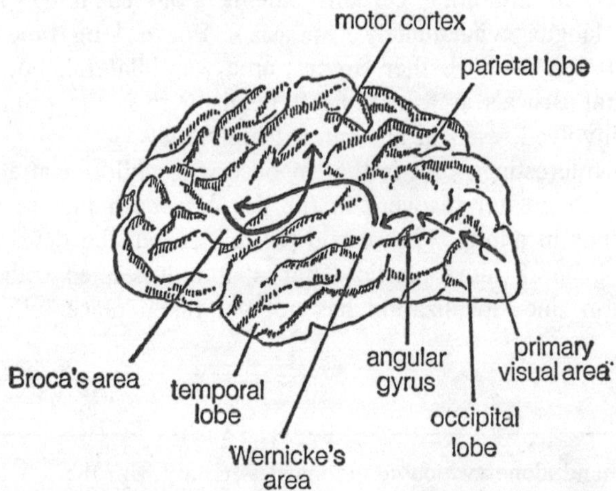

Fig. 5. Linguistic competence requires the cooperation of several areas of the cortex. When a word is heard (upper diagram), the sensation from the ears is received by the primary auditory cortex, but the word cannot be understood until the signal has been processed in Wernicke's area nearby. If the word is to be spoken, some representation of it is thought to be transmitted from Wernicke's area to Broca's area, through a bundle of nerve fibers called the arcuate fasciculus. In Broca's area the word

therefore, a much greater chance for the right hemispheric Broca's area to take over some of this function and permit normal expression of language. We might point out here that speech and language are not synonomous. Language involves the use of vocal sounds or written symbols to form, express and communicate thoughts and feelings. Speech is a more limited concept, related to the act of uttering sounds.

When a child does have a Broca's lesion, he speaks in a halting, slow manner and is apt to drop some of his nouns or verbs, or perhaps will use only one or two words to express himself. We call this condition *telegraphic speech.* At the same time the child may be able to sing perfectly. This curious fact makes it clear that telegraphic speech is not due to a paralysis of that area of the motor cortex that actually controls the use of the muscles, but rather that it results from a defect in the use of symbols and language (expressive aphasia).

The next great discovery was made by Carl Wernicke about fifteen years later. He found that a lesion in a certain portion of the temporal lobe still allows a child rhythmical, grammatical speech and articulation, unlike Broca's lesion, but that the speech is devoid of content. Jargon or unintelligible, garbled speech may characterize the child's vocal output. He uses many words to attempt to explain and describe what he cannot make sense out of. He may also speak of non-related subjects. When invited to participate in the ordinary conversational exchange "How are you?" "I'm fine," he has extreme difficulty. Normally, the stimulus (the question) passes through the ear apparatus and finally comes to the superior portion of the temporal convolution of the brain. At this point the sound is sorted and analyzed and begun to be put into shape. It then passes to the

---

evokes a detailed program for articulation, which is supplied to the face area of the motor cortex. The motor cortex in turn drives the muscles of the lips, the tongue, the larynx and so on. When a written word is read (lower diagram) the sensation is first registered by the primary visual cortex. It is then thought to be relayed to the angular gyrus, which associates the visual form of the word with the corresponding auditory pattern in Wernicke's area. Speaking the word then draws on the same systems of neurons as before.

Wernicke system where the syllables are organized into what we call *phonemes* and arranged and coded to begin to make sense out of what has been said. Finally, the stimulus is transmitted by a series of fibers back to Broca's area, from where a stimulus to the motor area produces the vocal response. This all transpires with enormous speed but here has been broken down step by step to demonstrate the chain of interactions that are involved. In a child with a lesion in Wernicke's area, this sequence of steps is interrupted somewhere along the way.

When a child is asked to spell, he starts out with the same circuit processing of the auditory stimulus, but in addition, he also uses the visual pattern of the word. The processing of visual patterns takes place in the angular gyrus. With this additional visual information the stimulus then returns through the arcuate fibers to Broca's area and he spells! The contribution of the angular gyrus system is to give us visual symbolization. Similarly, when a child is asked to read, he uses the visual area in the occipital lobe. This visual stimulus is passed on to the angular gyrus for a visual symbol, and finally to Wernicke's area for the auditory pattern. These are all associated movements, and that is what we mean by pointing out that the first zone receives material, the second sorts it out but the third zone actually does the integration. The third zone contains the deep fiber pathways that connect with other areas.

The process of writing brings in a new area altogether. We need both vision and spatial concepts to write accurately, and the area of the parietal lobe is particularly involved with spatial relationships. To develop these spacial relationships involves a number of steps. In the first place, to recognize a letter we have to be able to realize that the letter is made up of short components (lines). This ability to recognize structure is made possible by a functioning parietal area. Secondly, there is the sequential arrangement of the letters, and thirdly, the question of right or left orientation of the letters.

It has been shown in clinical experiments that when a youngster is asked to write, he will often times move his mouth and is auditorially involved in expressing the same word that he is writing. If his lips are sealed or if he is asked to keep his teeth over his tongue so that he can't move it, he may make more errors in writing than he would without the restraint.

This has demonstrated the correlation between the articulation of the word and the writing of it. In the process of writing, then, the child uses the articulating system and the spatial system, as well as the visual system. In addition, he uses the frontal area to shape a sequence that makes common sense. Otherwise the individual might write a lot of words without any integrated meaning. These are the essential points in the neurology of learning that must be intact for children to achieve academically. An intact reticular system permits them to focus their attention on stimuli while the sensory system analyzes and stores information and the anterior portion of the frontal area controls planning. Both short- and long-term memory are essential in the learning process.

While we have discussed the neurological scheme of learning, it is obvious, of course, that there are certain other factors that enter into the picture. The human brain is affected both by genetic inheritance and by environmental factors during pregnancy, at the time of delivery and afterward. Some examples of genetic conditions are Down's Syndrome (chromosomal), phenylketonuria and galactosemia (biochemical). Recent evidence suggests that to some extent the susceptibility to schizophrenia may be genetic. One of the environmental factors that is significant during pregnancy is severe malnutrition of the mother. In experimental animals, it has been shown that if there has been a severe lack of nutrition in the early part of the pregnancy, the offspring will have a deficiency in the number of brain cells.

On the other hand, if the lack of nutrition occurs later in the pregnancy, the proper number of cells will be present in the brain but they will not function as well. In the latter instance, good nutrition after birth does permit full recovery of function. The point is that when the noxious agent operates in the early part of the pregnancy, it is much more deleterious than it would be later. And we have evidence of the harmful effects of rubella (German measles) when contracted by the mother early in the pregnancy. Other noxious agents are congenital syphilis or the ingestion of a large amount of alcohol or excessive smoking by the mother or the introduction of drugs into the system. The development of the fetus is also affected by the lack of certain hormones.

At birth there can be the devastating effect of birth injury, and subsequent to birth there may be problems related to infection of the brain or trauma. After birth, environmental factors such as deprivation of parental love and lack of stimulation of the child can be devastating, but these factors affect the thoughts and emotions, not the brain itself. A child's whole social environment, too, is important; it is a fact that children exposed to a broader cultural background or better surroundings are going to learn better than those denied such advantages. Similarly, those who have not been malnourished will generally have an easier time learning than those who have. All children are genetically endowed with a specific inheritance. We try to improve social life, emotional climate and nutrition so as to enable them to utilize and derive the maximum from that with which they have been endowed.

The explanation given in the preceding pages is intended only as an introduction to the capacity, structure and operation of the central nervous system.[1] While much has been learned, much still remains outside the current body of knowledge. Investigation of specific mechanisms is ongoing and will continue, we hope, to assist us to understand these minimal dysfunctions that afflict the learning-disabled child.

[1] While this discussion has dealt entirely with the Central Nervous System, the reader should also be aware of the Autonomic Nervous System (ANS). The ANS consists of the sympathetic and para-sympathetic systems, which control involuntary actions, such as breathing or blinking. A detailed description of the specific functions of the Autonomic Nervous System is beyond the scope of this book.

IV. PEDIATRIC NEUROLOGICAL EXAMINATION AND TREATMENT

Any child referred to us for evaluation begins with a comprehensive pediatric neurological examination. We do this before any of our other evaluations because we wish to establish the physical and neurological condition of the child right from the onset. Since the basis of our work is dependent upon a careful, differential diagnosis, we have to be able to distinguish between the subtle varieties of conditions we encounter. Poor attention, for example, could be related to a petit mal form of epilepsy. A child who is unable to function effectively in gym might have a slight motor problem.

Pediatrics deals with the total care of the infant and child and the pediatric neurologist is a fully trained pediatrician. Medically, it takes up where obstetrical care leaves off after pregnancy and delivery of the newborn. In pediatric neurology we start with the broadest possible look at the child's general appearance, and then systematically narrow the focus of our examination to specific areas such as the senses, specific nerves and functions. The thorough, detailed physical examination helps us to recognize children suffering from neurosensory loss of hearing or vision, the child with mild cerebral palsy, mental retardation, the child suffering from posttraumatic or postoperative shock, the autistic infant, childhood schizophrenia or the child with a neurotic behavior disorder.

Overall, what we want to establish is whether the results of the neurological examination are normal or abnormal. If they are abnormal, we try to pinpoint the specific pathology. We want to be able to delineate whether the results are functional (i.e., emotional), physical or both. If there is an organic problem in a non-learning-disabled child, it is often limited to one side of the brain or the other. In the case of the learning-disabled child, however, it is less common to find neurological signs localized in one hemisphere; they are usually bilateral and diffuse.

Ordinarily, all examinations, even those in which children are found to have functional disorders, appear to fall within the normal range of neurological response, with the exception of some minor problems that we refer to as one or more of the "soft" neurological signs. These are sometimes difficult to elicit since they are minor or subtle. Some neurological signs are age related. Their presence is normal up to a certain age and abnormal when they persist after that age, such as a plantar (toe curling) reflex—also referred to as a Babinski reflex—in an infant over two or three years of age.

Of great importance, particularly when dealing with infants, is noting what the child can and cannot do in terms of the developmental milestones. These latter are demonstrated abilities that tend to appear in children at a given anticipated age or period of time and in a fixed sequence. Examples of such abilities are the capacity to sit up unassisted or to utter the first real words.

Our first procedure is to take a general history of the child, and this is perhaps the most important part of the pediatric neurological examination. We look for anything of significance that would involve the central nervous system (CNS) and cause damage or dysfunction in the brain.

We pay particular attention to the pregnancy, labor and delivery, and the period in the nursery. The birth and the few weeks afterward are designated as the perinatal period. We look to see whether or not this has been a stormy one, whether the child has had a difficult time during the birth process itself or in the nursery. We want to know whether the child required special care such as resuscitation or incubation to survive. The child's entire blood supply might have been exchanged because of Rh incompatibility with jaundice, or he might have had a case of meningitis or developed intracranial bleeding. All of these conditions can have a deleterious effect upon the brain. In brief, we want to know if any artificial means for supporting life had to be utilized during that time.

When we speak to the mother about the course of her pregnancy, we ask her about all sorts of subtle conditions that may have been neglected, such as mild elevation of blood pressure (hypertension), mild swelling of the ankles (edema), and the use of water pills, which might mean that she was toxemic during that time.

We also look for complications, such as a ruptured placenta, placental bleeding and so forth. We ask about her weight gain and if it was not too excessive (that is, under twenty-five pounds), we would not feel that it had been a contributing factor in any problems. However, if the maternal weight gain during pregnancy were excessive, then we would have to consider it as a possible cause of some problems during that time.

Toxemias of pregnancy are most often associated with hypertension. If such a constriction of the blood vessels does exist in the expectant mother, then the blood and oxygen supplied to the developing baby are also limited, and this could result in some type of brain injury or poor prenatal development.

Of course, we check for alcohol or drug abuse or rubella, but these are more readily identifiable conditions. Ordinarily, the mother will give us all this information as part of the history. In addition, immediately after birth the attending physician may see signs of the congenital rubella syndrome and some of the other conditions previously mentioned.

The value of the history depends a great deal on the historian, the person eliciting the information. He has to lead the parents, the mother usually, since they are not doctors or nurses. He has to describe clearly to them exactly what information is being sought and then they can be forthcoming with it.

We make note of the person or institution referring the child to us, first of all to make sure the interested party receives a report of our findings. It may be a physician or a school guidance counselor sending us a child, and since neurology, per se, is on a consultation basis rather than a primary-care basis, we refer the child back to the doctor who will take overall responsibility and who must have a complete record of our findings.

The history is developed both from the parents' account and from the hospital report where the child was born or treated. These are routinely requested and most often forwarded to us. In those instances where the reports are not available to us, we rely on the parents' statements and our own observations. Of course, many of the mothers have been given sedatives and anesthetics during the delivery, and they are not entirely aware of what actually happened, so that we have to gauge our impressions from what information we can gather. For example, it is routine in the United States for full-term, spontaneously delivered babies to be kept in the hospital for a period of three days, and children delivered by caesarian section for a week. Thus, if the mother informs us that she went home but that her baby stayed in the hospital for more than three days and was not delivered by caesarian section, we would conclude that there probably had been some complication, although we would not know the precise nature of it without a hospital report.

One of the things we look for in considering birth trauma is the presence of head injuries of any kind. We want to know how the child performed after delivery and if there were any seizures. Even though head injuries are often mild, in children they may be further complicated by a posttraumatic or postconcussion syndrome with psychological or emotional overtones. At other times, a head injury can bring about significant neurological sequelae. Of course, we are always interested in hospitalization for any reason at all, whether it is for elective surgery or an emergency admission. While we are keenly alert to neurological problems, we are basically concerned with the whole child and his total health status.

In addition to taking the history of the individual child, we also inquire about the family history, since many neurological syndromes are genetically determined. We look for relatives who have seizures, or are hearing impaired or who have a degenerative condition due to an enzyme deficiency. In the latter case, the child might seem to develop normally up to a point, and then show signs of deterioration.

Once all of this basic and very important information has been recorded we are ready to perform the physical examination of the child. This would normally begin with recording height and weight and head circumference, which we would evaluate according to the appropriate norms for the child's age and sex. Although we are primarily interested in neurological problems, we regard the child as a whole and examine him from head to toe. We look at his general appearance and try to gauge his mental state. The child's level of consciousness, his orientation, his ability to reason, and his developmental level are all tested. We want to know precisely what the child's awareness of himself and his environment is. Does he know, in an age appropriate context, where he is, what time it is, what day of the week, and what the date is? Can he name the various body parts? This portion of the examination consists of questions and answers and, of course, direct observation by the examining physician.

Part of the mental state is the child's concept of his own body. Let us say we ask the child to touch his left ear with his right hand and he successfully completes the task. This simple action gives us a great deal of information. First, it tells about laterality, that the child knows right from left. Secondly, it indicates awareness of body parts and comprehension of a command. Finally, it demonstrates the ability to execute a command in an orderly fashion.

In the case of the mentally retarded child or the infant who cannot answer questions (because of age), we test his awareness of the environment by seeing whether he reacts appropriately to a variety of sensory stimuli, such as the flashing of a light or the ringing of a bell. Once these general tests have been completed we proceed to examine more specific things, starting with speech.

Since we have already been speaking to the child or listening to any vocalizing that the infant may make, we have been able to observe the child's use of speech in a general way. One of the things that we look for is slurring of speech (*dysarthria*). This problem is usually neurological in origin, because the muscles responsible for speech production are controlled by the lower cranial nerves.

We are on the alert for a number of factors, but three in particular are of great importance. We want to see whether a child can construct sentences correctly, whether he can comprehend, and whether he can repeat. We also test his ability to name objects and to read and write. *Dysphasia* is the term that covers disturbance in language function because of injury to the higher cortical areas. Since language function resides in the left brain, we would assume some injury there if there is evidence of language disturbance.

Next, we try to determine whether *dyspraxia* exists; that is, the inability to execute skilled, learned movements for reasons other than weakness (paralysis) or sensory problems. We ask the child to perform a one-step action. "Pick up the pencil!" Then we give him a two-step action. "Pick up the pencil and bring it here!" Following this we ask him to perform a three-step action. We are looking for any inability on the child's part (excluding inability due to weakness or sensory problems) to execute the command. If he becomes confused and the process breaks down, we may be dealing with a dyspractic syndrome, which customarily involves the parietal lobe.

Next we ask the child to draw a person on a piece of paper. It is really up to the child to determine whether it will be an adult or a child, male or female. We do not offer any specific instruction other than to ask for a person. What the child will do is to execute a human figure according to his own concept of the body. Not what we think it looks like, or anyone else thinks it looks like, but what the child himself brings out of his perceptual set.

This is a very valuable exercise for us for several reasons. It helps us to determine the developmental age of the child, because there are established, age-related norms for various types of drawings. These norms take into consideration the number of details, the placement of the features, and the like. The drawing also gives us a clue as to whether we are dealing with an emotionally disturbed child. Such a child may render a highly distorted, sometimes bizarre human figure. Only after questioning the child about individual features are we able to determine what some of the details are meant to represent.

Another cerebral function related to the body image is the child's ability to identify his lateral parts—i.e., arms, legs, eyes—accurately as right and left, without confusion. This skill is not well-developed until the child is approximately six years of age. By age nine he should also be able to name correctly the examiner's right and left hand or eye upon request. If there is confusion about right and left, then perhaps this is one of the dyspraxias, or it might just be a lack of well-developed dominance, such as we encounter in ambidexterity. Such confusion only gives a clue that there may be some subtle or minimal impairment, but cannot be interpreted as a definitive sign of neurological damage.

To this point, the examination has been conducted through questions and observation of general tasks imposed on the child. Now we want to examine specific body parts such as the head, neck, spine and the organs of sensation.

Of all the senses, vision is the most important because we receive the greatest part of our knowledge about the world through our eyes. They have been referred to as the "windows of the soul," but on a very practical level they are windows of the body. Eye tissue is transparent, and with our instruments we can illuminate the inside of the eye and actually see the optic nerve, cranial nerve II. This is the only avenue through which we can directly examine a portion of the central nervous system.

There are twelve cranial nerves and they fall into several groups, which are primarily concerned with the proper functioning of the eyes, ears, nose and throat. The first group is comprised of the cranial nerves III, IV and VI. (The cranial nerves are always identified by roman numerals.) These respond to incoming visual stimuli and control the muscle movements of the eyes, so that when we ask the child to look to the left and then to the right, we are testing several functions at the same time. We look for any imbalance. For instance, when we hold up one finger to the right of the child, we observe that the eyes shift in that direction. At the same time we also ask the child how many fingers he can see. If he says "one" that is fine, but if he says "two" then we are aware that there is an ocular imbalance. Moving the eyes to the right and left is controlled by the frontal lobe of the brain. However, some children who can do this have difficulty with their tracking gaze; that is, following the moving finger, because this function is mediated by another area entirely, the occipital lobe at the rear of the brain.

We look at convergence by holding a finger directly in front of the child and moving it from a distance right up to the tip of the nose. In order to keep the finger in view it is necessary that the eyes move inward, toward one another, as the finger gets closer and closer to the tip of the nose. Conversely, when we ask the child to look into the distance, then the movement of the eyes should show a divergence as he widens the scope of his gaze to take in a larger field. The outward movement of the eyes is a more subtle action and it takes a trained observer to pick it up. Many people with increased intracranial pressure have some problem with the lateral muscles which limit the movement of the eyes. As a result, when they look at something far away, they see double because they cannot merge the image from both eyes on the same spot on the retina.

Before we look at the optic nerve, however, we run several other tests beginning with a standard eye chart examination. Usually, by the time that a child is five or six he has developed normal 20/20 vision. Decidedly lower visual acuity, particularly if there was some abnormality in the muscle function of the eyes, would cause us to refer the child to the ophthalmologist. We look at the visual fields to see whether there is any unusual condition present. Central vision refers to the area of the retina where the object that the individual looks at registers primarily, and the rest of the visual field takes in those areas that surround the central object and give us peripheral vision. If we do detect any abnormalities in these areas, the child could have either an eye abnormality or brain pathology.

For instance, if there were blindness or diminished vision in one half of the right visual field and one half of the left visual field, it is indicative of a dysfunction in the central nervous system almost 100 percent of the time. Because of the bilateral nature of the brain, we find nerve fibers from both eyes going to each of the two cerebral hemispheres, and such a symmetrical deficit would indicate that, in all likelihood, the eye itself was not impaired, but rather the brain. This difficulty could result in the failure of the child to see all parts of the blackboard.

The actual inspection of the eye concentrates first on the optic disc, which is the head of the optic nerve, and then moves to the retina, which is an extension of the nervous system. This inspection gives us a lot of information. For example, intrauterine infections may be revealed by abnormalities in the retina, and swollen optic nerve heads alert us to the presence of greater than normal intracranial pressure. If we observe hemorrhages in the eye, it may indicate some pathology occurring within the brain, although other conditions in the eye itself must also be considered.

The hearing examination is also important to us because if a child's hearing is impaired, he is at a definite disadvantage in the classroom; his inability to hear what the teacher is saying eventually leaves him behind in achievement. It is a popular, but erroneous, misconception that the hearing-impaired individual is not particularly bright. No doubt, the fact that such individuals did not respond to a vocal request with the appropriate answer was interpreted as a lack of understanding instead of a hearing deficiency. It wasn't that the person didn't know the answer. He didn't hear the question! Correct the hearing problem, and the child will benefit from normal instruction. We uncovered a particularly unhappy situation a number of years ago in which a child who was totally deaf had been inappropriately placed in a home for the mentally retarded for ten years. Unfortunately, we couldn't give him those ten years back, but we were able to set him on the road to a productive and rewarding future life.

The human ear can distinguish sounds in the range of twenty

to twenty thousand cycles per second, approximately. Hearing loss in the upper range can diminish consonant recognition, which is more debilitating than losses in the lower frequencies. A borderline hearing deficit requires that a child concentrate very intensively to hear what a teacher is saying. This requires a great deal of effort during the course of the day, and unless highly motivated, the child's attention is apt to wander and he will miss out on instructions. Children with very severe deficits in the upper frequencies are afflicted with speech impairment of varying degrees.

In our initial examination of hearing (cranial nerve VIII) we perform gross (not subtle) tests. In the case of the infant, we ring a bell and observe his reaction or lack of it, and his ability to trace the source of the sound by turning his head. We look for a reaction to whispered speech or the jingling of keys on a ring, sounds that reflect a lower level of stimulation. In the older child we test with a tuning fork, which is a much finer and more reliable test for hearing. With this examination we can detect whether there is any hearing loss in terms of air or bone conduction, since both can transmit sound. Air conduction is a much better medium, since a tone can be detected almost twice as long. We first place the finely vibrating tuning fork on the surface of the skin behind the child's ear where the mastoid bone is located (testing for bone conduction) and ask the child to signal us when he can no longer hear the sound. Right after that, we place it in front of the ear (air conduction). Usually the child will still be able to hear the tone. Individually, the length of time that a child can hear the sound when conducted by bone and the length of time that the child can hear the sound when conducted by air are significant. In addition, the relationship between the two amounts of time is significant. If the relative duration between bone and air conduction is abnormal, this may indicate a hearing problem attributable to middle-ear difficulty.

Testing taste (cranial nerves VII and IX) is very difficult and is not routinely done with children. Generally, alterations in the sense of taste are associated with neuropathological conditions which are rarely seen in children. We test the sense of smell, though the reliability of such testing is limited, particularly in children, because it may be interfered with by many factors, especially the common cold. Such testing is important, however, because in the case of head injury or trauma the olfactory nerve (cranial nerve I), which is the nerve that mediates smell, is most vulnerable to damage. We usually use coffee or any mild odor as a stimulus. We do not use perfume or alcohol or ammonia because these not only stimulate smell but the mucous membranes of the nose as well, and thus become an irritant.

The motor component of cranial nerve V controls the muscles of chewing and opening the jaw. In its sensory part, it mediates almost everything from the midportion of the head down to the angle of the jaw and out to the chin. From the sensory portion of this nerve we can test tactile and thermal sensation. We therefore determine whether the child can appreciate touch, pain, hot and cold. The tuning fork is also useful to us for general testing because the metal is cold and when rubbed in the hands warms up, so that we can gauge the child's broad reaction to heat and cold. Ordinarily, this simple test is enough to recognize a problem or lack thereof, but if we suspect any difficulty, we would then do further testing. As with most of the tests, when looking for a pain reaction, we do not offer an extreme stimulus to the child. We simply take a wisp of cotton and lightly touch the cornea of the eye, which should produce a blink bilaterally.

We further examine VII, which also controls smiling and facial expression. It stimulates muscles in the eyes as well as the mouth. It controls closing the eyelids, although opening the eyelids is controlled by cranial nerve III. Testing the seventh nerve is relatively simple and we usually ask the child to show us his teeth. We then look for facial asymmetry and mobility of expression.

Cranial nerves IX and X control a variety of functions, among them swallowing. For our examination, we determine that the palate is aligned with the uvula (that teardrop-shaped body that descends from the top of the throat). This is done by simple visual inspection. We also check the gag reflex at this time. A cotton applicator is gently touched to the back of the throat and we expect a rapid reaction. If the child is slow to gag, then there is some difficulty. Ordinarily, if the child was having difficulty swallowing, he or the parent would have told us about it and complained of frequent regurgitation. In addition to its function in this area, nerve X controls a number of the vital support systems, such as heartbeat and breathing.

Nerve XI controls the large muscles called the sternocleidomastoids, which stand out on the sides of the neck behind the ears, and other nearby neck muscles. We look for good strong muscle tone and we hold a hand to the child's jaw and tell him to turn his head against the resistance of the hand. As he does so we touch the sternocleidomastoid on the opposite side to gauge its firmness. The test is then repeated for the other side. This nerve also controls the shoulder muscles that keep the head oriented upright, and can be tested by asking the child to shrug his shoulders.

There are several important roles that these shoulder and neck muscles play. First of all, they keep the head aligned so that vision can function in a normal manner. These muscles also contain the receptors for the proprioceptive stimuli that facilitate the perception of spatial orientation. A combination of these impulses, along with the vestibular (balance) component of cranial nerve VIII and the dorsal columns of the spinal cord all work together to determine proper orientation and insure balance.

Cranial nerve XII is the last of the major cranial nerves. It controls the tongue, which is important for speech and for eating and tasting. The nerve is specifically motor. We test this nerve's functioning by asking the child to stick his tongue out, and it should emerge in the midline. Deviation to one side usually suggests damage to the cortex on the opposite side. We look also to see whether there is smooth movement of the tongue. A rippling of the tongue indicates that individual muscle fibers are contracting independently, and this should be taken as a warning sign. This test completes the examination of the cranial nerves and the various sense organs.

We next concern ourselves with the child's station and gait, by which we mean his posture in space and his walking ability. Frequently, if there is trouble in this area, a glance at the soles and heels of the shoes will reveal an uneven wear pattern, which suggests a problem even before we do any formal tests. When we look at posture, we are trying to determine whether there are any problems connected with cranial nerve VIII, the dorsal columns of the spinal cord or vision. The ability to balance depends on these three areas, and the individual can maintain balance with two out of the three intact, but not with only one.

We ask the child to stand with eyes closed and both feet together, hands dangling at the sides, in a steady position. There will be some slight swaying in most children. If the dorsal columns and the vestibular functions are working properly, there should be no real problems at all because of lack of the visual input. The child will be able to keep his balance. If there are problems with the dorsal columns and the child still has vestibular function and visual input, he will also be able to maintain balance. However, if we shut off the visual input of a child with a dysfunction in the vestibular system and the dorsal columns, he will begin to sway markedly. This is known as a positive Romberg sign and confirms the presence of the dysfunctions.

When we assess gait, we focus on the act of walking, the associated movements of the arms swinging to and fro, the foot positions, the pelvis, and the bearing of the head. In children with mild hemiparesis (weakness on one side of the body), there is very little arm swing on that side. We also look for foot drop, which causes the child to compensate by lifting the foot very high, as if he were going to cross a stream by stepping from stone to stone.

A broad-base gait occurs in several muscle diseases, especially diseases involving the proximal muscles of the extremities. To walk, the child has to shift his center of gravity from side to side; he is not able to maintain it in the midline as is usual. We also ask the child to walk on his heels and on his toes. Inability to heel walk means either that there is a peripheral nerve or a central nervous system problem, and we would try to distinguish between the two with further testing. Inability to walk on the toes usually indicates a peripheral nerve problem. We also ask the child to tandem walk, which is ordinary heel and toe walking along an imaginary line. Deviation from the line could indicate cerebellar trouble, since the function of the cerebellum is to moderate gross movements into finer, smooth ones by filtering out undesirable impulses.

The motor functions of the body consist of coordinated, appropriate muscular responses to stimuli. To test motor functions we first examine the large muscle groups, flexors and extensors, of the arms and legs. We ask the child to "make a muscle" and then gauge the tone by squeezing the biceps. We also look at the size of the muscles by simple visual inspection to see that they are as developed as we would expect for his particular age. Then we ask the child to hold his arm straight and not allow the examiner to bend it at the elbow, and in this way we derive a sense of the strength of the triceps. We are on the alert to see any differences between one arm and the other. By flexing the arm and asking the child to resist extension we test the biceps.

The young child between seven and ten years of age is reasonably strong and it can be difficult for the examining physician to overcome his power, so one can get a clear sense of his strength. With an infant, of course, it is entirely different and we look to see if one arm is markedly stronger than the other. If we observe this, it tells us that we have a problem in either the nerves or the muscles, and we would have to test further. We ordinarily expect to find more or less symmetrical development of the limbs whether a child is right- or left-sided.

Another important component in the working of the muscles is their coordinated use, and so we give the child a few simple tests to see how well coordinated he is. We ask him to touch the tip of his finger to his nose, to rotate his forearms showing us palms up and palms down, to touch each finger to his thumb in sequence, and maintain his arms stretched out in front of himself. If he is not able to do these tasks smoothly and accurately, it indicates some disorder in the cerebellum. An inability to place blocks on top of one another or to reproduce geometric figures with pencil and paper alerts us to another dysfunction that may be either perceptual or perceptual-motor.

Even before testing specifically for coordination, we have had a chance to see how well coordinated a child is by watching him unbutton and button his clothes and untie and tie his shoelaces. These are, in reality, tests of coordination, though they are not labeled as such. When we see a child able to do these things and to write his name in script he has already demonstrated a great deal of coordination. Clumsiness in and of itself may not necessarily indicate organic damage. We try to determine whether or not the child is nervous or uncertain of himself and whether this might be causing his awkwardness.

During this part of the examination we note any involuntary movements such as tics, which involve repetitive blinking of the eyes or constant facial grimacing. These may indicate dysfunction of a nerve or may only mean that the child is nervous, so we test further to determine which it is. Abnormal involuntary movements, called athetoid or choreiform, are jerky movements of the extremities that are repetitious but do not occur in the same area every time. Athetoid movements are much slower, more sustained, and of greater amplitude than choreiform movements. Both involve the extremities, especially the hands and the feet, as well as the trunk, neck and facial muscles. Athetoid movements disappear during sleep. Another group of involuntary movements are called dystonic movements and are more generalized, involving greater areas of the body simultaneously.

Now we test for reflexes, which are expected to be prompt and automatic. There are ten of them, including the well-known "knee jerk," and we look for symmetry in response from both limbs. We test the deep tendon reflexes by tapping the knee, for example, and we look for a muscle response. These responses are stress reflexes, first stretching the tendons and then immediately contracting them. These are normal responses that are usually depressed or absent if there is a peripheral nerve problem. They are very exaggerated when there are brain or various spinal-cord problems. Another reflex test involves stroking the surface of the skin to watch for muscle contractions (such as toe curling). In all of the above tests, the reactions are outside of the child's conscious control.

Another type of touch test is to see whether a child can display two-point discrimination, which requires a greater discrimination than simple recognition of touching. We apply two prongs to the finger, palm, or anywhere on the surface of the body and ask the child to tell us whether he has been touched with one or two points. More exact assessment involves varying the distance between the prongs. It is the function of the peripheral nerves and the dorsal columns of the spinal cord to transmit the stimulus, but the individual needs the brain (parietal lobe) to make the discrimination. An intact transmission network is only part of the identification process. The impulses have to be sorted out by the brain.

These tests are getting at finer cortical functions. We look for other kinds of touch recognition (stereognosis) by giving the child familiar objects, without letting him see them, and asking him to identify them. A house key or marble or coin are frequently used for these tests. The child with parietal-lobe damage will not be able to identify the objects with his eyes closed. He feels the object because his sense of touch is functioning, but he will misidentify it or not be able to hazard a guess. We also might ask a child to tell us which of two objects is heavier or larger, and if he has parietal-lobe damage, he will not be able to do so. This condition is called astereognosis.

The autonomic nervous system is concerned with tearing, perspiration, salivation, and the color and temperature of the skin. We note if there is excessive perspiration or an overall skin color that we characterize as "blanch" or "blush," depending on whether it is excessively pale or ruddy. These abnormal states are caused by a malfunction in the autonomic nerves that control the blood vessels of the skin.

By the time that we have completed the standard pediatric neurological examination, we have a pretty good picture of the functioning of the child's central nervous system as well as his general well being. However, if there are any areas that require further exploration, we may ask for chromosomal or chemical tests to screen for toxic agents or enzyme deficiencies. The EEG test will give us evidence of seizure disorder, and a CAT Scan (Computerized Axial Tomography) enables us to examine the brain for lesions and tumors with greater clarity than ever before. Finally, cortical, auditory, visual and spinal cord evoked potential techniques have been developed which help us in testing for vision, hearing and somatosensory disturbances, respectively, when conscious responses are difficult to obtain.

❦

The tests described in this chapter stimulate precise, measurable neural responses from specialized portions of the central nervous system. They provide us with objective data. The two following case histories demonstrate the types of deficits that are detected during the course of the pediatric neurological examination.

Michael, an eleven-year-old in the eighth grade, was referred to us by a private pediatrician because of hyperactivity and behavioral problems in school. The school reported that he was constantly distracted by other children and couldn't attend to an academic exercise on a sustained basis. In addition, he annoyed the other children.

His birth history was normal. He was the product of a full-term gestation and spontaneous birth. He had an uneventful medical history, though he was always an active child. Our examination revealed nothing out of the ordinary. The cranial nerves were normal and everything else in the way of reflexes and muscle tone were normal. An electroencephalogram was taken and revealed some mild abnormality, but did not identify any specific pattern. He had been treated with Dilantin and Ritalin for two years previously by the private pediatrician without any success in controlling the hyperactivity, and so the medication was discontinued by us.

We found that he was in the average range in intellectual functioning with an IQ of 101. He had been held over in the first grade and his disruptive behavior prompted the Committee on the Handicapped to call for an academic evaluation when he was in the third grade. It showed that he was slightly below grade level in reading and a year behind in math—not good, but not all that bad either.

His diagnostic category was not clear, so he was assigned to a preplacement class to attempt remediation before making a definite placement elsewhere in the school system. It was a form of crisis intervention.

Our diagnosis was that he was hyperkinetic and impulsive, and in need of supervision. We recommended a special class along with some psychological counseling, and we reinstituted drug therapy. We placed him on Dexedrine, a drug that had not been tried previously. Checking the teacher's response subsequently we were informed that while medicated, Michael's hyperactivity was brought under control. He was still easily distracted, but he could sit still and his attention span was up to about ten minutes. Without medication the hyperactivity had been uncontrollable and he could not concentrate on any classroom material.

The child was now able to maintain classwork. The drug dosage was reduced in slow stages and a new level sufficient to control the hyperactivity was found. Michael advanced to the seventh grade and performed at the expected level in his special class. His medication was discontinued during the summer, but was resumed at the beginning of the following school year when he entered junior high school.

School reports indicate that he was attentive and prompt, participated in oral reading, and was good in spelling. At times he was frustrated, but he learned quickly and could usually perform when the task was explained to him. His independent written work was

1. Establishing a good rapport is an essential first step.

2. The pediatric neurological evaluation, which is at the core of the work-up, is concerned with the *whole* child rather than isolated parts. In the picture on the left, the pediatric neurologist looks for any slight alterations in balance as the child tries to walk on the white line.

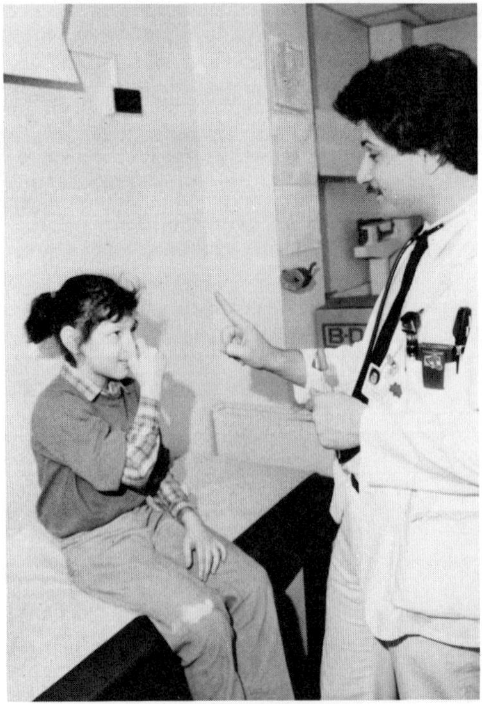

3. This young girl is being tested for the integrity of her visual perception and motor-planning abilities.

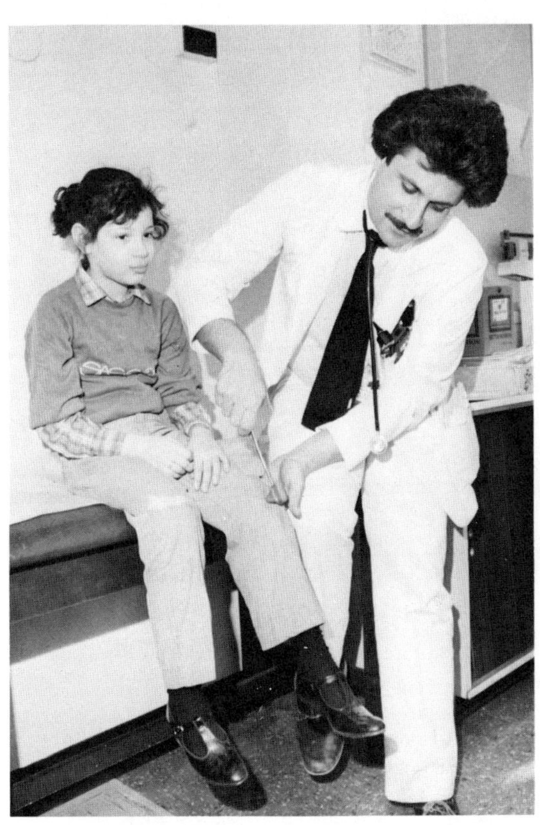

4. Testing for deep tendon reflexes.

5. The pediatric neurologist evaluates the child's ability to imitate movements requiring fine finger coordination.

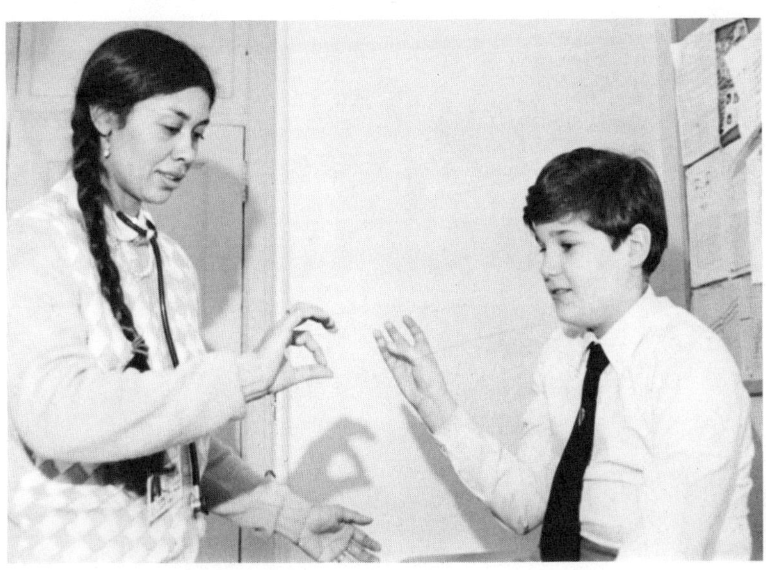

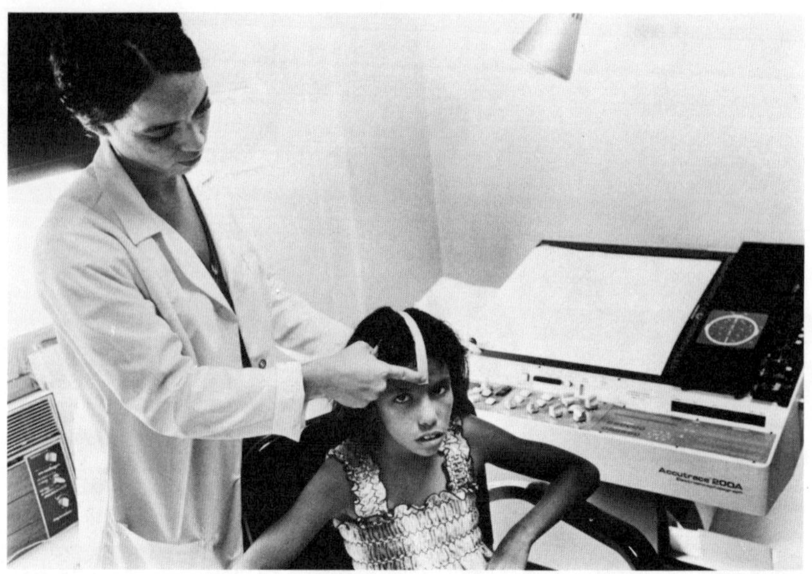

6. Taking an electroencephalogram (EEG) is a painless process that generally lasts from thirty to forty-five minutes. Parents are frequently more apprehensive about the procedure than their children are.

7. The psychologist evaluates the child's abilities using standardized tests of intelligence as well as certain projective techniques to assess personality development.

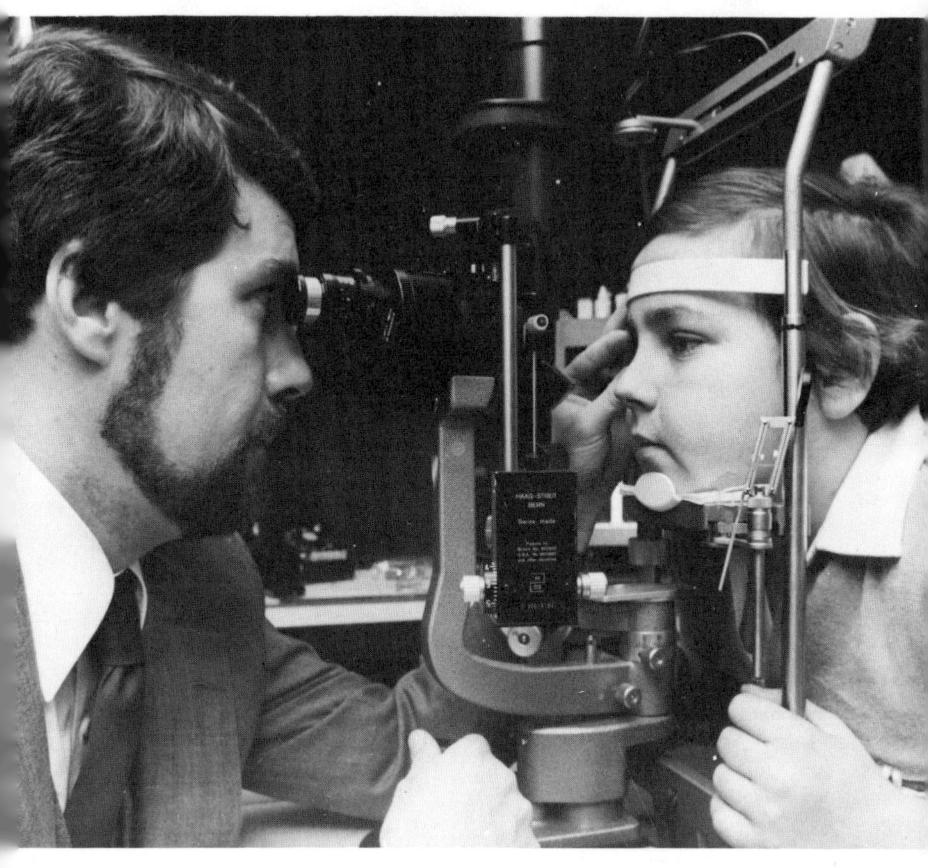

8. A comprehensive eye examination is a crucial part of the medical evaluation.

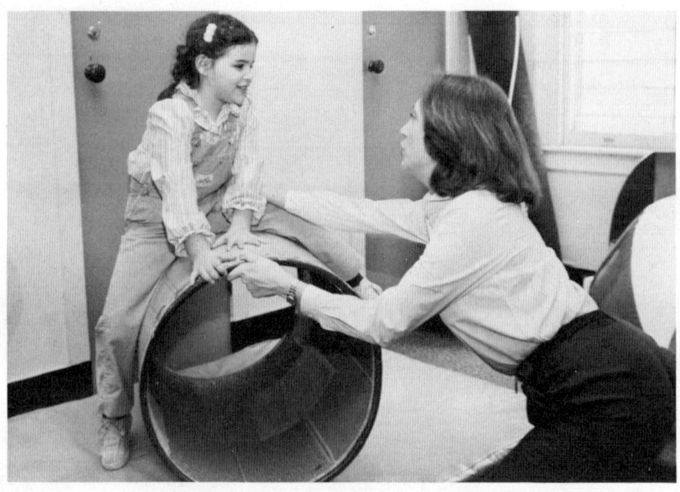

9 & 10. Work disguised as play. The methods of sensory-integrative therapy shown here are designed to improve coordination and sense of balance (above), and to strengthen vestibular function through the use of the bolster swing (below).

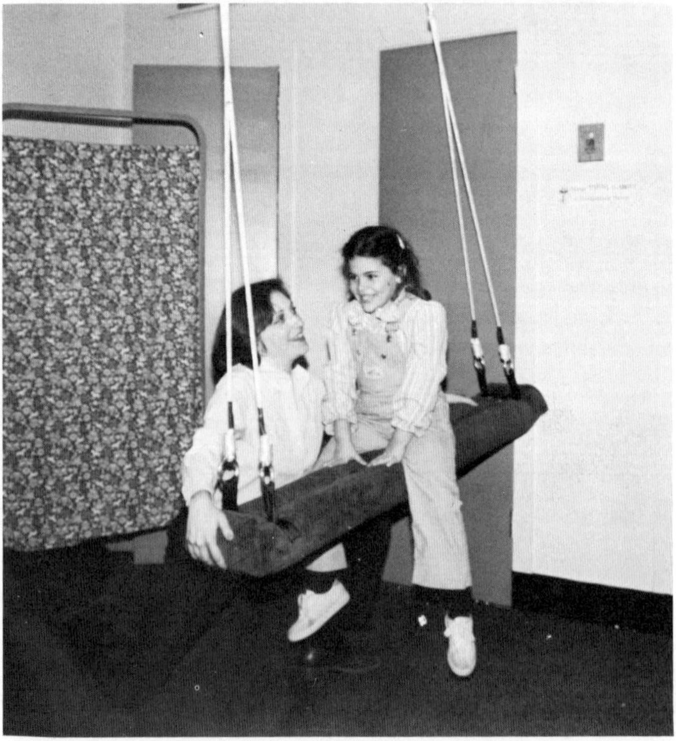

11. The child above is working on an exercise that facilitates gross-motor coordination.

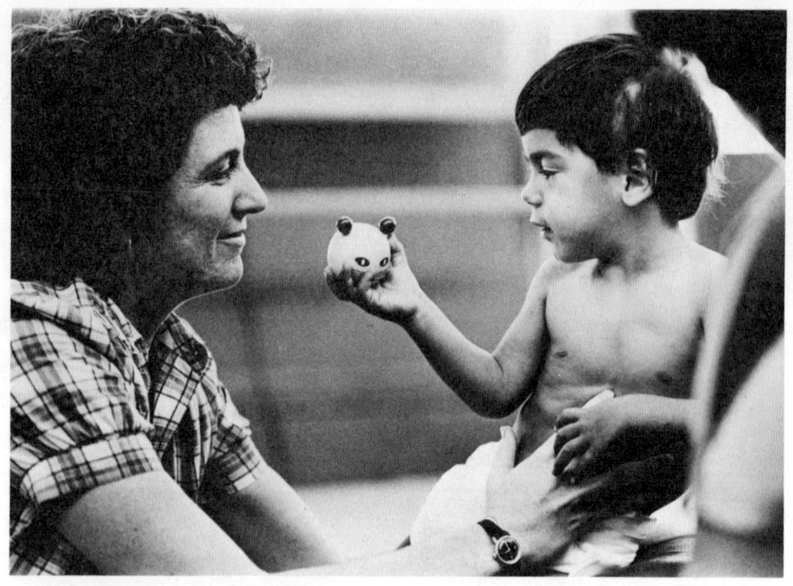

12. Learning to feel and enhancing tactile awareness.

13. A parent-oriented training program that focuses on increasing the child's attention span.

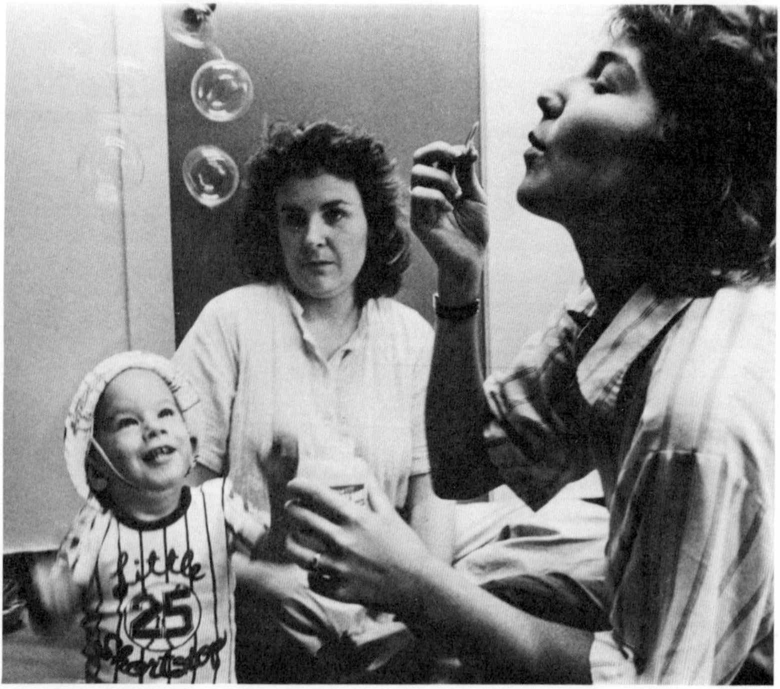

satisfactory. He still had some problems and left his seat to tease other children, but the disruptive behavior occurred much less frequently and Michael continued to receive the medication at a reduced dosage level.

❦

Eva was referred to us by The Long Island College Hospital outpatient clinic at fourteen months of age because she was having problems walking. In addition, the foster mother also reported that she did not talk or babble, but did cry.

The medical history revealed that Eva was born to an eighteen-year-old mother who had smoked more than a pack of cigarettes a day during pregnancy and consumed alcohol regularly during the gestational period, though no overt features of fetal alcohol syndrome were observed. Her birth weight was 4 lbs. 13 ozs., which was low for a full-term baby.

She was placed in foster care at five months and showed normal developmental milestones in terms of head control, a social smile, and the ability to sit up unassisted. She stood with support at eleven months. There were several hospital admissions for gastroenteritis and asthma, and an iron-deficiency anemia was noted. She had congenital bilateral dislocation of the hips but could walk with support and was developing normally up to the age of nine months.

There was no verbalization at all during the examination. She appeared to hear, and the cranial nerves were intact. Her deep tendon reflexes were normal and the initial general physical examination uncovered nothing abnormal. Her chemical tests were normal, as were her skull X rays and CAT Scan.

A physical-therapy examination noted instability in sitting and creeping and that her equilibrium was impaired, causing her to walk unsteadily. The occupational therapist reported that Eva was four months below age level overall, though muscle tone was within normal limits. Visual tracking and sound location were found to be deficient. She did not like being touched on the hands and her play was immature, being characterized by mouthing and dropping of objects. Although she attended to toys visually, her physical interaction was limited.

At the diagnostic conference, the chairman felt that the developmental delays were questionable and asked further about her hearing.

In the initial exam she had appeared to hear, but a full audiological examination then indicated that she had a significant sensorineural hearing loss. She was almost deaf. Eva was then referred to a school for the deaf for treatment. Once again, we see the extent to which severe hearing impairment influences normal growth and devolpment, including behavioral manifestations.

V. PSYCHOLOGICAL EVALUATION AND THERAPY

The fundamental purpose of the psychological evaluation is to determine a child's capacity for intellectual growth and development and the potential for satisfying interpersonal relations. This involves the assessment of both cognitive skills and the various emotional factors that may affect the child's ability to use those skills effectively in the learning situation. We look at any discrepancy between the child's abilities and his current performance in the classroom. From this we differentiate several broad diagnostic pictures; mild mental retardation, normal intelligence with a pattern of underachievement for some other reason, or a learning-disability profile.

Most psychological tests now in use were designed before the term "learning disability" was widely used. As constructed, they were concerned more with the idea of general intelligence rather than the specifics of learning styles or learning mechanisms. Over the past ten years, however, we have learned to correlate certain test profiles with case histories of children who are ultimately diagnosed as having a learning disability. While we have not derived precise statistics, the process has lead to a fairly workable diagnostic model.

In addition to the objective observations that we make and the interpretation of the test results, the role of the psychologist involves the correlation of this information with what is known to be available in the way of resources in the community. Situations arise where we might find ourselves asking for the creation of a new resource depending on how strongly we feel about its necessity. We are always weighing the possibility of getting some helpful and more appropriate placement for the child even if we cannot get the optimum.

With each of the children who come to us we start the psychological testing with a test of general intelligence. (We define intelligence pragmatically as that collection of skills which allow for successful learning.) Assuming that the child is of school age and that there is no sensory or motor deficit, the test of choice would be the Wechsler Intelligence Test for Children-Revised. The test is broken down into ten different sub-tests. It is not based on any particular model of intelligence other than the fact that intelligence is assumed to be a general trait, and the average individual would function in each of these areas at about the same level within the range of expected statistical variation. In constructing the test, the tasks were picked to meet that assumption. In other words, theory would cause us to expect high correlations from one area to the next as well as a high correlation of individual test results with the total score.

Each of the tests is constructed with age parameters in mind. The age placement for items are sequential and the criterion to pass is that three quarters of the children at a given age level in the validation sample answered them correctly. The test is appropriate for children ages six through seventeen years. The test is composed of five verbal sub-tests to examine how well he receives and responds to verbal items, and five performance sub-tests that are perceptual and require written or manipulative responses.

Test 1. The child is asked for common sorts of information that he could have learned at home as well as at school. (It is no longer assumed that the test is tapping native intelligence alone!) The questions are verbal, and the child responds verbally. When evaluating a child with a peripheral speech problem we bend the rules and allow him to write his answers, but this is exceptional.

There is a qualitative aspect to these tests as well. For example, we would want to see whether the child is responding immediately or whether he has a long retrieval time. If the latter is the case, we would then want to know if this was caused by slow internal processing, or whether it was an anxiety manifestation or perhaps a strategy employed trying to tease the answer out of the evaluator. In each portion of the test we look to see that the child is meeting the expectation. On the information sub-test, for example, one might assume that an eight-year-old, say, would get the first several items in the sequence correct and then start failing consistently. But if an inconsistent pattern emerges in which the child answers one item correctly, the next one incorrectly, and the next one correctly, that puts us on the alert to look for specific problems. This might be indicative of test anxiety or some environmental factor rather than intrinsic factors interfering with optimal performance.

The manner in which a child approaches the various test items can yield valuable information that is not revealed by the instrument itself. This is the essential argument for investing the time to conduct individual assessments as opposed to group testing. In group testing we can derive scores that point up an inadequacy, but are unable to determine the source of the failure.

Currently, the sub-test sequence alternates between the Verbal scale and the Performance scale items. But it was not always administered that way. In the first edition, all of the verbal material was administered first and then all of the performance sub-tests. It was later determined that this procedure worked to the detriment of the child. If the child has a language impairment and is given all of the verbal material, he would become discouraged quickly. Secondly, switching back and forth between the two types of test adds some variety to the testing situation and helps to maintain interest.

Test 2. Picture completion is a sub-test in which the child is shown a drawing of a familiar item with one detail missing. He is asked to identify the missing portion. He doesn't have to name the missing element, it is sufficient to point to the area where it should be with his finger. If there is any doubt as to whether he pointed to the right place or indicated the right place for the wrong reason, then the evaluator is allowed to question him a bit about it. Typically, an item would be an everyday article such as a chair without one leg. The items increase in complexity as the test progresses. Normally, aphasic children who would be at a disadvantage in a language sub-test are able to demonstrate the missing item through gesture, indicating that they have picked up the error visually despite their inability to describe it verbally. In general, when evaluating performance on this test, we are rating the child's visual attentiveness and his ability to organize a whole image with its component parts. Some children who are either perceptually deficient or generally impulsive would not be able to perform well on this test. They could organize the gestalt (whole image), and they could probably even re-create it for the examiner, but either perceptually or behaviorally, they have no interest in the detail.

In the classroom, a child like this might not copy a homework assignment. He would know when it was time to do so, but just would not have the perseverence to attend to each point in the process. We might predict that in reading he would be a whole-word reader rather than a phonetic reader who breaks the word down into syllables, or that in arithmetic he would be a memorizer rather than an analyzer.

Test 3. The similarities sub-test asks the child to form verbal analogies. This measures the child's verbal reasoning ability, and it looks for the level of abstraction achieved as well. It comes close to the heart of what we consider intelligence to be, which is the ability to abstract verbally. All of the items are graded "zero," "one" or "two." If a child is shown a violin and an accordian he would be graded "zero" if his response is that they make noise, a "one" if his response is that "you can play a song," and a "two" if he classifies them as musical instruments. Again, in addition to an overall score there is a great deal of qualitative information to be derived. There are some children who can complete all of the items and achieve an average score with all of the responses graded "ones." Such a child is working at a very concrete and descriptive level and not at the more advanced abstract thinking level. On the positive side, this kind of performance tells us that the child has good memory and retention and has acquired a lot of knowledge. However, he is processing it at a descriptive rather than at an analytic level.

Test 4. The picture arrangement sub-test consists of a string of cartoon pictures in a random sequence. The child is asked to rearrange them in a proper sequence so that they tell a story.

This gives us some insight into linear-, logical- or visual-sequencing ability. If other scores are high and this one is low, it would offer us a clue that the child has some deficiency in the sequencing of images. Since people tend to assign a verbal content to these pictures by making up a story (which they may not even utter) the test does have some verbal content. It is analogous to the way that we speak of reading as being a form of silent speech.

Test 5. The arithmetic sub-test is essentially measuring school-based knowledge. Initially, we present a card to the child with nine objects on it and the child is asked to name them and tell us how many there are. At a higher level of complexity we would present the child with a problem verbally. An example would be: "A boy has twenty-five cents and apples cost five cents each. How many apples could he buy with the money he has?" Here he has to understand both what the verbal context is telling him and the process of division. We do not allow the child to do any computations on paper in this test. So again, we are measuring multiple factors: Has the child memorized his multiplication tables, how good is his verbal reasoning, and how attentive is he? We often get a clue to his attentiveness or lack thereof when a child will ask us to repeat either the whole problem or just a portion of it.

Something we have noticed over the years is that numerical operations are very sensitive to stress factors, so that test anxiety could affect this score. At times, after the test is over and the child has relaxed, we will administer this test again and the child will do markedly better since the "official" testing is over.

Unlike the other verbal tests, this one is timed, but it has been our experience that the time limit is generous. Thus, few of our learning-disabled children are penalized in this respect. On the easy items such as simple addition and subtraction, the child usually responds within a couple of seconds. If it is not too anxiety provoking and we see that the child is working on the problem, we will allow him to use the full thirty seconds permitted.

The situation might be that the child does not have all of his number facts (e.g., memorized the multiplication table) at hand and is in reality counting on his fingers to work out the problem. We often want to see whether a failure is the result of inaccuracies in basic operations or inability to remember the stimulus items. If it becomes obvious that the child is getting upset, we would ask whether he had come up with the answer. If his response is "No, I can't," then we would pass on to the next item. We have this discretion because there is no requirement that the full time allotment be used, as there is on other elements of the test.

Test 6. The block-design sub-test offers us some insight into the child's ability to reason abstractly in the visual-perceptual sphere. Like the similarities sub-test (of which this is the non-verbal equivalent), the block-design test measures an ability that comes close to what we think of as the essence of intelligence. This abstracting ability is one of the primary skills lacking in a child who is having learning problems. The test also assumes a bit of manipulative ability, since the child is asked to move blocks around physically. The child is shown a card on which is drawn a design in two colors—red and white—and he is asked to match the design with red and white blocks.

The simplest tests use four blocks and the most complex, nine. The child is not allowed to place blocks over the design, but must reproduce it independently. One thing that we have to ensure is that the card is kept squarely in front of the child. Some of the items in the test are printed in a rotated position, and it would defeat the purpose of the test to allow the child to "right" the stimulus. Such a test will prove difficult for the child who has trouble maintaining perceptual constancy; that is, the ability to understand vertical and horizontal relationships. But, of course, that is what we want to uncover. The fact that a child would want to "right" it is an indication that there may be something wrong.

An added bit of information that emerges from this sub-test is an insight into the degree to which the child is working intuitively as opposed to the child who methodically plods along segment by segment. Also we look to see how rapidly both of these types of children integrate the segments. It is possible for a child to complete this test successfully on a strictly rote basis, having no concept of the overall design but just visualizing mentally that this block must look this way and that block must look another way. Such a child will not use any of the context clues to organize the design as a whole. The child will receive credit for assembling the design in this manner but the style tells us something about his ability to think abstractly.

Test 7. Vocabulary has always been considered to be the best predicator of overall intelligence and, in fact, has often been used as a screening item for grade placement since it calls upon such a comprehensive set of intellectual factors. Again, we observe the manner in which the child approaches the test items, which are at graded levels of abstraction. It is possible to have a child take the test right through to the last item but receive only partial credit for each. This occurs if he fails to utilize an age-appropriate level of abstraction and only gives correct responses limited to concrete examples. The interpretation of this sub-test score requires considerable judgment when it is administered to a child for whom English is a second language. As is well known, people conceive objects in different ways, and some of the items on this test would not make much sense to some children whose primary language is not English.

If the vocabulary test is poor but other sub-tests yield average or superior scores, the original principle that vocabulary should be the best predictor of overall IQ is violated. One possible explanation would be that there is a language or a cultural problem, or that the child just did not possess a particular fund of information.

In interpreting the levels of abstraction we do not consider any one meaning of a word to be more valuable than any other. A word like "join" could refer to membership in a group, meeting a friend at a particular place, or fastening things together. All of these responses are equally valid, but within each one we look for the level of abstraction that is displayed; i.e., the child's ability to generalize rather than be bound to concrete specifics. An illustration of a one-point response would be, for example, "I joined my friends," but a definition such as "to bring together" would be graded "two," since it represents a higher level of abstraction. We have occasionally encountered responses that were atypical but valid and highly original. In these cases the examiner is called upon to extend the test manual guidelines and comment on the child's particular creative strengths.

Test 8. Object assembly is a performance test in which we ask the child to work with meaningful rather than abstract designs. The child is given a set of puzzle pieces which, when assembled, will represent something familiar like a face or an animal. Performance on this test can be compared with performance on the abstract block-design test, and we can begin to develop an insight as to whether the deficit involves general perceptual functioning on the sensory side or whether it is specifically related to cultural aspects of the data.

Most frequently we encounter scores in which the abstract block design is lower than the concrete object assembly score. This tells us that the child is able to make use of the contextual clues that go along with known objects. One of the four items that comprise the object assembly test, however, does not offer many context clues, and even when correctly assembled merely gives the outline but none of the individual object's characteristics. It is, in large measure, "abstract." A child could succeed on the other three items and fail on this one. Typically, in this situation the abstract block-design test score is also very low. Such a correlation constitutes confirming evidence that a true perceptual problem is present.

Test 9. Comprehension is a sub-test that sometimes can be very useful in assessing responses to everyday experiences. The original intent of the test was to uncover the degree of the child's socialization. Has the child incorporated the norms for behavior that would be compatible with his age level? The child is asked simple questions such as, "What would you do if you cut your finger?" The response is graded according to whether he would take care of the situation on his own or seek help. The more self-reliant answer is awarded the higher score. On certain items the child is asked to give two correct answers; one a practical, day-to-day useful answer, and the other more generalized. We have found that children will frequently give multiple answers, but they are all from the same realm, the practical. In this test we are allowed to cue them by commenting that what they have said is a good idea, but could they think of another one.

There are some problems connected with interpreting this test. A child from a lower socioeconomic group may have problems with some of these items. To a great extent we tend to look at this test as more of an experiential gauge than an analytical one. It tells us what the child has absorbed from his culture. If we know that the child is in a good home environment with good stimulation, yet hangs on to one response, then it would be tempting to make the hypothesis that the child is rigid or inflexible. But one always has to be wary. There have been striking cases where the profile was normal and this sub-test score was low. Theoretically, such a low-scoring child has been exposed to the information but he is not processing it at all. In other words, when the question asks him what he himself would do, he is not willing to take on any personal responsibility. This might be typical of an antisocial response.

Test 10. The final sub-test is called the coding test. This involves a large number of rapid judgments and gauges accuracy in transposing visual data. The child is asked to match symbols that are attached to each number from "1" to "9" by drawing in the correct symbol under the corresponding number each time it appears in the grid of numbers that he is given on the printed page. He tries to do as many as he can manage in the two minutes allotted for the test.

We have encountered children who are able to memorize all nine symbols and go through the test without even glancing back at the sample. This, however, is not very common. If we see that a child is failing and not doing the test correctly, we stop him and explain what the task is and then let him proceed again. Other children will fail to master the task at all. Qualitatively, we are looking at the level of memorization, how frequently the child refers back to the sample grid, and whether or not he has trouble transferring information from the grid to the test boxes. Sometimes we see that the child will point to the box with his pencil and then when he goes to fill it in, his eye slips and he enters it in the next box. Then, we try to determine where, in the transfer process, the child is falling down. Visual-motor association, speed and accuracy are the primary skills at which this test is aimed.

Having completed all of the sub-tests we take the new scores and convert them to scale scores. These scale scores are designed to have a mean (weighted average) score of "10." The average child would be scoring approximately "10" on each one of these tests. When they are all added up ten "10" scores equal "100," and that would translate into the average IQ score of "100." When we are finished what we look for is the pattern of these scaled scores and whether the variation between them is more than that which would be expected on the basis of chance alone. The kinds of conclusions that the psychologist draws in the end are based more on the overall profile than the performance on individual sub-tests.*

In general, we examine the pattern of the scores to develop a profile. The lack of strong cognitive abstraction is one common pro-

* We know that these scaled scores have a mean average of 10 and a standard deviation (anticipated and recurring variation) of 1.5, so that if two standard deviations or less are taken as the boundary for the average range, then any score which is "7" or less would be examined to determine why the child's performance was less than average in that functional area. If the mean for the profile (the full scale IQ) was 85, which is one standard deviation below the mean, then we would look to see whether there were sub-tests that were two standard deviations above or below to identify specific strengths and weaknesses.

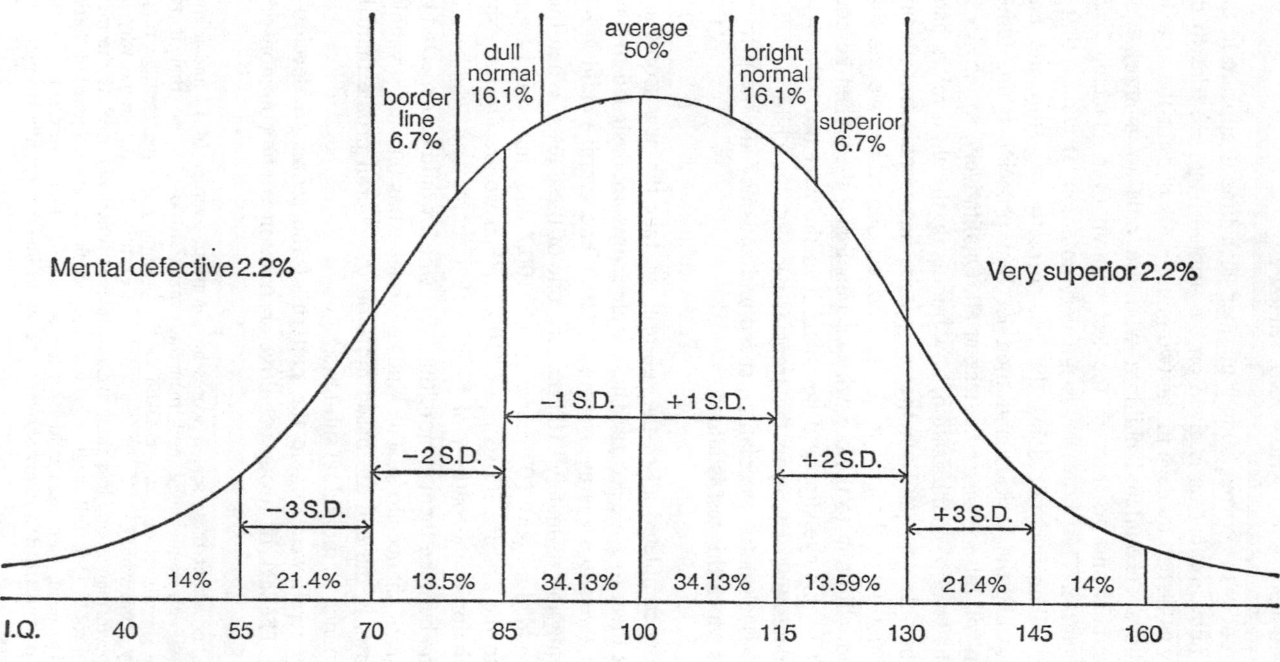

Fig. 6. Distribution of IQ scores in the general population (S.D. = standard deviation).

file we encounter with learning-disabled children. Theoretically, there could be a lesion in one hemisphere that was affecting abstract visual processing. Again, theoretically, in terms of teaching strategy, if one could teach verbally without calling on the visual skill of the child, he should be able to proceed normally. In other words, if his information could be transmitted using all verbal stimuli with no requirement for reading, no requirement for analyzing diagrams, he should be able to acquire the same body of knowledge as the perfectly normal individual.

The problem is that there are very few children who show only a deficit in a single area. We have come across a few, but not very many. The majority of children are more likely to show deficits on both the block design and similarities sub-tests, as one example. That is why the assumption has to be that the pathology is more spread out and not just limited to one hemisphere, that it is a general abstraction problem, but that the child has compensating strengths that give him structure and a lot of feedback and reinforcement. He is able to do other things on a less abstract level, and his deficit does not preclude the acquisition of his general fund of knowledge or vocabulary or carrying out associative operations. It is just the degree to which he would integrate it on his own that is missing. That would be the most common profile for a learning-disabled child.

There are other profiles in which the suspicion is that the fundamental problem is not one of cognitive abstraction but some underlying process, and the most common one is memory. If we suspect this, we can give another sub-test in which the child is told a string of numbers and asked to repeat them as he heard them and then in reverse. If he does poorly on this digit span test we would suspect a deficit in auditory memory. The literature on the subject indicates that if a dysfunction is present, the child may do well in the first recitation, but be severely deficient in his attempt to recite the numbers backward.

We do encounter children who conform to this pattern, but more often we see deficits on both digits forward and digits backward. On the rest of the test he is typically achieving scores of "8" or better while on this sub-test he may be at "6" or less. At this point the examiner has a pretty firm handle on a special sort of problem If the problem were one of visual memory, we would use another test in which the child is asked to reproduce a series of designs from memory.

The more typical profile of the learning-disabled child is that he will begin failing early on the similarities sub-test. Another basic profile would be the one in which we find inconsistent strengths and weaknesses, due to the fact that the child has teased the answers out of the examiner, since the terms of the test administration do allow us to give limited cues. Thus, one typical profile for a learning-disabled child based upon language deficit involves his doing poorly on the verbal items as well as the picture arrangement sub-test, while the rest of his performance is normal.

Relating the arithmetic sub-test to the profile, if we find that all the verbal elements are up and this test is down, we would wonder why he was not benefiting from instruction in this area, and we would want to keep in mind any concern about his attention. If the overall test score is strong, the results of the vocabulary sub-test can be helpful in a number of ways, whereas if there are a number of deficits throughout the testing and it is not apparent what they stem from, then this test is not helpful in pinpointing problems either. In all cases we look for atypical scores on individual sub-tests, relative to the overall score, to try to determine the exact area of the deficit.

Another test (Bender-Gestalt) that we commonly use is one that tests visual performance and lets us determine whether a problem is a receptive or an expressive one. We then compare the scores for the WISC-Revised block-design sub-test and the Bender-Gestalt test (described below). If the latter is low and the former high, then we know that the problem is a constructional one rather than a receptive one. If both scores are low, then we are left trying to judge the qualitative aspects of motor performance. If we feel that the child's motor abilities are satisfactory, then the difficulty probably lies more on the receptive side.

In administering the Bender we tell the child that he will be shown nine different patterns one by one, and that we would like him to copy them as neatly and as carefully as he can. The first pattern is used as a demonstration sample and does not count in the scoring. There is no time limit for any of the items. The child can take as long as he needs to complete the task. He then simply tells the examiner that he has finished, and is presented with the next design.

This test was originally developed for use with adults, but more

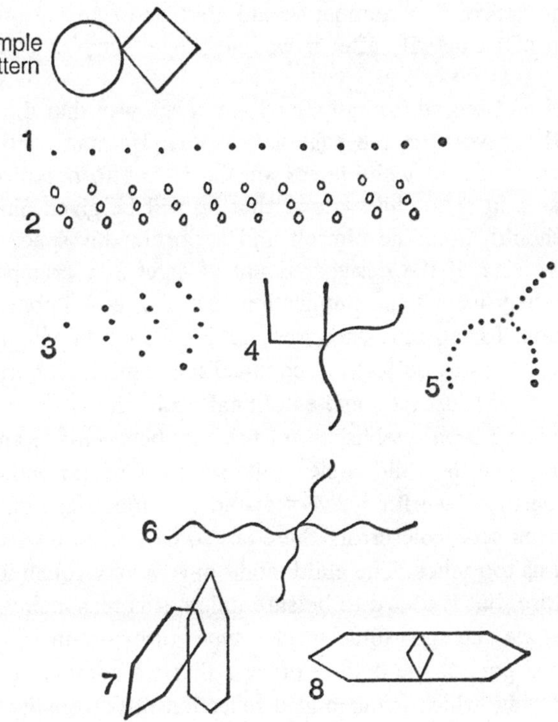

Fig. 7. The Bender-Gestalt Test.

recently children's norms have been established. There are an average of three to four criteria for each design. Some of them examine whether the figures are integrated. Others are concerned with the angulation of the figure to see whether it is intact, or whether the whole figure is rotated or is in proper position. Depending on the qualities of the design, we would use other appropriate criteria. A line of dots that the child continued to repeat even after he had drawn the appropriate number would alert us to perseveration—the repetition of an activity after it was no longer purposeful or appropriate.

Though not scored formally, we look at the way that the child has organized his work on the page as a whole. He starts with a blank 8½″ x 11″ sheet of white paper and he is free to organize it however he sees fit. The child knows that he will be given nine designs and he should discipline himself and apportion his space into nine areas. The size of the designated areas—irregular, cramped or expansive—may have some implication, but the most important thing is that room for all nine exercises has been apportioned. If we saw that everything was perfect but confined into one small corner of the page, we would suspect some emotional problem.

Norms have been established for the ages between five and eleven, and by the time the child is eleven he should perform without error. Normal performance for a five-year-old is thirteen errors, but even with thirteen scoreable errors there are some overall test scores that don't tell us too much. The child might have a very rough idea of the total picture, but it's hard to be sure unless it is reasonably well executed and we can spot some specific types of errors in it.

The final part of the battery of tests that we administer is human figure drawing, which is taken as a reflection of personality organization, emotional factors, and general intelligence. It also provides some differential information in comparing what is demonstrated by the figure drawing vis-à-vis the WISC-Rev. Our emphasis in the figure drawing is to concentrate on the intellectual factors while taking the social dynamic factors into account. If the WISC IQ is low and the figure drawing IQ is high, we look for an emotional problem. We ask ourselves why the child is not using the endowment that the figure drawing tells us he has. We have many children who have WISC IQ's in the 60s and figure-drawing IQ's in the 80s.

A typical drawing by an average child would consist of a complete figure, perhaps missing some elements of clothing or lacking proper proportion in the fine details—an outsized ear, for instance. When we then ask for an identification to determine who their idol or authority figures are, we normally don't get a very satisfactory response. They are often likely to say that the drawing is nobody. Then, if we pursue it, we usually get the name of someone the child knows from school.

We are obviously interested in the correctness and precision of the child's response, but we are also very interested in how he arrives at his associations and any comments about himself that he may volunteer. Sometimes children are prompted by some item on the tests and will start to talk about themselves or a situation that is bothering them. This becomes valuable information to us.

Children are surprisingly blasé about these tests. We might anticipate that many children would be somewhat nervous, but generally they seem to take the tests in stride. There is a small percentage of very shy, bashful children who require perhaps ten or fifteen minutes warming up, getting them used to the examiner and letting them know that they are not being threatened. The average younger child, on the other hand, can pretty well get down to business right away. Adolescents pose a special problem, in that they have a better idea of the importance of the test and will even comment along the way about it and be more defensive about their failures.

In a way, the child who is aware of his failures is ahead of the game compared to the child who is unaware and doesn't self-evaluate, because it indicates that he could benefit more from a teaching strategy that is going to give him more individual feedback. He has shown himself open to the process.

Thus, the psychologist contributes significantly to the total evaluation by identifying specific areas of strength and weakness. With this information remedial strategies may be designed and implemented. Additionally, where emotional factors may be interfering with the learning process, therapeutic intervention may be recommended. The purpose of psychological testing, therefore, is to uncover problems in the areas of innate ability, achievement and emotional behavior. The following cases concern children who, because of difficulty in one of these areas, were having difficulties in school and did not seem able to progress. Our task was to find means so that they could begin real achievement.

❦

David was referred to us by the school guidance counselor, who suspected that David had learning problems when he was nine and in the fourth grade. The school reported that he was failing language arts and reading, and that he studied hard but showed little improvement, even though he was being given some remedial help at the school.

His full scale IQ was 107—Verbal 114 and Performance 99—and the examiner felt that the child was anxious and might have done even better were it not for that factor. So we had a paradoxical case in which a child has a high average verbal IQ and despite this he was failing language arts.

He was a very pleasant child in terms of his behavior, but the school noted that he was becoming frustrated. When we spoke to him, it was obvious that he had a tremendous investment in wanting to do well. He was terribly disappointed in himself, and his fear of failure before a test was extreme. Something was preventing him from using the knowledge that he possessed.

He tended to exaggerate the difficulties of the material and anticipated the worst. Ordinarily, he entered the test situation well prepared, although he himself could never feel well prepared enough. He became overwhelmed and tended to freeze up during the test. He would be able to get through the whole test within the time limits, since he wasn't slow, but his anxiety prevented him from concentrating on it.

David was preoccupied with feelings that he couldn't do the work and was going to fail. His fantasies didn't even stop with the test situation itself but became broadened into a climate of general catastrophy. If he didn't know the answer to one question that gap quickly grew to "I am going to fail the test," "I am going to fail the subject," "I'm going to be left back," "It's all over!" His anxiety was blown out of all proportion.

When David was seven, he woke up one day with muscle spasms in his neck. Because he became afraid that the spasms would reoccur while he was sleeping, he started to experience difficulty falling asleep. Medication was prescribed to help him fall asleep, and this worked for a while. The mother reported that the sleeping problems began to reappear in September, the month that school opened.

In this particular school the fourth grade started to become somewhat more departmentalized than the previous grades. There was more than one teacher, and there was more pressure. Some of the teachers he found hard to deal with, and in talking about the various subjects, it seemed that tests administered by certain teachers generated a lot more anxiety than other subjects in which he did well. He was aware that some subjects were harder for him because of this.

There was another factor that was part of the problem. Two older, high-school brothers were not particularly outstanding, but had passed through the school without problems. However, there was an older sister, aged eleven, in the same school at the same time, and she was a phenomenal student. David was forever comparing himself to her, and since it was a small school he sometimes encountered a teacher who taught his sister and had similar expectations of him.

Rather than use a generalized, psychotherapeutic approach, we worked on the specific problem of test anxiety. Other issues we would take up with him later. The first step was to construct a hierarchy of situations dealing with all the problems involved in test taking. We determined what was the most stress-provoking part of the process by examining all of the steps—finding out about the test and preparing for it, then the actual test period itself, and finally the period between finishing the test and receiving a grade. Then we assessed his skills in study and test taking in general in terms of sufficient preparation or a possible deficit in his approach to study. Basically we found that his preparation was fine, and it was just the anxiety inspired by the test situation itself.

David's parents were supportive and his mother would test him the evening before an examination. She noticed that a stomachache would develop when he was studying certain subjects. He felt quite insecure in general. He felt loved, but one of his fantasies was that his parents' love depended on his success in school, too, so that not only could failure destroy his academic career but he could also lose his family's support and affection as well.

After identifying the test itself as the main problem area, we then developed a hierarchy of anxiety-producing situations. This therapeutic approach is called *cognitive behavior therapy*. All of the items were arranged in order, starting at zero—an item which produced absolutely no anxiety at all—to one hundred, which was the worst situation he could imagine. For David the worst situation he could imagine was a test in his worst subject, which happened to be science, and a test specifically on plants, on which he knew none of the answers. Another dangerous area was a situation in which he was not sure of certain questions, and if he missed one, then he started exaggerating.

We began working on relaxation training with David. We taught him to relax his whole body starting with certain groups of muscles. To put him in touch with what anxiety feels like physically, we asked him to first tense and then relax the muscles of the forehead and jaw, for example. He relaxed so quickly that the therapist sometimes wondered whether he was asleep or not, and at one point actually asked him a question to verify that he was awake.

We asked him to think of a very pleasant image that he generated for himself. We then asked him to think of other specific situations, beginning with the item in the scale that produced no anxiety and proceeding up the hierarchy to successively more anxiety-producing situations. If he experienced anxiety when imagining a situation, he raised a finger to let the therapist know. We didn't want him to talk because this would interfere with relaxation. We would tell him to return to the comfortable image and relax, because relaxation is the opposite of tension. When one is relaxed, it is more difficult for anxiety to arise.

Cognitive restructuring enabled him to say positive things rather than critical ones when he was feeling anxiety. In David's case it was to think that "It's only one question. It's not the end of the world." He has learned to handle the anxiety in the therapy sessions and has been promoted to the fifth grade where he has settled in successfully.

José, referred by his day-care center when he was five, lacked secure control of bladder or bowel movements, both during the day and at night. He had been toilet trained early by the age of one but now had regressed. He was not speaking at all in the center. One of the ideas that was being entertained was that, perhaps, the child was retarded.

He went through the work-up speaking only an isolated word here and there to any of the examiners. He did participate in the non-verbal tasks of posture imitating and drawing. Given the limited nature of the information he provided us, we had to be guided by performance items, not verbal items, in our tests. Psychological testing showed him to have a performance level of 111. This represents a high-average score, and so retardation was ruled out. During the work-up and during subsequent remediation he did not display the lack of bladder and bowel control that had been reported at the day-care center and at home.

The father, we learned, was a disruptive and violent individual. The parents were separated and the mother reported that there had been violent episodes in the house and elsewhere that had been observed by José. Once she had been walking in the street, arguing with José's father, and the father bent her fingers back far enough to break two of them. José may have come to associate talking with violence in a way that his little sister who also witnessed the incident, did not. In any case, he was silent most of the time, and his condition is called selective or elective mutism.

The child spoke at home, according to the testimony of his mother, and did not speak at the day-care center, according to their testimony. While remaining silent during the bulk of our examination, he unexpectedly responded to the questions of the diagnostic conference leader, demonstrating his ability to speak. His responses, however, betrayed a lack of comprehension.

In general he did not speak to people outside of his own home. Even in the home he wouldn't speak to a stranger or even his grandmother when she visited. And in a public place like a bus or a park, he wouldn't speak to his mother. She frequently took him to the park with the hope that one day a little child would come over and José would start to speak to him and then the problem would all be over.

Because of this refusal to speak he suffered substantial losses at times. One time during treatment, he was playing with his sister and she was taking every toy away, right out of his hands and he let it all happen. He didn't say a word. He was very very stubborn and would sometimes refuse to come down the hall to enter the office for treatment.

Something profoundly negative is happening to a child who won't speak, who, essentially, is withholding himself from the outside world. Part of José's difficulty came from his toilet training and his fear of sitting in the bathroom by himself. His mother would not take the time to accompany him, although this had been suggested to her.

Before starting treatment, we observed him to see whether he would speak as he became accustomed to the therapy sessions, and to establish a base line of his behavior. When he decided to say a few words, he often would just echo what the therapst had said without any comprehension. For the most part, however, he wouldn't say anything at all. We noted each time that he spoke. According to the mother, he liked candy, and since the therapy we had decided to use involved material reinforcement, every time he said anything, he would be rewarded with a piece of candy. He very quickly lost interest in the candy, but was attracted by various puzzles and a toy car.

He was allowed to select a car that he was interested in earning. Whenever he said a word, he was rewarded with a "happy face" drawn on a piece of 8½″ x 11″ paper. When the entire page was covered with "happy faces" José was allowed to take the car home. He had played with it during the therapy session and now was allowed to take it away with him. Generally it took him two sessions to "earn" each vehicle.

He began to respond with increased frequency after the first month of therapy. Two months after initiation of therapy he had moved to a higher level of response, although even this was variable and could drop in any given session, depending on his mood. After he started to speak he progressed to the point where he would not only respond but would spontaneously say things.

Unfortunately, the therapy never progressed to the point where he could begin to talk about the reasons for his silence. We really did not have the understanding cooperation of the mother throughout much of the therapy. School started and José began to attend kindergarten. When he spoke at school his mother figured that the desired result had been achieved and she terminated José's therapy.

Although treatment was stopped prematurely, José had certainly changed as a result of the sessions. He was now speaking to strangers outside his home. However, he still needed speech therapy to bring his language skills up to an age-appropriate level. This now was a realistic goal because he had overcome his elective mutism.

Christopher was nine and a half years old and in the third grade when he was referred to us by the guidance counselor of his school. Christopher had repeated first and second grades. The school report indicated that in addition to problems in reading and mathematics, Christopher's concentration and motivation were poor. He was not attending school regularly, and frequently looked unhappy.

Christopher's father was interviewed prior to the testing session. He explained that he recently gained custody of Christopher because of the poor home environment provided by the mother. Christopher's birth and early development were reported to be within normal limits.

Christopher was a nice-looking boy who was cooperative but somewhat anxious during the evaluation. He seemed interested in performing well on tasks, but had a tendency to respond impulsively.

Formal testing revealed an intelligence quotient in the low-average range. Christopher's social awareness, vocabulary and memory were within the average range of functioning. However, the profile indicated weaknesses in areas that could affect learning. Christopher had difficulty solving problems that involved the manipulation of objects and other manual responses. His ability to deal with relatively abstract stimuli was also poor. Christopher's learning problems were also seen on tests of visual-motor performance. He had particular difficulty integrating designs, orienting them in space, and copying angles.

Tests of personality structure and organization revealed a somewhat anxious, depressed and angry boy with strong needs for love and affection probably stemming from emotional deprivation at home. Christopher also felt inadequate regarding his failures at school.

Christopher was referred for psychotherapy and occupational therapy at the Institute. He attended sessions for approximately eight months. In psychotherapy, Christopher explored feelings related to familiar relationships. As his home situation stabilized and he gained understanding and self-acceptance regarding his learning difficulties, his sense of self-worth improved.

In occupational therapy Christopher worked on visual-motor coordination and learned to recognize geometric forms and designs more efficiently. He was helped to control his impulsivity and to take the time to study the various components of a visual pattern.

Christopher passed his exams at the end of the school year and was promoted to the next grade. He was even beginning to smile occasionally and to engage in satisfying activities with his peers.

Luis, a fifteen-year-old adolescent, was referred by his school for evaluation of poor school performance. At the time of referral, he was attending a special day school for students who are socially maladjusted and emotionally disturbed. Luis had been in special education (CEH) since third grade, following a drug overdose.

On the Wechsler Intelligence Scale for Children-Revised, Luis achieved a full scale IQ of 70, placing his overall functioning in the borderline range. His verbal IQ of 52 (moderately retarded) was significantly lower than his performance IQ of 91 (average).

A detailed analysis of the sub-tests revealed that all of Luis' verbal skills were severely deficient. They ranged from approximately a 7- to an 8¾-year level. In distinct contrast, Luis demonstrated visual-motor skills that were age appropriate or extended beyond age-level expectations. The one area of visual-motor deficiency he exhibited involved sequencing stimuli. This task involves inner language, and is therefore related to his overall lack of language development.

The psychological evaluation served to pinpoint the etiology of Luis' lack of academic success. He had severe learning problems that were linguistically based. Luis' problem was not primarily emotional, but rather a reaction to his chronic experience of failure. It was therefore recommended that Luis receive intensive remediation in both occupational therapy and language therapy. A change in class placement was also recommended.

A follow-up after six months showed that Luis' language skills had improved significantly and that his ability to appropriately sequence incoming stimuli had improved. His behavior was much improved, his school performance was better and he was no longer viewed by the school as emotionally disturbed.

None of the foregoing is to suggest that all of Luis' problems were resolved, but there is ample evidence that we are moving in the right direction and that progress is being made.

VI. PSYCHIATRIC EXAMINATION AND THERAPY

With the psychiatric examination we strive to achieve a clear picture of the child's personality and to determine how he is functioning in terms of his own personal psychological characteristics. We try to see whether he is depressed, fearful, anxious or overburdened in any way that would hamper his ability to function up to the maximum of his ability.

We derive the information needed to make this assessment through an interview with one or both parents (usually it's the mother alone) and the child himself. If we are unable to talk to the natural mother, then we will speak to the foster mother or father or grandparents or any adult who will be able to furnish us with the information that we need. However, the natural mother is usually the best informant that we have.

In the course of a typical psychiatric examination we ask about the child's sleeping habits—whether or not he sleeps well, what time he goes to bed and does he go to bed willingly or is it a continuous struggle to avoid bedtime? Is going to bed a protracted process that starts at eight o'clock and is still going on an hour later? During this time, does the child fight or scream? Conversely, we would want to know whether he just goes to bed and sleeps right away because he is very tired. We want to know how long it takes him to fall asleep, whether immediately or several hours later.

Now, there are few children who willingly go to bed as soon as they are asked, so that in discussing the bedtime pattern we are looking for behavior that goes beyond the normal resistance that the average child will offer. If we find extreme reluctance, behavior that turns bedtime into a regular problem, then it may indicate that we are dealing with a very stubborn child or one who has a great deal of energy. On the other hand, it may simply mean that the mother is putting the child to bed too early. Another possibility is that the mother does not have adequate control over the child, so that when she announces bedtime, the process becomes a power struggle and the child proves that he is the boss by going to bed much later than he was instructed to.

The child who is so tired that he falls asleep right away might really be going to bed too late, or it might indicate that the family has a certain dependable routine and the child expects to go to bed at a certain time and he just does. Children sleep better when they have a routine. It is possible that a child who has screaming fits about bedtime will exhaust himself and sleep right away, but ordinarily the arguing, whining and fussing that go on are not conducive to sleep at all. We like to know about the quality of the child's sleep, but usually the mother finds that hard to gauge, although she can report whether he was restless or showed a pattern of waking up during the night, perhaps complaining of bad dreams.

It is important to know whether or not the child wets the bed at night and how frequently. Again we have to examine all of the possible explanations. It could mean that the child has a bladder or kidney infection, or a congenital abnormality. In this case, he usually has trouble in the daytime as well. In the winter time a room that's too cold can cause bed wetting because the child doesn't want to leave the warm bed. Aside from these factors we have to determine if we are dealing with a child who is told to go to the bathroom by the mother but stubbornly lies in bed and urinates there instead. This is a conflict between the child and the mother and is another aspect of the struggle for control.

Eating is another area that we discuss thoroughly with the mother. We want to know whether the child is cooperative, or does he have to be forced to eat? Will he feed himself, or does he require the mother to feed him? Does he require a great deal of coaxing? Extremely difficult behavior regarding eating could be an indication of conflict between the mother and the child, but the diet itself is important. If, for instance, the child refuses to eat meat, he may be missing important nutritional elements. We find often among autistic children an avoidance of meat unless it is blended with other foods so that it hardly resembles meat.

When the child will only eat when he is fed by the mother, we try to determine if the mother is fostering a type of dependency in the child by babying him. Is the mother refusing to relinquish this role?

Many times we see this situation in the case of the youngest child in a family where the mother is reluctant to have the child grow up and become less dependent on her. We are always interested in who gets the biggest piece of cake, the drumstick, or other favored morsels. Does it alternate between various members of the family, or is it always the same person? If it is always the same person, we try to determine if this is a sign of favoritism, or if one of the children is a bully or manipulative and always grabs the prize.

Behavior like this tells us a great deal about the structure of the family. When the child gets older we would like to know who it is who helps to set the table, and who helps to clean up after the meal by clearing the table or washing and drying the dishes. In the case of a girl we would want to know whether she has started to learn to cook. It is not our intent to perpetuate stereotypic sexual roles, but in the real world of the eighties, traditional roles are still very prevalent. Of course, all of these activities are subject to cultural differences, and we would only regard them as significant in as much as they differed or conformed to the mores of the culture the child comes from. For example, in some families, boys are taught to cook at the same age as girls.

Play and play activity in general are where the child's fantasies, thoughts and feelings come out. Little children are not very verbal, and it is only by inquiring about the quality of their playing that we can make some observations about what is really going on inside. As an example we might find a little boy playing with a fire engine constantly to the exclusion of other toys because he is extremely frightened that the house will burn down at night and that is the reason that he cannot sleep. The anxiety is revealed when we talk to the child, but it was the fire engine that furnished the clue and drew our attention to the source of the difficulty.

We want to know how he plays and who he plays with, or does he prefer to play alone? Things that we are on the lookout for are cooperation with other children or, on the other hand, non-cooperation in the form of fighting. Does he play with his brothers and sisters or with the neighborhood children? How long can the child play before fighting and bickering break out? Does the child share? Who is the leader in the play? Who is the follower? Does he play with children much younger than himself? Does he play exclusively with boys or with girls, or does he play with children older than himself?

In the latter case we might surmise that he wants to be tough and grown-up.

We are always interested in extreme behavior. Normally, children will play alone or with others depending on the circumstances. If the child prefers to play alone practically all of the time, it makes us curious to know why. In the same way, if we encounter a child who cannot stand to play alone and always must find some other child to play with, we want to know why. Both of these kinds of children are not flexible.

We ask the mother to furnish us with all of the particulars concerning the child's favorite toys. This information can help us to pinpoint fears or fantasies (as in the case of the boy and the fire engine), but we also want to consider their appropriateness for a given developmental age. For example, when other children are playing team sports such as football and baseball, is he still playing with toy cars? Situations like this may indicate that he is behind in his play development. Bicycle riding is an activity that we are very interested in. We want to know whether the child can ride without training wheels by the age of nine or ten. Another aspect we want to know about is whether the child can take care of the bicycle, since it is often the first large and expensive item a child owns.

Sometimes we find boys who are not interested in bicycle riding at all, which may be a sign of dependency on the home or parents or fear. We would then determine if the boy was inclined to shy away from football or baseball. If so, perhaps the child is afraid of being hurt. We would want to find a pattern. If the boy played these games but was not interested in bicycle riding, then perhaps it would be a question of a lack of coordination.

In baseball, one can stick a child in the outfield and if he misjudges a ball, it is usually no great tragedy. It is quite something else with bicycle riding where a lack of balance or coordination could result in a real fall with immediate pain, even serious injury. Of course, before one begins to speculate on any of the reasons for a child's inability or disinclination to ride a bicycle, one first has to be very practical and determine if the family can afford to buy a bicycle for the child, or if there are the opportunities for the child to ride regularly in the neighborhood he lives in. For example, some neighborhoods might be too dangerous for bicycle riding.

Sometimes parents are the ones who prevent a child from learning to ride because even if they can afford it, they will not buy a bicycle for him. It may be that they are afraid that it will be stolen from him or that he will ride too far away from home or will be in an accident. These may be legitimate fears, but then one has to think about the number of older children crossing the street who are struck by cars each year. The parallel is that the possibility of an accident is not a good enough reason to avoid crossing streets, and if a mother is still holding a child's hand by the time he is ten, there is something wrong in the relationship unless the child is handicapped in some way.

In the dynamics of the family, the relationship of the child to the parents evolves constantly. In the beginning, the relationship is one of total dependence on the mother. As he gets older, the child gradually becomes more and more self-reliant. The word to emphasize is *gradually*. Slowly, little by little, the child begins to take over the chores that previously were done for him such as feeding, dressing and getting around. At first the child is taken to school, and later on makes his own way there by being able to cross streets alone and remember directions. He acquires the security of being able to do things for himself and this security develops in stages. The child does not simply have everything done for him and then, at the age of eighteen, announce that he is ready to leave home.

The wise parent aids this process in a variety of ways. Money, for instance, is something that children start to learn about by handling small allowances that can be increased step by step. The child can learn about choosing clothes by being asked to select between two or three shirts that have been chosen for him; later on he will be allowed to buy his own shirts.

Money is something that a child will be dealing with throughout his entire life, and we like to see how he is learning to handle it. We want to know how money is regarded in the family. Is it treated as a gift, is the family very tight with money or is the money used to buy his cooperation? If there is allowance money, in whatever amount, is it given at a regular time each week? Is the child totally responsible for it himself? It's very important to know what the child does with the money. Does he save it? Does he spend it all immediately? Does he put part of it away to save up for something that is more expensive? Does he just put it in the bank and do nothing with it at all? Does he give it to a friend or attempt to buy friendship?

Once we have determined the method of disposition of money, we then have to find out why the child behaved as he did. Take the case of the child who went out and spent it all right away. On the face of it, one might conclude that he squandered it. However, he might have an older brother who would take it away from him if he still had it. So he decides that one good fling beats having nothing at all. Then again, he might be a child with a very short attention span who feels that everything has to be done right away. Such a child can't wait for the future and tends to act impulsively. He might want to buy a football but just can't organize himself to put a little bit away each week. A child who is able to defer gratification shows a greater degree of social maturity than the child who is not able to impose this discipline on himself.

Opposed to this sort of behavior we might have a child who takes out a bit of the money for immediate use and puts the rest away in a savings bank. This would seem to be prudent, praiseworthy behavior and we would try to find out what he was saving the money for. He might tell us that he was saving it for college or he might not have any specific reason; he just squirrels it away. Then again, while his parents give him the money, they may also march him right down to the bank and effect what are compulsory savings, so that we don't have a real sense of what the child would do with the money if left to his own devices.

Another area of interest is the type of television programming that the child selects. Most children spend more time in front of a television set than they do in school. Studies have shown that many children watch at breakfast and at dinner, after school and on weekends, over holidays and during vacations. On any particular day they may attend school for six hours and watch television four hours, but since the child attends school approximately 180 days, this constitutes only half his year, so that overall the child logs a great deal more television hours than school hours. We look to see also whether the child selects age-appropriate programs. If a child is nine and is still watching "Sesame Street," which is geared to five-year-olds, then something is amiss. This does not mean that watching it occasionally is odd, but only if he does it on a regular sustained basis in preference to other programs. Then again we might find a nine-year-old watching a late night movie after midnight, which is not common nor particularly good for that age child since he needs his sleep.

Children like cartoons when they are younger but by fourth or fifth grade they should move away from them and become viewers of comedy shows that are made with a children's audience partly in mind. There are male and female preferences that have to be taken into account. It is not surprising that a little boy might spend some time watching baseball and football programs, but we would not expect to find that these programs had much appeal to most little girls. If they did, we would want to know why. The fact that the child watches anything is only the starting point; the reason why the child watches is the most valuable piece of information. If the little boy is watching soap operas on a sustained basis again, we would want to know why; it might reflect some confusion as to his sexual identity, or may simply be that he is following his mother's preference. Just watching is not proof of a problem, but it could be a clue to one.

Obviously, one of the areas we are concerned with in talking with parents about learning-disabled children is the quality of the child's school experience. We try to find out how much contact the parent has had with the child's teachers. It is possible that because of shyness, embarrassment or preoccupation with other activities, the only contact that the parent has with the school is the report card. We try to find out if the parent goes to Parent-Teachers Association meetings and is open to contact with teachers in other ways. We are also interested in the parents' awareness of the volume of homework that the child has, and whether or not they supervise it. This would be a positive step, but we have also found the unprofitable situation in which the parents actually do the homework for the child, which really does not help him at all. The child simply ends up copying over that which the parent had done for him.

We like to determine what the parents' basic attitudes toward school is. Is it an encouraging attitude or is it a punitive one? In the latter case, we might find that a child who failed a spelling test with 60 percent would be denied dessert that evening or might not be allowed to go out to play or to watch television. Repeated punishment of this sort begins to give the child a negative attitude toward school. The child starts worrying and develops a real dislike for school. Another child might come home with the same failing grade and the parents might neither criticize nor give him much encouragement to study harder. Their response betrays a kind of indifference to school. A third type of parent would pick up on the fact that the failing grade of 60 percent means that the child got six out of ten answers correct and would encourage him to work on the other four. The third type would be the most helpful for motivating the child to do better.

It is important for a child to have an adequate place to work on his homework. If the only place is the kitchen table with a nearby television going, he's starting with a handicap. A quiet spot with good lighting will be to his advantage. Do the parents read regularly and set an example for the children? If reading and discussions are not part of the parents' lives, then the child may conclude that reading comprehension is not too important. We would want to know what the child's grade is and whether or not he is performing at grade level in addition to his reading and math skills. And if he is not performing at grade level, how far below is he?

Up to now we have spoken to the parent, and now we would want to speak to the child himself to try to gauge how he sees the situation. If the child is older, we would certainly ask the parent to leave so that we might talk privately, but if the child is younger we might have the parent remain. Ordinarily, however, we ask them to leave for at least part of the interview, since this separation offers us some information about the child's reaction. He might have a temper tantrum or become silent and fearful, or he might become friendly. In some cases he might not even appear to notice that the mother left.

The child who throws the temper tantrum might have an overdependency on the mother. She may rush back in to hug and comfort him and refuse to leave the room, or the mother may say to the child psychiatrist that the child has tantrums like this and it is nothing to worry about, since it will be over in a minute. The parent may bawl out the child and threaten him with punishment if he does not behave. The child who does not appear to notice the mother's departure is indicating that the examiner who remains in the room is just as adequate as the parent who left. This may indicate trust and a good judgment. Or it may indicate that as far as the child is concerned, people are interchangeable. This may mean that the child is autistic and that any adult who can respond to his needs by giving him attention, food and the toys he requires, is satisfactory. It might indicate retardation. The parentally abused child may relax and become quite friendly. But whatever the reaction is to the parent's separation, it provides us with some information about the child and helps us to come to a conclusion about his particular psychological state.

One of the first things we ask the child is what he would like to become. And we frequently hear that he wants to become a bus driver, a policeman or a fireman, especially from the younger children. As they become a little older, getting into their teens, they may want to join the army, work in an office or department store, become a doctor or a lawyer, or still a policeman, fireman or bus driver. There is a far greater range of responses as the child grows up. And, of course, we ask him why he has selected the particular job or career named. What is there he likes about it? The little child who has said "policeman" will tell us that he wants to get a gun and shoot it, the slightly older child will tell us that he wants to catch crooks, and when we ask the pre-teenager that question, typically, he will tell us that he wants to help to protect people.

After we have talked about what the child would like to do when he grows up, we discuss what it is that he likes to do now; what his favorite activities, games, and sports are. The responses again depend on the age of the child, his socioeconomic background and whether the child is male or female. A typical seven-year-old boy might tell us that he likes to watch television, play with his toy cars or play with his brother. Now these are indoor responses, so we would ask him about what he would do if he went outside. He might tell us that he likes to run around or toss a ball, or he may tell us that the kids are too big or that he would rather stay home with Mommy. The fact that the child would rather stay home doesn't tell us anything until we find out the reason why. It is possible that the child lives in a terrible neighborhood and he is forced to stay home. On the other hand, if he lives next to a pleasant park and never goes into it, we would inquire further as to the reasons for staying indoors.

One of the things we look for throughout the interview is the correspondence between the child's answers and those that had been given to us by the parent. If they do not corroborate one another, we wonder whether or not it might indicate that he is living in a fantasy world or trying to cover up a particular aspect of his life. He might say he is the greatest baseball player in the world and believe this in his own mind, but yet the mother has told us that he doesn't play baseball very much or very well. If the child really believes it, it is a bad sign and could mean that he is not in touch with the world as it is.

We first try to find out just how much he really believes his own statement, which may differ significantly from the parent's assertion. We might ask him what would happen if he couldn't play baseball well. What would happen if he struck out instead of hitting a home run? What would happen if his team lost? What would happen if he was with a group of boys and didn't play well enough to get on the team? We want to see how the child handles these possibilities. He might still assert that he is the best baseball player and that he regularly hits home runs. On the other hand he might say that he would feel terrible and very sad if he played poorly or his team lost. Then again he might threaten to beat up anyone who wouldn't let him play on the team. These varying responses indicate the type of personality lying behind the fantasy. Of course, there is the other possibility that the child's history is more accurate than that of the parent.

It could also mean that the child is lying and telling the questioner something to make a good impression. He knows that he shouldn't be staying home all day while the other boys are out playing baseball. In another example he might be doing poorly in school and yet he will tell you that he receives good grades. In the latter case he knows what he should be doing and is concealing the fact that he is not doing it. In both cases the children are trying to protect themselves, but the child who has mistaken fantasy for fact is in far greater difficulty than the child who knows reality but covers up his problem defensively and consciously.

Ordinarily, we expect a child to have a best friend because it is important for his development. Working closely with another person helps the child to develop trust and cooperation. The best friend also helps the child by teaching the concept of sharing, whether it be secrets or common projects and experiences. They have to support one another, take turns and play and work together, and these things are essential to help a child mature. The absence of a best friend is an indicator of possible problems. It may mean that the child is a "loner" or that the child has difficulty in making friends, whether it is because he is too aggressive or too shy or unskilled in social abilities.

Parents sometimes hamper the formation of best-friend relationships because they criticize all or most of the friends that the child brings home. They find one is too rough, another may be too rich, and still another is too poor. The parent may seize on almost anything to inhibit the formation of a best-friend relationship. This eventually carries over to the child and he gets the idea that no one is worthy of him, and he starts looking down on others and criticizing them. And it is a fact of life that one cannot have a best-friend relationship and be overly critical at the same time.

Another way that parents may block the formation of a best friend is to keep the child home and discourage telephone calls. Or when the child announces that he is going out to play baseball they find a task for him to do before he leaves, and this ultimately makes the child miss the activity, or at least be late. They might also refuse to have other children come to the home to visit. They say that it is too small or too messy or that the other children will mess it up. All these roadblocks are directed toward preventing the formation of the best friend. This may be because the parents want to keep the child dependent or because they are paranoid or suspicious of everyone outside the family, even a little child. Or perhaps they have a superiority complex and think they are better than everyone else, or perhaps they are just fearful and apprehensive that something bad will happen to the child when he leaves the house.

On the subject of food, we inquire as to what his favorite dish is. Frequently the child will name a special dish that his mother makes, but sometimes a child will comment that he cannot stand the food that the mother prepares. The former child indicates a possible closeness to the mother and home that is perhaps lacking in the second child's response. We also look to see if the child will name a wholesome food or junk food as being the favorite. We also like to know what he selects to have after school as a snack, just to help us get a picture of the child's eating habits.

Just as we had spoken to the parent about money, so do we bring up this subject with the child. We ask the child concrete questions first—what does he spend his money on, for instance—and then we go to a more hypothetical level and ask what he would do if he had more money. If the child is receiving $1.00 each week, we inquire as to what he would do if he were to receive $5.00 or $10. With the larger sum, he would have the discretion to buy things he would like right now, and his answer would give us an insight into what he was really interested in, such as clothes, sports equipment, records or having a party with his friends.

We also ask children what they would do if a friend were to ask them for money to buy a candy bar just after they had received their allowance. We want to know if the child would give the money to the friend, or lend it to him with the expectation of getting it back, or would refuse to lend it at all. The child who would give the money makes us curious as to how often he does that. If it were once a year then there would be nothing amiss, but if it were more than once a week, then in general it would not be a good sign, especially if the child were handing over a substantial portion of the allowance. It might indicate that his friend is a bully and the child is afraid, or that he is so desperate to make friends that he is willing to try to buy them.

If the child lends the money and doesn't have a pressing need for it and the friend is usually reliable about paying it back, then there would be nothing wrong with the transaction. On the other hand, if he does want to buy something for himself and puts off doing so in order to lend the money to the friend, it could indicate that he puts a higher priority on his friend's needs than on his own. Again, if this happens once in a long while there is nothing wrong with it and it is rather generous, but if it is a regular occurrence and he is constantly placing his friend ahead of himself, that may be a negative sign. It may mean that he lacks confidence and perhaps feels less worthy than others and doesn't deserve things, or that he is fearful of others. In general, it could indicate that he has a poor image of himself, but it could also indicate shyness, passivity or that he is easily led.

In discussing school, we find that most of the children say that they like it, but we like to get beyond that into the specifics. We inquire about what subjects, teachers and classmates they like most or least, because few children, even the best students, like everything about school. We automatically begin to suspect that the child is not being frank with us, if he says that he likes everything. We try to penetrate that blanket statement in a friendly way, perhaps telling him that he is the first person that we have ever encountered who liked *everything*. We encourage him to mention anything at all that does not please him, and gradually he will admit that he is not all that happy with math or something else. Once the child gets the idea the average person has some dislikes then he begins to feel free to voice some of his own annoyances which he has been holding back for one reason or another. The child may just want to get the interview over with as soon as possible, and so he just says nice things, or perhaps he doesn't like the idea of a psychiatric interview and is protecting himself from being labeled unfavorably. We find that most children, however, are able to go through the interview with little difficulty.

Sometimes if the child is shy and is having difficulty speaking freely, we ask him if he would like to take a piece of chalk and go to the blackboard and draw a picture. Then, depending on what he drew, whether it is a car or a person or an airplane, we could begin to talk about that. Gradually, the child will relax and we can get on with the other items that we want to cover during the interview. If a child is full of hostility, he may draw a picture with people shooting and stabbing one another, and this is another source of information reflecting the child's state of mind. We usually don't direct the child to draw any specific thing but leave the choice of subject up to him. However, asking him to draw a person is often informative.

Also, we observe the behavior of the child during the course of the interview. The hyperactive child will be up and down, in and out of his seat running back and forth. The child may look through the desk drawers or open a closet. On the other hand, the child may sit quietly with hands folded almost as if he were in the classroom, afraid or apprehensive and timid. We try to deal with each child individually, encouraging the timid ones to speak out and trying to calm the hyperactive ones to see how they respond. As a rule, children will talk about money, television, and play quite easily, but find it more difficult to talk about why they were expelled from school or why they were punished by their parents. These are areas where they have experienced failure of one sort or another, and they usually try to protect their own image.

The natural tendency for everyone is to not bring up negative aspects about themselves in public, but children are often even more reluctant in this respect than adults. An adult comes to a psychiatric examination with the idea that he can be helped, and that the quickest way to be helped is to bring up frankly and openly the problem that is troubling him. The child doesn't understand that psychiatric counseling can help him just by talking. Children are accustomed to taking aspirin to relieve a headache, or to receiving an injection to cure a more serious malady, but talking as therapy lies outside of their experience and they are dubious about its efficacy.

We attempt to reconcile all of the information that both the mother and the child have given us to determine if counseling, for the parents or the child or both, is indicated. It is difficult to predict exactly how much therapy may be needed, because some fairly major problems can be resolved rather quickly, given the right circumstances, and yet certain apparently smaller problems can persist.

We look at the child basically to see if he is able to function at the level that would be anticipated for children of his specific age and circumstances. Does he have the social capabilities to match his intellectual capabilities? There are rough norms for "appropriate" behavior, but they can change as the society changes. For example, the appropriate age for dating has been lowered and children and teenagers are dating at an earlier age. The child's environment also contributes to normative behavior; in the suburbs it is perfectly normal for a child to be taking driving lessons at the age of sixteen, but that is not the case, ordinarily, for the child living in the city. We try to look at the child as a whole, in the context of his entire background and environment, rather than focusing on just particular symptoms.

In the psychiatric evaluation we are trying to find out what is happening within the child and with the child in relationship to his family. We develop within the context of the family, neighborhood and school, and we want to gauge the child's position in these structures. Is he the tyrant or the pawn, or does he occupy a healthy middle ground?

Usually, anything that a child wants to talk about can be a rich source of information about his social maturity as well as other functioning. When we speak of games we want to know if the child can win and lose with grace. It is quite normal for a child to cheat at games and find it unbearable to lose when he is very young, but then around the ages of seven and eight he has to be able to learn to lose as well as win. This indicates that he is learning to play by the rules and is a sign of social maturity.

Hobbies, which are a voluntary activity, give us insight into the child's interests and his personality. Hobbies are not like schoolwork, where the child is compelled to study a set number of subjects. By choosing a hobby the child expresses an opinion, just as he does when he selects games that he enjoys. We would look for a pattern. Does the child start many hobbies only to drop them almost immediately, or does he select one or two and pursue them with great vigor? This latter would tell us that he is displaying a significant degree of self-discipline, which is part of the maturing process. We would be curious to know if he shared the activity with his father, mother or sibling, which could be a further demonstration of a sharing ability and maturity. If the hobby were stamp collecting, he would demonstrate more maturity by joining a club and going to meetings rather than just confining his activities to ordering them from a catalogue by mail with no social contact. These signs are not hard and fast, so we always look for the pattern in the whole context of the child's interactions both in the home and beyond the family circle. And the way that we uncover the pattern is by talking to parents and children about everyday activities and observing their reactions and listening to their responses.

The seriously disturbed children may be helped with counseling or drug therapy or both. With the less-serious problems, counseling sessions alone can suffice. Frequently employed techniques involve individual and group psychotherapy, family therapy, counseling and/or psychotherapy for one or both parents, medication of various types, play therapy and role simulation.

The following case histories are presented in order to emphasize the importance of carefully observing the child's response to medication. It is not uncommon to try several different medications in varying dosages, until the right combination is found. In addition, the beneficial effects of medication together with psychotherapy are described.

Henry was an eight-year-old boy referred by the third grade teacher of the public school which he attended. He was described as inattentive, impulsive and hyperactive in the classroom. At home, he lived with his mother and was described as fairly well behaved but "nervous and unable to sit still." He was the oldest of four siblings in a fatherless home. Because of various medical and other realistic problems, the mother could not bring him regularly for psychotherapy on a weekly basis. It was then that we decided on a trial period with medication. First, Hydroxyzine, (Atarax) 10 mg. twice a day was prescribed, but the mother noticed no change whatsoever. Then he was tried on 25 mg. of Hydroxyzine twice a day and the mother complained he was a little sleepy. Next, he was tried on 37.5 mg. of Pemoline (Cylert) every morning with no improvement noticed. The dose was increased by 18.75 mg., and he was slightly improved. When the dose was increased again, to 75 mg. each morning, his school behavior and performance improved significantly. He was kept on this medication during the school year with continued good results. He did not take the medication on weekends, school holidays or school vacations. No significant side effects were noted.

❦

John was a nine-year-old boy who was referred by his pediatrician for distractability, mischievous behavior in the classroom and difficulty sitting still. The pediatrician had tried various medications including Hydroxyzine, Thioridazine (Mellaril) and Methylphenidate (Ritalin), with no significant improvement. He was given individual psychotherapy, and counseling for the mother was initiated. However, the therapist found that he was too distractable and overactive to attend to the psychotherapeutic sessions, which consisted of talking together with opportunities for drawing, puppet play and games. Since he did not have side effects when he was on 10 mg. of Methylphenidate in the morning and again at noon, it was decided to combine the medication with psychotherapy. Significant improvement was noted. The therapist reported that he could understand and learn during the therapy sessions.

Subsequently, the teacher reported that he seemed to understand how to handle the other boys who tried to tease him and get him into trouble with the teacher. In addition, his attention span and motivation to do his schoolwork both improved.

VII. OCCUPATIONAL THERAPY EVALUATION AND TREATMENT

All children experience some difficulty at first in tying their shoelaces, buttoning a jacket or closing snaps, but in a relatively short space of time they learn to accomplish these little tasks of everyday life. Being able to dress themselves becomes a source of pride for most youngsters, and they enjoy being praised for being "grown-up." Soon they pass on to more complex tasks quite naturally and are hardly aware of the considerable dexterity they display. There are, of course, differences in proficiency between various children in their ability to complete these tasks efficiently. The span of time that it takes most children to accomplish these tasks is described as the normal time span.

A small percentage of the children will be much quicker than the others, and another group of about the same size will be significantly slower. Among these latter children will be those who find it extraordinarily difficult to accomplish these tasks and may not be able to do them at all. They just seem to lack the coordination required to tie, insert or fasten things together and will need remedial help in order to acquire the skill that others picked up quite naturally. Later on, reading and writing in school may pose another set of difficulties for these youngsters.

In the occupational therapy evaluation we pay special attention to the process of *sensory integration,* as evidenced by the child's ability to perform purposeful activity. The term sensory integration has been extensively used by A. Jean Ayres and her associates to describe the interaction of two or more functions or processes in a manner that enhances the effectiveness of the brain's response. Her work has been based primarily on the findings of Charles Sherrington, an outstanding neurophysiologist who stressed the importance of the central nervous system in organizing and interpreting environmental stimuli. We are primarily concerned with evaluating the basic skills that underlie all of the more complex activities, such as learning in school or the ability to play games. For example, if a child has faulty eye-hand coordination, he will never be able to play baseball well. If there is a flaw in his visual space perception, he may have difficulty in learning how to read. In each case the difficulty is obvious only in the end result, which is failure.

The occupational therapist meticulously examines each task, breaking it down into its component parts in order to identify the problem link in the chain of activity. This involves two distinct types of examination. First, we talk to the child and ask him to take a series of tests, and then we take a careful history from the parent. Both provide essential information.

When the child first comes for the evaluation we ask his parent to wait outside while we conduct the testing, explaining that we will speak to the parent subsequently, once the various tests have been administered. We look to see whether the child separates easily from the mother and vice versa or whether there is some type of emotional scene. We observe the child's behavior throughout the evaluation, taking special note of the way he responds to the tests, whether he is interested and cooperative, or anxious and withdrawn. We gauge his attention span to see if he is easily distracted, and we observe whether he approaches the various tasks in an organized manner. We also make note of his ability to communicate—does he comprehend and converse?—and we judge whether his activity level is normal, overactive or lethargic. These are clinical observations that do not contribute to the child's test scores, but do help us to evaluate the type of child we are working with. In noting these various behavioral characteristics we jot down examples of a particular action, such as tapping the table repeatedly, to indicate a certain nervousness. We do not simply note "anxious."

We begin the actual testing with a written test of visual-motor integration, which simply means translating a visual stimulus into a movement. We present the child with a test booklet and a pencil, which is placed right in the middle of it, so as not to influence his use of either hand. When he has picked up the pencil, we ask the child to write his name in the booklet and to open it to the first page, which contains six boxes. The three top ones have simple geometric designs in them, and we ask the child to copy them exactly, in the empty boxes below each one. There is no time limitation on the task

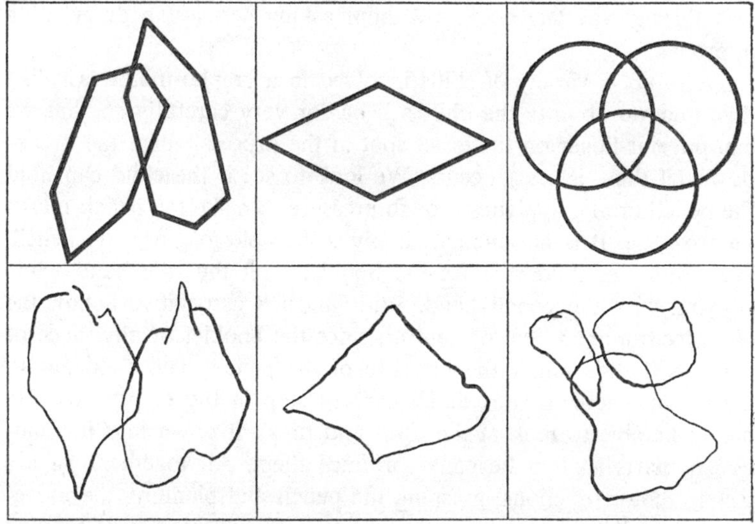

Fig. 8. Copying designs. The designs in the lower boxes have been copied by a child with a normal IQ, but with visual-motor problems.

and the child proceeds at his own pace. The only limitation that we do place on the child is to instruct him not to erase anything.

Children develop a certain rhythm doing this test and many will spontaneously complete the three figures on one page, turn to the next page, and proceed to the point where it becomes too complicated for them. We are alerted when a child will sit and wait each time for approval before continuing. It may mean that the child is insecure, or that this type of test makes him uncomfortable for one reason or another. Normally, most children become so motivated by the task that they forget the presence of the evaluator and simply work their way through the test booklet without asking permission or awaiting approval.

There are a variety of skills involved in a grapho-motor task like this, and we observe the child's behavior very carefully so that we can put our finger on the exact spot in the process where the breakdown (if there is one) occurs. We look to see if the child can hold the pencil firmly, applying enough pressure to make the pencil marks on the page. It is not enough simply to be able to grasp the pencil. We see if the child steadies the booklet with the free hand while copying with the pencil hand. Without such associative action the child loses a great deal of control, since the booklet or any piece of paper will slide under the pressure of the pencil. The child has to figure out where to start and where to stop in the empty box. He has to be able to look at the form and break it down into its component parts so that he can reproduce them. All together, we are testing motor functions, grasping the pencil and planning the movement, as well as a spatial perception function with this simple copying task. The test is scored by norms established for various age levels. Some of the other things we notice are which hand the child favors, any problems with switching hands, his ability to organize himself when presented with a task, his distractability, and basically whether or not writing is a problem for him.

The specific sensory-integration assessments are made with a variety of sub-tests, of which we may give a few or all, depending upon the child's attention span. The first of these also involves copying a figure, but the child has to impose the design on a grid of dots, which is a more complicated task. This requires a higher order of spatial manipulation, including visual scanning back and forth between the design and the grid to make sure that the lines are going

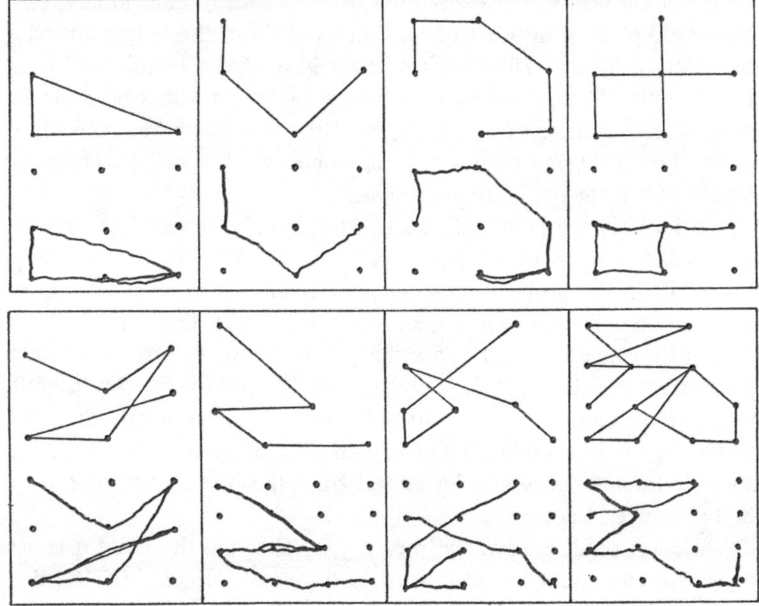

Fig. 9. Having a child copy patterns of connecting lines between dots is another way of assessing visual-motor problems.

in the same direction as the figure being copied. We ask the child to make the lines as straight as possible. The test is graded both for accuracy in reproducing the design and also for the precision of the execution, so that instead of receiving a score of "two" for a figure that was accurate but not as precise as it should have been, the child will be graded "one." Failure to copy it at all would be graded "zero."

In the next sub-test we present the child with a list of words and ask him to copy them as accurately as possible and remind him that he is not allowed to erase anything. If he wishes to change anything, he should place it in brackets and then put down the corrected letter or letters beside it. Here we get some idea of the child's ability to form letters. There is no aspect of language being tested because the child does not have to be able to read the words, just to copy them correctly. The same would be true for anyone asked to copy the letters of a language he didn't know.

We look to see how well the child forms the letters, the amount of spacing that he leaves between them, and whether he can align his words in the proper order. Since he scans the word at the top of the page and has to reproduce it on a numbered line on the lower half of the page, we want to see that all of the words are copied onto the correct numbered line. We also look to see how quickly a child works. No matter how beautifully he forms his characters, this skill would be of little practical use to him if he were too slow in doing so. The homework would be erased from the blackboard before he had a chance to copy it.

We get a reading of visual memory by showing the child a series of words, each on a separate word card, one at a time. After turning each word card face down, we ask the child to circle the correct word from a series of four possibilities on the page in front of him. As in the previous test, the child need not be able to read the word to pick it out, but can simply memorize the sequence of symbols.

Now we introduce a matching test in which the cue card remains face up. We show the child a word and then ask him to pick out the same word from a series of four possibilities, three of which are incorrectly spelled. The words that are used in this test contain the letters that are most often confused by a child with some form of reading disability—"u" and "n," "b" and "d," "p" and "q." In each case a rotation, or a reversal, would change the letter completely and, of course, the spelling of the word. Another manifestation of a reading problem is the transposition of letters so that the simple word "thing" becomes "thign." In this case the child will match this incorrect spelling. We get a great deal of information about the child's visual processing ability from this sub-test.

Next we give the child a slightly harder task to do by showing him a number of figures, and ask him to copy them from memory after being able to look at them for five seconds. Similarly, we give him a sequence of letters, remove them, and ask the child to reproduce them himself. Here we may see that a child who had good letter formation when he was copying from a visual model might begin to experience difficulty when he has to rely on his memory for the image. We also might pick up rotations and reversals that we wouldn't get when a child copies from the page. The numbers "6," "9" and "3" are all potentially troublesome.

We now go one step further in testing the child's ability to reproduce letters, by simply asking him to do so verbally. This means that the child has to retrieve the image from memory, because he has had no visual cue. Even when we were making it more difficult for him by showing it for only five seconds, the child still had something to look at. Now he does not. We might find that the child could manage letters, but that when we gave him a whole word, he could not spell. These children have a difficulty in forming the visual-auditory-motor sequence—that is, associating the sound with what the letter looks like and how to write it—that is necessary to complete this task successfully. We are very interested to see whether there is a difference in scores between the visual and the auditory test. In some cases there is and in others there is not. But if a child does show marked strength in one channel (for example auditory over visual), then we would plan any remedial work to take advantage of that fact.

A further test of auditory perception related to reading is given by saying words, and then asking the child to repeat the first or last letter and then to write it down. We are interested to see whether a child can focus in on a single part of a word.

To get a sense of his auditory association we say a word and ask the child to pick it out from four printed words.

In examining visual skills in relation to forms, we use a series of tests timed by a stopwatch. Up until this series of tests, there has been no time pressure. These timed tests are quite straightforward and consist of asking the child to select the correct shape, of the two offered, to match the example shown. We instruct the child to figure out which of the shapes is the correct one before touching either of them, because the first one he chooses will be graded as his answer. (We want to make sure that the child solves the relationship visually, and not by manipulation.) We are interested in the time it takes the child to process the visual information. There are several types of visual perception skills being tested here, and we are interested to see whether the child makes his errors in simple form differentiation or in the orientation-in-space section or with the mental manipulation items. If the child is having difficulty, we want to determine whether the difficulty stems from the process itself or the time limitation. A child's performance on this test would have implications for his mathematical skills, his ability to read maps, his mechanical ability, and would correlate positively with his IQ.

To determine the child's ability to distinguish between the figure and the ground (central importance vs. background), we present him with a line drawing in which three figures are overlapped, along with a series of individual drawings without any overlapping. Then we ask him to pick out of the individual group the figure which is included in the overlapping one. The child has to be able to perceive the central figure despite the distraction of the background figures. We want to see whether he can retain the gestalt (perception of a whole form). The figures offered include both representational objects, such as a stool, and abstract geometric shapes.

The test we employ to measure a child's conception of position-in-space uses non-representational figures exclusively. We show the child a circle with the first quadrant (12–3 o'clock) missing, and then another circle with the fourth quadrant missing (9–12 o'clock). We then present the child with a third circle, which also has a quadrant missing, and ask if it is like the first one. We do the same thing for the second circle, and continue to accustom the child to the test with a series of similar examples which we leave in front of him. Ultimately, the items become very complex and we then introduce the factor of memory, by covering the examples while continuing to ask the child whether or not the test figure represents the one that he just saw. The skill demonstrated here is related to reading ability, for if the child cannot differentiate between rotated non-representational forms or maintain a visual memory of a sequence of forms, he may well have difficulty doing so with letters and words.

Fig. 10. Drawing of a clock by a child with a visual perceptual problem. *Perception* is the area of difficulty here; this is what the child actually sees.

By this time, we have made enough clinical observations of the child to form some idea about whether his level of attention is average or short, and whether he is easily distracted. We would now like to determine whether the child is more easily distracted by auditory, visual or tactile stimuli, because people differ in their susceptibility and any program of remedial help would have to respect this.

We begin a series of physical tests to determine eye preference, hand preference, and the mobility of the eye and hand in a series of simple tasks. For example, we would roll up a sheet of paper and ask the child to look at something through it. The eye that he used would indicate his preference. If there were any doubt or hesitancy we would offer him a second piece of paper, from which the center had been torn out, and again ask him to look through it. The second observation should confirm the preference.

Moving a pencil back and forth shows us how well the eye tracks, an essential movement in reading. And we would not want to see the head move, because that would be exhaustive when reading. Since the brain is divided into two hemispheres, we test to see whether the eyes move smoothly across the imaginary mid-line, just as we test for the hand movement. Convergence and divergence would be observed as we moved the pencil closer and closer to the tip of his nose, and then away. This test and many others overlap with those given in the pediatric neurological examination, but here we concentrate more on the physical skills that would be of most use in a school situation. We examine closely those skills that are basic to the acquiring of information. We are interested to see whether or not the processing systems are operating in a normal manner so that learning can take place without any interference. It is an examination of the means rather than the ends that we concentrate on, so that we break down physical movements into their finest parts to see exactly where any problem may be.

For example, we are very interested in motor planning, and ask the child to imitate a series of movements that we demonstrate to him. The child, who is sitting in the opposite chair, is told to imitate the positions as quickly as possible. The examiner performs these movements rapidly, so that the child will not have time to examine the process. Instead, he will be presented with the final position and have to figure it out himself, and exercise his motor-planning function in a clear and unambiguous manner. At times, the child will respond to the fast movements of the examiner by being equally quick, and the examination turns into a game of sorts. Most children do respond to the tests readily and work their way through them with some degree of interest. If the child is able to achieve the correct position in under three seconds it is scored as a "2," under ten seconds a "1," and over ten seconds a "0." As with all of the other tests, we add up the individual scores and compare them to standardized norms to determine whether the individual child scores at the average, above average, or below. We are interested to see how well the individual child can coordinate the movements of both sides of his body, and how well he can execute controlled, purposeful movement.

To test automatic movement, we ask the child to imitate the movements of the examiner, who once again is facing him, by responding as if he were looking in the mirror. If the examiner raises the right hand to the right ear, then we would expect the child to touch the left ear with the left hand. We are looking here to find out the child's internal consciousness of laterality. We expect that most children would pick up on the rhythm of the test fairly easily, though there are times when the child has some difficulty with this automatic response, and we would note that this basic response is deficient. Since it is a fundamental response, we would anticipate other difficulties in movements that rely in part on such automatic responses. Oftentimes, the child who confuses the "b" and the "d" or who has difficulty distinguishing right from left will also have trouble here. These responses are internal and automatic and do not depend on thinking; they reflect a built-in sense of right and left. Thus, a problem in this area may lead to hesitancy, confusion and clumsiness.

To get a sense of the cognitive understanding of right and left, we ask the child to pick up an object in his right hand and place it in the examiner's right hand. Or we ask a child to show us his right hand by raising it. Here we are concerned with the length of time that it takes a child to perform the requisite action. It may be that he has simply taught himself that he has a freckle on the right hand and when he hears right, he thinks of that mark and raises that hand. He really doesn't know it instinctively, but he has thought about it. And we do find that children devise all sorts of clever strategies to help themselves to get along. It is our job to see through whatever strategies may have been developed so that we know where to begin with remedial help. We pay particular attention to the length of time it takes a child to perform any of these verbal requests to determine whether he is thinking his way through it or doing it automatically.

Tactile, kinesthetic testing is done in a variety of ways and one of the simplest is to touch a child's ear or hand and observe whether or not there is an adverse response to it. Does the child complain of itching or does he appear to be very uncomfortable? We call this tactile defensiveness, and it is an indication that the nervous system is not functioning properly. Theoretically, there are two types of tactile systems. One is the *protective* system, which makes the child or adult pull a hand away quickly, without thinking, from a hot object. The second is the *discriminatory* system. That is the system that allows the child to explore things with the hands and not be in a state of "fight or flight." It is believed that when we encounter tactile defensiveness, the protective system is dominant and therefore the child does not explore. He responds continually as if he is being threatened. Being in a classroom is a horror for such a child, because there is always another child walking near or brushing up against him, and he is beset by defensive reactions. This is a condition that goes far beyond the normal, occasional feeling of not wanting to be touched that most everyone experiences from time to time.

In all of these tests, we are looking at the integrity of the nervous system. The tests are designed to elicit what we call "soft" signs as compared to "hard" signs. A "hard" or definite sign would be obvious spasticity, while a "soft" sign only implies that there is cerebral dysfunction, but it cannot be proved. And we look for these "soft" signs in connection with a problem. If there is no learning problem and a child is clumsy, it simply means that the child is clumsy and nothing more.

We ask the child to do rapid alternating movements, such as slapping the thigh with the palm and then the back of the hand, to see if the child has good coordination and picks up the correct rhythm. In addition, we look to see if the child uses the whole arm, or just the forearm, which is all that is required, and if he can strike the same spot consistently or has a tendency to wander up and down the leg. Looking further at coordination, we ask the child to touch the tips of the thumbs with each of the fingers in sequence, one hand at a time, and then both together.

Fine motor coordination is demonstrated in such tasks as threading tiny beads, tying shoelaces, and cutting paper with scissors. We might also toss and catch a ball for a while. Each of these tasks should be accomplished relatively easily and precisely.

We are also concerned with basic muscle tone. To test this we ask the child to flex his biceps, and then we move the arm back and forth, looking for the normal ability to hold the position. We would also ask the child to jump and hop and skip, as well as to walk, so that we can check his gross-motor coordination. During this testing we look for both coordination and the purposefulness of the movement. The body has to be able to make the necessary changes in muscle use automatically. This holds true for a task as fine as handwriting as well as the larger movements of walking.

It is important to determine if a child can stand with eyes closed, extending his arms in front of himself, and maintain the position comfortably. Some children make little balancing flutters with their fingers, and others really have to struggle to maintain the position. Still others lack the strength to keep the arms extended for the short time required. After a few moments the tester will turn the child's head to one side, to observe whether this has a disorganizing effect on the posture.

A variety of equilibrium reactions are checked while the child is lying face down, kneeling on all fours and sitting. This permits us to see that the basic systems are intact. One test consists of standing a child on a rotating board and turning him completely around ten times. Then we stop the board and look into his eyes to count the number of small glancing movements of the eyes that persist, after the rotating has stopped.

These small eye movements are called *nystagmus,* and since in this case they are taking place after the child has been turned about several times, they are referred to as *post-rotary nystagmus.* These motions of the eye are normal, and, theoretically, there is something wrong with the vestibular system of those children who do not display these movements. Some investigators have reported a lack of *post-rotary nystagmus* in up to 50 percent of the learning-disabled children they have tested, but in our experience the percent has been significantly lower. When a problem is identified, we use techniques involving swinging activities and scooter board activities to improve balance and equilibrium. These are valuable methods of treatment and should be viewed in relation to the discussion of dyslexia (p. 000) and the section on the brain's role in learning disabilities (p. 000).

We look for strong vestibular bilateral integration, and when it is deficient it means that the child is not moving his body correctly. This is reflected in the postural tests and the lack of eye movement ordinarily observed in post-rotary nystagmus, among other signs. In practical terms, it means that the foundation for learning as it relates to his body is deficient, and if the lower level of vestibular integration does not function adequately, then the higher levels—for example, the activities of the cortex—are influenced adversely.

Another cluster of problems has to do with *apraxia,* which means difficulty with motor planning. Another would have to do with visual problems. In each case we would combine our clinical observations with the actual test scores achieved in the various areas to draw a coherent and logical conclusion. We always try to refine our observations to focus on the precise portion of the system that is causing the difficulty, so as to be able to apply our remediation efforts with the greatest efficiency.

After we have spoken to the child and administered the various tests, we interview the mother while the child waits outside. We ask the mother what she thinks the primary problem is. This history is similar to that taken by the pediatric neurologist, but from the occupational therapist's special perspective it is necessary to delve into the question of the child's handedness in somewhat greater detail. We are particularly interested in right/left preference, and coordination in general. An uncertainty in handedness will contribute to hesitancy about how to begin a task, and if a child has other learning problems, this can be very disorienting. As infants, children use one or another hand normally, and we try to find out when the child started to use one hand more than the other. We routinely ask which hand the child uses to eat with. We pursue this back as far as we can go to see whether he always used his right hand when he was younger, or whether there ever was an indication that he might have been left-handed, and was forced to use the other hand. Compulsory switching was routine in schools in the thirties, and cases of it still crop up. Historically, it is a very controversial issue since sinistrality (left-handedness) has traditionally been regarded with some suspicion.

We discuss the school with the parents—where it is, what grade the child is in, and how he is doing—in order to derive a feel for the parents' understanding of the school situation. Some of these points are covered in other specialists' histories, but we think that it is important to look for consistency, so these questions are repeated by different disciplines.

We talk about any problems the child might be having at home. It is important to determine whether the problems are the same or are different from those in school. If they are different, then we might begin to think of environmental factors as being important. On the other hand, if they are the same, we are led to think that the problems are probably within the child himself.

We like to know how the child gets along with his brothers and sisters and the parents themselves. We are also interested to know whether he has any friends outside of the immediate family circle, to get an idea of how social a person he is.

To determine whether the child can take care of himself, we ask whether the child can feed and dress himself and handle other activities of daily living such as toilet training. We like to know whether the parent is still feeding the child and encouraging dependency by being overly protective, or if the parent is feeding the child because he cannot complete a meal by himself since he is so distractible.

Dressing can offer us further clues. We ask whether he has trouble putting on clothes and inquire about any reversals that might occur, such as the wrong shoe on the wrong foot. These tasks that are so routine for most children can be troublesome to a child with a learning disability. He might have extreme difficulty in buttoning a shirt in the right sequence, and thus display a perceptual problem.

Another area of special interest to us is whether or not the child participates in chores. Does he take out the garbage or help carry the packages at the supermarket? These may seem like simple things, but they involve a whole range of central-nervous-system activities and a breakdown anywhere along the way can cause trouble. To carry groceries, the child has to hear and understand the request. He must pick them up in a coordinated manner using his motor-planning sense, and then remember where to take them. If he is ascending a flight of stairs, he must rely on his vestibular system to let him know where his body is in space so that he does not stumble, and finally he must complete the task by placing them on the proper table without spilling or dropping. The child who is disorganized will not be able to do such a task. In fact, the disorganized child makes life more confusing with his efforts to help.

We ask the parents if the child knows how to handle money. Can he take public transportation by himself, paying his fare and descending at the correct stop? This latter instance would tell us in an operational way whether the child has problems in understanding direction or sequence or has an inadequate sense of time. It also gives us some insight about any possible retarded mental development, or about his level of maturity.

We ask the parents how he uses his hands in general, and we are on the alert for any mention of clumsiness or weakness. The sort of clumsiness that is significant consists of a regular pattern of dropping things—not the stray accident. The dropping of objects and spilling of glasses and cups makes us aware of a lack of coordination. And in this respect we would want to know if the child rides a bicycle and is able to play the games that other children of his own age are engaged in.

These tasks and games that we take for granted are compilations of very complex skills. Through the conversation with the parents and the child and the fine series of tests that we administer, we try to make a determination that will tell us whether the child really lacks the necessary skills or whether there is another factor operating. If his skills are deficient, then we try to design remedial programs. Precisely how much success he will have depends on the age when the deficit was discovered, its seriousness and the child's whole situation. For example, if a child is in the second or third grade and has a reading problem, it is very important that we actually work on reading recognition. If the same child gets to the tenth grade and nothing was done, then the priorities have changed. We might think more of vocational training, although for the truly dyslectic child the intellect may be superior and he may have developed compensatory mechanisms that allow him to pursue and benefit from higher education. Stories about prominent and successful individuals who overcame the problems of dyslexia have become legendary.

In every case we would work with the child's assets to correct or ameliorate his difficulties, and to maximize his potential for success. The three case histories that follow demonstrate the training approach specifically geared to the problems faced by the individual learning-disabled child.

Peter was first seen at the age of nine and a half when he was in the fourth grade. He was referred by his school because of behavior problems and poor academic achievement. His attention span was poor and he seemed sullen at times and uncooperative. He was called stupid by his classmates and was frequently involved in fights with them.

He was described as being disinterested in achievement and as having severe difficulty with reading and writing. When presented with something new he would not even attempt it on his own. He was unable to express himself in writing at all. However, he was reported as having come prepared for his lessons, and his mother always helped him. He was very bright and his family was extremely supportive.

He was very cooperative and motivated during the evaluation and seemed very aware of his reading problems. He was unusual in that he was able to describe specific problems that he had and the ways that he had developed to compensate for them. When presented with the letter "h" he knew that he didn't know the name of the letter. "Oh," he said, "that's the one I don't know." He wasn't able to rely on his memory of the symbol, nor was he able to integrate the sound and the symbol, which indicated that he had perceptual problems to a severe degree.

When he was asked to read words without comprehension, that is, simply to decode them, he had great difficulty establishing any sound-letter relationship. He didn't even know the names of the letters with any consistency. He relied very heavily on conceptual cues—for example his comment, "That's the one I don't know." He used a cognitive concept to compensate for the perceptual problem. He had difficulty matching identical printed words, even when everything was in front of him on facing pages.

Identifying letters was very laborious for him, and as we did more of these he became much more anxious. Of course, since he couldn't read the words he couldn't write them either. It became apparent that he had developmental dyslexia. He didn't have problems in any other areas of functioning.

He seemed to process information better through the auditory-vocal channel, so we attempted a phonetic approach in remediation rather than using the whole-word approach. We contacted his schoolteacher and confirmed that he did have a learning problem and that he was not lazy or a bad child. We felt that he should be given the opportunity to receive information verbally and asked that he be allowed to use a tape recorder in class to record the lectures and instructions.

This enabled him to listen to these notes and do whatever assignments were required, even to give reports from television or radio. We also asked that his mother be allowed to read his assignments to him. Then he would answer verbally and she would write the answers down. In this way Peter would at least be able to benefit conceptually from the instruction. His teacher was very cooperative and said that while she could not devote as much time to Peter as she would like to, she would try to accommodate to his needs.

We began remediation by teaching him ways to remember vowels from a conceptual base. These letters present the greatest difficulty since their sound is subtle, while consonants are more concrete and more easily recognized. We began by telling him that when he saw an "a" to think of an apple. When it is cut in half it roughly resembles the letter "a." We had to teach him to listen in a concrete way, to break up the letters. We worked with objects at first. We had Peter hold a pencil in his hand, even though we didn't ask him to write anything. Holding something such as the pencil helps to anchor attention. We call this a multisensory approach.

We placed three objects on the table in front of him and we asked him to start with the middle object which represented the vowel. The objects were a banana, an apple and a top, and the word represented by their first letters was "b-a-t." The task we set for him was very concrete, and we created a very rigid learning situation for remediation. It appeared that he needed the firm structure if the sessions were to work effectively. We asked him to look at the object, pronounce the final two letters "at" and then add the first letter "b" to get the complete word "bat." Even if he forgot a letter, the corresponding object was still there, and he began to build up the associations.

We started at the most basic level with three-letter words and then changed the first letter to introduce other words. The substitution of a car for the banana changed the word to "c-a-t." When we established the sequence of the sounds in the visual-auditory-vocal process, we asked him to make words to reverse the process and to go from auditory to visual; we said the word and he had to match it to the objects. We progressed through all the vowels in this manner. As he was able to grasp more words he was able to retain them, as well, and finally he was truly able to really read for the first time in his life. Previously, the letters had no meaningful sequence, they were a "jumble," as he described it.

He was good in math and science and was able to do well in those subjects when he was tested orally, and so he continued to advance in school. He failed language arts, but he did so well in other subjects that he was able to be promoted to the next grade. After the pressure was off, the school clearly saw that he did not have a behavior problem. We progressed from objects to printed words at the same basic level, and after six months, to sentences. At this point his facility with word recognition was improving steadily though slowly. Fortunately, his new teacher was very cooperative and helped him, as had the previous year's teacher.

After about three years of remediation he was up to a fourth-grade level in reading and was finally not threatened by reading a page of text. He continued to work by himself, and then we saw him after a year's break. As a result of his mother's extensive support and his intelligence and motivation, he had continued to make gains in reading, but spelling still posed a problem for him. He was graduating from grade school and had to find a high school. We wrote to the school he wished to attend, explaining that he was exceptional and that if it were possible for him to take the entrance examination orally, they could better judge his ability.

Presently he is attending high school and reading whole books. The big problem is still his speed, and reading is laborious. He was thirteen and a half before he was able to pick up a book for pleasure. We secured access to a library for the blind so that he could benefit from their spoken books program. He intends to go on to college and complete his degree. We have every expectation that Peter will do just that!

❧

Joseph was described by his school principal as being easily distracted, disorganized, prone to day dreaming, fidgety and having poor writing skills. We saw him when he was seven years of age, and during the evaluation he did show some of the signs of the distractibility described. He was cooperative and pleasant, but did need prodding to continue the tasks of the evaluation.

His overall IQ score put him on the borderline of the average range of intellectual functioning. However, we noted that he was pulled down by the performance items, and it was felt the score did not adequately assess his potential. This is very common among children with sensory-integrative difficulties.

His mother reported a history of hand switching, so that it wasn't clear which hand he was going to prefer even at age six. During the evaluation he tended to use his right hand but often reached for things with his left hand. His mother also reported that he had difficulty with learning to dress himself, though he was able to manipulate buttons. She reported that his distractibility interfered with his ability to watch television.

He had some difficulty in carrying out instructions, and when asked to indicate changes in what he wrote by bracketing the word that he wanted to change, he made a series of brackets one after another, instead of enclosing a word or a portion of a word. The normal eye flickering (post-rotary nystagmus) did not appear after testing, indicating that he had dysfunction in his vestibular system, which is very important in organizing a person's functioning. The visual-motor skills necessary for copying designs were delayed, the level of these skills being about those of a five-year-old. He was the older of two boys and in many ways the four-year-old brother was more advanced than Joseph when he first came to us.

Joseph's distractibility interfered with learning almost immediately, so we first worked on improving his sensory-integrative skills so that his attention level would improve. He didn't need much work with dressing, but needed more work with fine-motor tasks that involved lacing and tying, so we stressed those. We were pleased to note that he improved quickly.

We determined that he really was right-handed and began to prepare him to write by introducing structured, directional writing movements. We had him make circles and diagonals to improve his pencil pressure, and then we progressed to moving in the correct direction across the page. Once these skills were established we went to work on sequencing, making a large line and then a small one, and developing the rhythm of writing, and these were all preparatory to actual writing exercises. We took special care to get the sensory-integrative process working rather than just have him repeat one specific shape over and over. Slowly, the hyperactivity began to diminish as he began to experience success in these activities.

We also introduced word recognition activities. He could recognize three-letter words, but larger ones were more difficult. He guessed at them and would mistake them completely—"book" he read as "down," confusing the word in large measure because of his directional error in reversing the "b" to a "d." We began to focus on reading and spelling. He had some symptoms that one would see in dyslexia, but he had a whole slew of other problems, including the distractibility and poor motor coordination. It was not pure dyslexia.

After remediation, his reading did not pick up immediately, but he was more organized and was better able to receive information and act correctly on it. His behavior improved greatly when given structure- and sensory-integration help.

There was a question about whether he would have to go into a special class, but he was able to hold his own and he advanced to the third grade with his classmates. We told the school the types of remediation that we were attempting and alerted them as to what to watch for and reinforce. Joseph's mother understood the nature of his problem and was able to work with him each day at home, and this helped him a great deal.

Joseph was highly vulnerable and ran a high risk of failure. Any disturbance at home, for example, could have caused him to fail at school. The skills he was holding onto would break down under stress, but his mother, who was a teacher, was very supportive. He probably will always have problems remembering things and will have to continually find strategies to help himself, but he has made a good beginning. We recommended continuing family therapy to strengthen and maintain the necessary support systems.

Billy came to see us when he was six. His mother had first noticed a problem when at the age of four, he was not speaking well and was having difficulty in making himself understood. At first she thought that this might reflect the fact that she was overly protective since he was the baby in a large family. As time went by she realized that this was not the case. In kindergarten the teacher remarked that he "was not quite right."

He had difficulty in fine-motor coordination, including such tasks as holding a pencil, forming letters, zippering and doing up his belt. In dressing he had spatial difficulties in placing the right buttons in the right holes, and he became very frustrated. While he had motor problems affecting his ability to dress himself, he acquired an emotional overlay, which is not uncommon, in that he wanted his mother to dress him.

His peer relations were reported to be good, but because of his immaturity were not all that they could have been. During the evaluation he was initially shy, but he separated from his mother and warmed up quite quickly. But he appeared to be very anxious, wringing his hands, which is unusual at that age. He tended to doubt his own abilities, gave up very easily, and didn't really seem to understand tasks. However, he did take a great deal of satisfaction when he correctly completed a task.

At times he became fixated and repeated things over and over in a perseverative manner. He would become "stuck" in a groove and not able to switch out of it. He had trouble organizing himself and also he physically tended to hang onto objects, almost as if he were trying to "ground" himself. His muscle tone was roughly within normal limits, but his ability was limited when asked to assume and hold certain postures.

His balance was poor and he didn't move fluidly; almost as if his body were not attached to his arms. He couldn't maintain a sequence, and the fine-motor tasks of touching the tips of the fingers to the thumb rapidly one after another was too much for him. He also had severe difficulty in coordinating the two sides of his body. He didn't have a sense of his center and his bilateral-motor coordination was poor as a result.

Basically, sensory integration was the main problem. The two goals we set were to work on the activities of daily living as well as writing skills. First of all, our approach was very structured and we started in the grapho-motor writing area, working on pressure activities. We used silly putty and asked him to erase things so that he could develop the ability to squeeze but in the context of an activity; simply to give a child a pencil and tell him to press harder does not work. Through working with the putty, he developed a sense of how to push, and he could transfer that ability to activities of daily life, such as taking off his shoes where one has to push down on the heel. When we started with Billy he could not get his shoes off. For dressing we gave him tubes of cloth, like sleeves, so that he could get used to the parts before trying to put on his jacket. As far as buttoning went, we gave him loose buttons and told him to place them in a shoebox that had slots.

First, he just dealt with the isolated task of figuring out how to orient the button so that it would fit into the slot. We began with the simple task before starting the multistep buttoning task he found so difficult.

He was a very appealing child though he was immature. We saw him for a year and began to introduce more and more complex tasks. We went from pressure to working with a crayon. By this time he had entered the first grade but was having problems, so we recommended to the diagnostic team conference that he go into a class for children with neurological impairments. He developed a more focused approach, though he was still distractible and would get disorganized. Then we began to work on sequential memory tasks and physical tasks. For the latter we used an obstacle course that required planning, and he began to develop some real skill at this.

The fact that he could organize himself to imitate movements was just amazing, considering the difficulty he had with his first attempts. He continued to attend a special class and became able to take care of himself at home and was almost independent. He still had significant learning problems and will have to continue to work on them, but he's traveled a long way from where he started.

VIII. EDUCATIONAL EVALUATION AND REMEDIATION

Under the law, each child is entitled to an education that is appropriate to his individual needs. We, therefore, are requested to do educational evaluations from the age of three right up to the age of twenty-one. What we attempt to do is to direct children to the type of class that will give them what they are missing with the hope that there will be successful remediation and that these children will eventually be able to enter the mainstream. The recommendation for a specific type of class emerges from the reports of the various special disciplines and from the educational evaluation itself.

When a child is referred to us by a guidance counselor in a school or brought to us by a parent for an evaluation, we try to secure from the parent and the school exactly what types of problems the child is presenting. We also want to know how well the child is getting along with other children. This information is secured either through a direct call to the teacher or the guidance counselor or by having a standardized form filled out by the school, or both.

Basically, this evaluation (as each of the previous evaluations) falls into two parts: the informal observations and the formal standardized tests. (The school report is considered part of the informal observations.) In the informal or introductory part of the evaluation we look for eye contact, whether or not the child is cooperative during the session, and whether he is distractible or has a short attention span. When we talk about eye contact we are referring to the normal conversational situation in which people address one another and ordinarily look at the person to whom they are speaking, indicating interaction. If a child simply will not look at you and instead is throwing glances all around the room, that either indicates something about that child's relationship with other people (e.g., extreme shyness), or it may be a symptom of distractibility or a short attention span. Another child might answer you but look downward at the top of the desk or table, thus avoiding making eye contact. In such a case one would want to check the reports of the psychiatric or the psychology departments since such behavior could suggest an emotional problem. Of course, one always has to be aware of cultural differences. As for instance, in the case of many Hispanic children such behavior would be more or less normal since they have been told to look away as a sign of respect to an adult. In any case, these are "soft signs" that are included in our informal impression of the child.

In this informal area we also have to examine whether a child is bilingual or not. We should find out which is the dominant language and test the child in that language. Some of the children obviously speak one language better than another, and others speak both languages with about the same degree of proficiency or deficiency. We ask ourselves if the child is having difficulty learning the two languages. Is there simply confusion, or is there a true language disorder? At home children may speak Spanish and at school they may speak English. We find that in many tests designed to query them about school-related material these children may only be able to answer in English, despite the fact that they are Spanish dominant.

That does not mean that they have poor skills in Spanish! For instance, if we ask the child to recite the alphabet in Spanish, he can't do it because that is totally school related. It simply means that he has not learned the alphabet in Spanish since, typically, it is not the sort of thing that parents would drill him on. Rather it is the sort of material that the school would handle.

For the formal portion of the evaluation the examiner has a variety of tests to choose from and will select the most appropriate one for each individual situation. Since children differ in their responses to tests we are always alert to note any skills that they may demonstrate that are not specifically sought by the tests. Before we begin the formal testing procedure though, we begin by eliciting some general information.

In this informal area we look for language skills such as serial language. That is, being able to count to ten or to recite the alphabet, enumerate the days of the week and the months of the year. Also we ask what day of the week it is and try to ascertain if the child has a general idea of his surroundings. Of course his ability in this area is dependent on age. If the child is five we can't anticipate that he will know all of these facts, but if he is ten, we would expect that he would. When we don't find such serial language in the child it indicates to us that he can't put two related elements together. If there is difficulty with concrete language, it may indicate that he will be hampered in his use of creative language.

Another thing that we are interested in observing is the ability to identify colors and shapes. We would also want to see how well the child can identify body parts and was able to relate the numbers of fingers and toes, etc. The child would be asked to name which hand he was writing with. Again, this could indicate that either there was a language deficit or a more serious problem if he could not distinguish between right and left.

We are also interested in determining whether the child has mastered the time concept of before and after. If the child knows the alphabet or if he knows how to count, we would ask what number comes before "5" or after "8," or what letter comes before "M" or follows "r." Of course, if the child does not have such serial language, then we would have to try to test this concept in another way. For example, we could place two objects on the table in front of the child and ask him to touch the pencil after he touches the pen. Chances are that this is a harder task than responding to the request for the letter before "M," and it would only be used to try to determine the presence of the before and after action in the absence of serial language skills. These tasks are all language related.

The final part of the informal assessment is a writing task. The child is asked to write his name, birthday, address and telephone number, the alphabet in its entirety, and the numbers from "M" to "10." In this task we are first of all looking at the overall appearance of the child's handwriting and seeing whether there are letter reversals which could indicate a problem area. All children reverse some letters when they are learning the alphabet, but this phase passes by relatively quickly so that it is significant if it persists in an older child. It may indicate some problem in the central nervous system and may point to a lack of organization or an inability to integrate material.

Writing that is extremely small or large may indicate an emotional problem to be further investigated by the psychologist. The child is permitted to write script or print, whichever he feels more comfortable with. Sometimes children will mix up the two, but if they are younger and just learning how to write there is little significance to such switching.

This handwriting exercise also, of course, helps us to determine how much the child knows about his own environment. Again this is general, normative information, and we make allowance for the fact that in some of the larger, lower socioeconomic families children may not be aware of the exact date they were born, although they would know their age. Simple questions about the family are asked, such as who is in the family, the number of brothers and sisters, their names, and whether they are older or younger. This all gives us a sense of the child's orientation, his sense of who he is and where he is.

We ask the child whether or not he watches television, and since most children do, they are asked to relate a story of a program that they have seen. From this one can get an idea of how they relate a story, how they comprehend and what they see. If the child does watch television and cannot tell the evaluator anything about what he has seen, it is a warning sign for some type of language problem. It can be indicative of two things: Either the child does not understand what he is watching, or he can understand it but is unable to express it. With the exception of the writing task, all of the observations are directed toward linguistic ability as demonstrated in everyday commonplace situations. From this we derive an informal impression of the child's abilities, and we must stress the word informal. Only subsequent testing by means of standardized examinations will yield a firmer clinical picture. Very often, however, the child's responses in this informal situation will indicate which tests of the many available would be the best to use for the formal evaluation. It may indicate that the evaluation should place emphasis on testing language skills rather than academics.

Moving to the formal tests, children are asked to complete a puzzle to get a sense of their visual-motor skills. The complexity of the puzzle selected is determined by the age of the child. If he is very young, then the puzzle is correspondingly simple. We even ask high school students to complete a puzzle if the situation warrants it. It really depends on the reason for the child's being referred to us. If he is here because he can't read, perhaps it is because he has a great deal of difficulty in processing visual stimuli. One of the things that would be helpful to know is the degree of skill that the child has in integrating visual forms. With the older child we might use a block design rather than a puzzle. We give him a selection of geometric forms of various colors to choose from. Then we present a card with a design printed on it, using exactly the same colors as the blocks that have been given to him, and ask him to replicate it. In the beginning these designs are simple, such as a green square, a red square and another green square side by side, but they increase in complexity and difficulty until we are asking for some quite complex designs. In addition to the primary information about the child's ability to integrate visual forms, we also are able to observe his facility in using his hands.

Sometimes we encounter a child who uses both hands, the right one for writing and the left one for any kind of manipulative skill. This is something that neurologists and occupational therapists also always look at to see whether the child has established dominance in one hand. It may or may not be meaningful in the case of any individual child, but since dominance is the norm, we are alerted to be watchful when in the presence of a deviation from the norm.

To get a further look at the child's ability to integrate visual forms we ask him to place simple geometric shapes into a board with the corresponding cut-out shapes. This is a geometric sorting test, requiring hand-eye coordination and manipulative skill as well. We don't consider a small amount of fumbling as indicative of anything out of the way, but the persistent attempt to place a shape in the wrong hole tells us that the child is having some visual-perceptual difficulty.

There is a drawing test that we also use to determine visual-motor skills. We give the child a pencil and ask him to reproduce the shapes that he sees on the page opposite, in the appropriate empty boxes of the page closer to him. These figures start with a line, go to the flat-plane geometric ones and progress to complex three-dimensional figures. There are norms that define a correct response to the figure offered.

Usually, if the score indicates that the child is just a little bit off (6–8 months) the examiner will look back to see what type of errors were made. If they were not significant but lowered the score, a note regarding the situation will be made. The evaluator who was there may have seen that the mistake was due to carelessness rather than lack of perception. This is where the interpretive skill of the trained expert adds a dimension of understanding to the dry score.

With respect to academic skills, we briefly go back to writing tasks. If we are dealing with an older child, perhaps the examiner will dictate a sentence and check the spelling. Ordinarily one finds poor spelling in a child who has difficulty reading. Handwriting also draws on the ability to replicate a form from memory. We find, frequently, that a child will see his street name on a sign every day and will not be able to reproduce it. Perhaps if a child is having difficulty with the name of the street, the evaluator will dictate it letter by letter to see whether the child can write letters from dictation.

We test the child's mathematical ability, another academic skill. Both his mathematical conceptual development and his ability to do simple arithmetic functions such as $3 - 2 = 1$ are tested. Depending on the age of the child, different standard tests are given. If we are dealing with a child in the first or second grade, we would use a test that asks the child to identify a number by finding the one that corresponds to it from among a group of numbers on a facing page in the test booklet—a simple matching test. Later on a child would be asked to determine from the number of candles on birthday cakes which child was the older of those celebrating their birthdays. One of the precursory skills required to be able to read is to be able to match visually.

Conceptually the child will be tested by being asked to select the largest object or the shortest object, or the examiner will ask a question that requires a child to add together two numbers, come up with the correct answer and then indicate the number among those printed. For example, "Billy has two apples and his mother gives him another one. How many does he have now?" Without using pencil and paper the child should pick out the number "3" from the four numbers shown as possible answers. All of the items in the test are numbered and we know what grade level they represent, so that if a fourth-grade child is being examined, the evaluator would start with material that a third grader would be expected to know. Then depending on the child's performance we would continue either forward or backward to assess the exact grade level of accomplishment.

After we have tested mathematical concepts, the child's ability to perform simple arithmetic functions is measured with a standardized written test. Perhaps the child will do very well on this portion of the evaluation, whereas he did not do at all well on the previous test, which was given orally. To the evaluator this would be a warning sign that perhaps the child was having a language difficulty. He does not understand or is not processing the question. He can deal with mathematical problems on a concrete level, but he cannot deal with them when presented orally. And, as we all know, much of the material that students receive in the classroom is presented orally. This is particularly true for the more advanced grades.

The next area to be tested is the child's ability to read. With the younger children we are again asking them to match and to pick out the correct letter from the four that are printed on the page, and in this way to make an assessment of the child's reading recognition skill, visual recognition and visual matching. We progress from the simple letter to small words.

What the evaluator specifically wants to do is to find the exact point at which the child's ability to read the word breaks down, and to determine if he can figure out a strange word using some kind of phonic strategy. Frequently, children have extreme difficulty (beyond what we would expect), trying to figure out an unfamiliar word, and this might indicate some sort of reading deficiency.

Up to this point the evaluator has concentrated on reading recognition. The next area of skill to be explored is that of the ability to read a sentence and to comprehend the meaning of that sentence. Again, a standardized test presents a series of sentences graded in their complexity. The child is asked to read them to himself and then respond to them by selecting one of a series of four pictures that fits the description or question posed. This type of test distinguishes between the simple ability to read and the ability to understand what is being read. Sometimes, children can rattle off a sentence and not have the faintest idea of what it means. Let's say that a child's reading recognition level is at a fourth-grade level, but that he does terribly on the comprehension test, scoring at a low second-grade level. He can *read* all the words, but he doesn't know what they represent. This would indicate that the child does not understand language very well and one of the reasons that he is having difficulties in comprehension is because it is a language-based problem. Let's take a simple example: "The toy fish is close to the baby." Perhaps the child doesn't know what "close" means, so he cannot possibly make sense out of the instructions to indicate the picture in which the toy fish is shown to be close to the baby. Yet he can read the word perfectly well.

Another area to be assessed is spelling, again with a standardized test. We have at this point examined the child's visual-motor skills and some of his academic accomplishment, and we have, as a by-product of the testing, been given some information about the child's language ability. For example, a child might read an instruction, turn the page to find the correct answer and be stumped because he completely forgot what the question was. This tells us that he is having some language trouble in the visual-memory area, since he cannot retain what he has just read, and when we test various other language skills we would be alert to any deficiencies in this area. Both the educational evaluator and the speech and language therapist will be testing the child quite thoroughly in language and their examinations will overlap to some extent. In the same way the occupational therapist will also test some motor functions that the educational evaluator examines, and their observations will also partially overlap. This serves the child well in obtaining a very extensive and comprehensive evaluation.

One aspect of language testing that the educational evaluator is particularly interested in is receptive language. One way to test the child's receptive vocabulary is to show him a sheet with four pictures on it and then instruct the child to indicate which of the objects pictured corresponds to the word that the evaluator has just said.

The child is also instructed that if he does not know which is the correct picture then he is to guess. This gives him a little leeway and lets him know that he is not expected to be familiar with every single word he will hear. This will tell us what the strength of the child's single word receptive vocabulary is. From simple words like "book" we progress to more complicated ones like "ceremony."

Again in interpreting the results of this test we do not worry unduly if the child scores a year below grade level. Language is a shifting and changing thing, and certain terms included in this test are no longer used to designate the object. Some groups say "bucket" and others, equally correctly, designate it "pail." So, as with all standardized tests,* we rely on the background and experience of the evaluator to interpret them in the most meaningful manner.

Another area that is of special interest to the educational evaluator is auditory memory span, since so much of the instruction given in school is verbal. There are a variety of tests that we use to measure this ability. Some use actual words, and we instruct the child to listen carefully and then repeat as many of them as is possible. We start with two unrelated words such as "cat" and "ice" and then continue up to the point where we are asking the child to repeat eight such unrelated words, which is quite difficult. The child does not have to repeat them in any special order but just give back as many as he can remember. The important thing is to demonstrate auditory memory span, not to display any special sequencing ability. The child is asked all of the items in the test and the grade achieved then translates into an age level.

We also use visual methods to test memory. The evaluator presents the child with a sheet that has two illustrations, allows the child time to look at them, and then removes the sheet from view. The child is then asked to name the two (or however many) illustrations. The number of items are increased to as many as eight.

We evaluated a fifteen-year-old girl who had extraordinary auditory difficulty remembering anything beyond two items. She tested out at a five-year-old level, which was considerably below what one would expect. During the course of the testing, she mentioned that she liked to sing and was encouraged to do so by the evaluator. She demonstrated an exceptional ability to remember the words of popular songs, so she was obviously not deficient in her auditory-memory span, despite the finding of the test. This is why it is important to look beyond the formal test. In this particular instance it was valuable to learn that she used music as an aid. That information would be

* Standardized tests reflect the average abilities of the population they are administered to. Test designers do not set out to find the brightest or the slowest children but a good cross section that is representative of the country as a whole. This means that a representative sample of people is chosen to set the norms of that test. New tests are gradually developed and introduced into our evaluations, but there is always a gap between the state of the spoken language and the establishment of standardized tests of it. This lag results from the time necessary to validate test items on thousands of individuals.

14. Although she is an excellent student in arithmetic, this twelve-year-old has to struggle in reading to keep up with her seven-year-old sister, who is reading at an age-appropriate level.

15. A multi-sensory approach to improving reading that uses visual, auditory and vocal channels.

16. Examining for language competence. The child is scanning pictures for appropriate visual and auditory sequencing of a six-part story.

17. Identifying and using letter-sound clusters is a crucial skill in reading. The same sound (in this case "an") in a new combination is frequently unrecognizable to the reading disabled.

18. Strengthening directional writing skills with a child who demonstrates visual-motor difficulties.

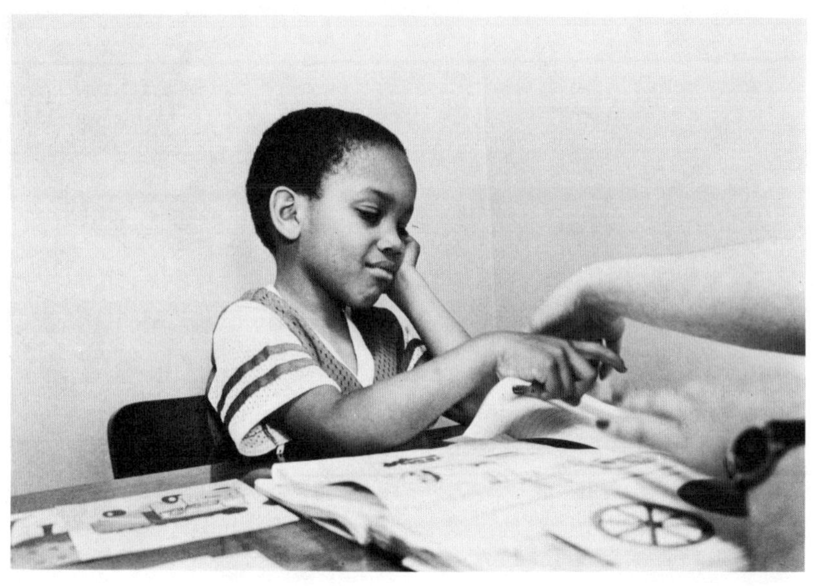

19. This preschool youngster is identifying sounds that he was unable to articulate correctly.

20. This life-size talking doll (which speaks with the therapist's voice) is used to improve speech and language functions.

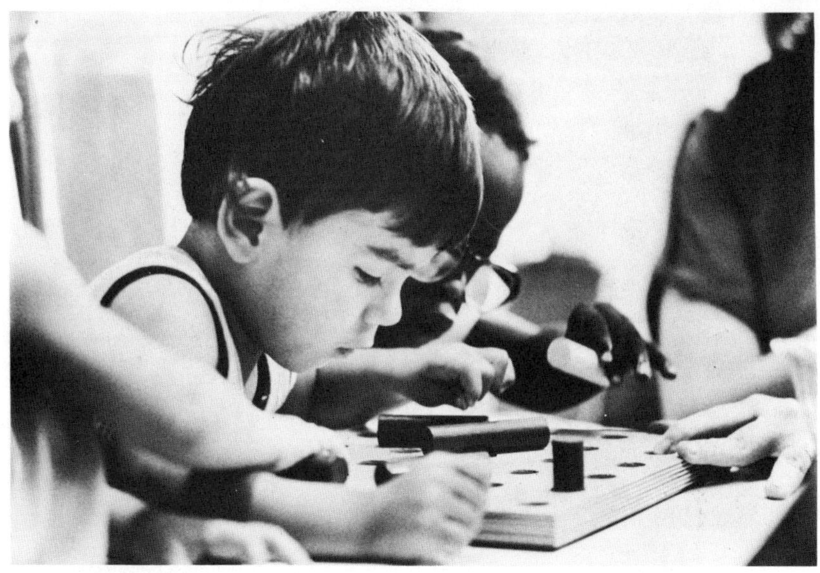

21. Practicing manipulative skills.

22. Group play activities have an important role in improving attention and promoting cooperative interaction.

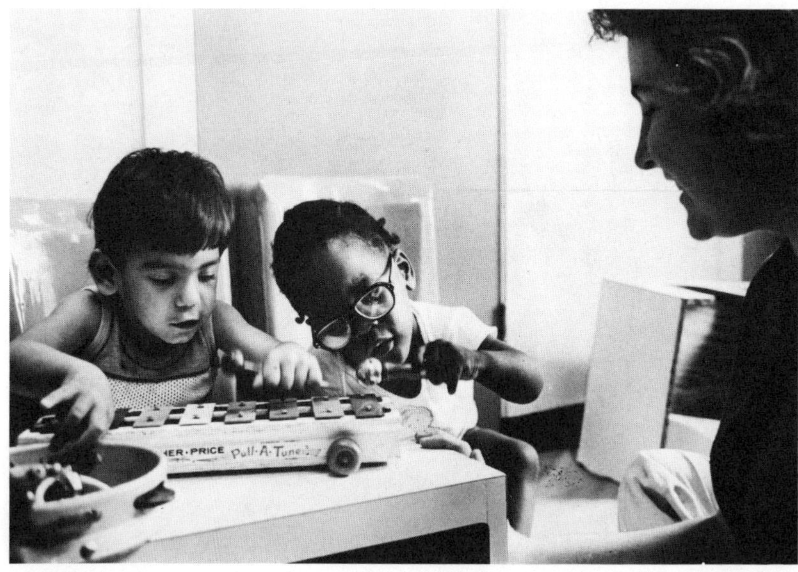

23. A computerized system of case management insures that all scheduled work-up components are completed in a timely manner.

24. After all of the elements of the work-up have been completed, the entire staff meets to establish a diagnosis and to initiate an individualized treatment program.

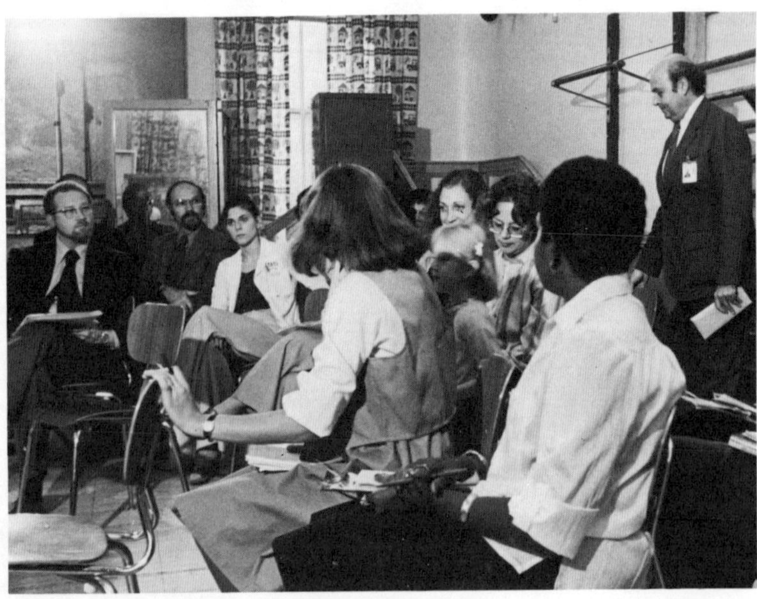

25. Sharing the conference findings and recommendations with the family.

26. Supportive counseling for the parent or parents is an integral part of the treatment process.

27. "I'm really much better now at getting my hands to do what I tell them to do."

passed on to anyone who was going to help her with her auditory memory.

Another area that we would look at regarding language is expressive vocabulary. With an older child we could use a test that asks the child to give the opposite word to one offered by the evaluator. This sort of test obviously could only be given to a child who grasped the meaning of "opposite" so that if the evaluator proposed "hot" the child would respond "cold."

Over all, the evaluator is interested in determining how much the child understands the language and how much he can express. Picture cards can be offered to the youngster, who is then asked to describe the story in the picture. This sort of exercise gives us a sense of the child's ability to handle the language grammatically. After the testing the educational evaluator should be able to name that area that is presenting the greatest difficulty to the child and holding back his progress in school. Does he have a language disorder? Does he have visual-perceptual problems? Does he have sequencing difficulties? If the child is not learning in any area and has what we call a "flat picture," the evaluator would want to know from psychological testing whether the child has the intellectual capacity to learn.

In the case of a mixed picture where there are some good skills and some deficits, pinpointing the problem allows the school system to transfer the child to a class that is geared to handle those difficulties. If the problem is less severe, the child might well be able to remain in his class and catch up with the use of remedial assistance in the weak area. In either case, the evaluator has not only participated in the diagnosis but has suggested a form of management to help remediate the problem. We feel that it is vital for schools and institutes such as ours to work together closely by sharing information, first of all, and then by understanding the programs available, so as to match the child with the best available care. A few examples of this cooperation are included in the following case histories.

Richard was identified in the nursery as an "at risk" child. The combination of a small-for-gestational-age infant and a young mother were the reasons for making this diagnosis. He was the product of a full-term pregnancy, but he weighed under five pounds.

Richard had begun therapy at age two and a half, but then we lost contact with him for two years. Then, when it came time for him to go to school, the mother returned when she realized that he would not be a candidate for regular school placement. At this point he was four and a half.

What the evaluation revealed at this time was a severe language delay and some behavior disorder. The placement question then became a choice between two possible programs. Ordinarily, we would like to see this child enter the preschool program for language-impaired children run by the Board of Education of the City of New York. However, there were indications that there had been some curtailment in the scope of this program so that referrals might not be accommodated.

The other alternative was a "readiness" program, which is a program that encompasses children with a variety of learning difficulties but not specifically geared to the child with language problems. The educational evaluator was aware of this dilemma, but on the merits of the case, decided to play an advocacy role and ask that the preschool for language-impaired children give special consideration to this child. Without such intervention from an evaluator working closely with us within the framework of the school system itself, such a placement would be less likely to have been made.

Eduardo was referred to us by a social worker from one of our associated clinics in The Long Island College Hospital. In the course of her work, she identified a school problem and realized that we were the resource to take care of it.

Though in the fifth grade, the child was reading on the second- to third-grade level. Math was at grade level, which led to the suspicion of a specific learning disability. Speech and language evaluation showed mild receptive and moderate expressive impairment. The occupational therapist also identified the reading problem while reporting that the other skills were roughly normal.

We uncovered a moderate to severe language impairment and a reading disability that was above and beyond what could be accounted for by the language impairment. That placed Eduardo between categories of remedial classes offered by the Board of Education. He would not be appropriate for assignment to a class for the language-impaired program. He might be suited for a resource room, but with some special services added to that program.

In this case the educational evaluator, employed by the Board of Education and working with us, advocated a resource room but also added the provision of speech therapy. Two periods each day were recommended in the remedial reading program since it was felt that Eduardo would have a good prognosis with the other dimensions of care. Ordinarily the resource-room program would only provide one period a day, and in this instance that really might not have been sufficient to aid Eduardo.

❧

Jacquile had been classified as an educable mentally retarded child by an outside agency. (This is an educational term which has been adopted by family courts and others and is now in general use.) She was seven when she was first referred to an out-patient pediatric clinic at The Long Island College Hospital and then to us. She appeared to be retarded following the first work-up, but this was a tentative diagnosis.

Her teacher was the first to note the fact that she was doing work beyond what would have been expected of a mentally retarded child. She was in the educable mentally retarded class and the teacher saw that her academic skills were above those of the other children and asked us to restudy her. We did so again at the age of ten.

We would have expected that, with an IQ of 60, which we had originally estimated, at the age of ten she would have had a first-grade reading level. She was instead reading at a mid-third-grade level at that time, so she was clearly above her anticipated level. She still showed some deficits on IQ testing, but there were specific areas in which she had improved.

The first time around all of the areas were depressed, a pattern that we commonly associate with retardation of one level of severity or another. She had made progress on the performance IQ, so that she was now in the borderline area overall, but there were specific sub-tests in which she was in the low-average range.

Interestingly, in the educational evaluation her formal testing was still a bit lower than her academic achievement. The interpretation of the discrepancy between the formal testing scores and her actual achievement was that there was a significant emotional component contributing to it. She did have a third- or mid-third-year level on reading and math, so our recommendation was for a transfer to a resource room. The reason for such a recommendation was that she had been given a trial period of mainstreaming in a third-grade class and was performing at that grade level. This trial was arranged on an informal basis between the teacher and the principal of the school, and the reevaluation changed the informal, voluntary action to a mandated one.

She was in a traumatic home environment and was able to pick herself up by her own bootstraps. So in addition to the recommendation for the transfer, there was also a recommendation for psychotherapeutic intervention. This situation validates our routine procedure for reexamining clients on a regular basis. In this instance, coordination between an alert teacher and our educational evaluator drew attention to the need for an immediate reevaluation. With it we were able to measure, in objective terms, the progress which Jacquile had made. This, in turn, led to an upward revision in our estimate of her academic potential.

The New York City Board of Education had established two preplacement classes at The Long Island College Hospital under the direction of the Lamm Institute for Developmental Disabilities. The classrooms are separated by an office with one way mirrors through which activities in the classroom can be observed without disturbing the children.

The school had a maximum capacity of twelve children, and its major assets are its unique, non-threatening, learning environment, and the availability of clinical services. These include individualized speech therapy, physical therapy, social service for both parents and children, and for some children, occupational therapy to aid in group interaction and task planning.

Teachers and clinicians are able to discuss planning and progress. Formal conferences are frequently held at which time the entire staff discusses the children's progress and alternatives for permanent placement. This team approach has significantly helped both the teachers and clinicians plan a curriculum that meets each child's educational and social needs.

IX. SPEECH AND LANGUAGE EVALUATION AND TREATMENT

In this section of the work-up we want to establish an age level for the child's receptive and expressive language and articulation skills, and the first step in assessing and diagnosing speech and language disorders is the parent interview. During this interview we ask parents detailed questions relating to the background history of the child, especially regarding speech development, although we ask about other developmental milestones as well.

We ask about crying, whether it was weak or strong, excessive or relatively scant. We want to know whether the child had a strong sucking ability or whether he gagged or choked on liquids. We try to determine the age at which babbling appeared and whether it was expressive, purposeful and directed at others.

Insofar as possible we try to ascertain exactly when the child said his first words, phrases and sentences. We are interested in the child's ability to understand and follow directions and answer questions. We also try to determine exactly how the child communicates. Does he use words, sentences, gestures or emotional behavior?

We then ask the parent what they see as the specific problem, when it was noticed and how it affects the child. We also try to determine whether any other member of the family has similar problems. For example, if a parent reported that the child began to coo and babble at three months and then completely stopped at seven months, we might suspect a hearing loss.[1] A history that indicated that a child began to speak normally and suddenly stopped at around eighteen months could make us suspect infantile autism. If a parent stated that their child was home alone all day with a baby-sitter who spoke a different language, it might indicate that the child was not receiving adequate stimulation for normal language development.

[1] As indicated in other sections of this book, a complete hearing work-up is essential in the evaluation of any speech or language problem.

The focus of the evaluation now turns to the child himself. We generally request that the parent leave at this point so that the child can perform optimally and without distractions. With the younger child, and even with some older ones, this is not possible, and the parent is allowed to remain in the testing room.

There is no standard set of tests that we administer to each child. The tests administered are determined by the child's age and level of cooperation and, of course, the specific skills that we wish to evaluate. In almost every case where the child is testable, though, we give the Peabody Picture Vocabulary Test. When we say "testable" we mean that the child can understand the test procedure and has an adequate attention span. We find that most children are cooperative and enter into the testing and evaluation process quite willingly.

In the picture vocabulary test, we present the child with a thick spiral bound book of line drawings and turn over one leaf at a time, giving the child an opportunity to look at the pictures. Each page has four pictures, and the therapist asks the child to pick out the one that represents "spoon" or "catching," for instance. No modifying definite or indefinite article is used, so as not to offer any clues, which would happen if the objects were in the plural or a verb form.

We proceed through the book starting at different levels, depending on the child's age. If he is able to identify the first eight consecutive items correctly, we continue to present items until the child fails to answer six out of eight correctly. If, on the other hand, the child is not able to answer the first eight items in the appropriate-age category, then the examiner starts to work backward in descending order until the child is able to identify eight consecutive items. We compute a total number of correct items which we then convert into an age score. In this manner we learn if the child is at, above or below age-level accomplishment. Frequently, the examiner will tell the child that the pictures become more difficult, so that the child doesn't become upset. Insofar as is possible, we want the child to be comfortable so that he will give us an accurate picture of his ability in this and all other areas.

This particular test reveals single-word vocabulary in the receptive (as understood) mode only, and it gives us an approximation of the child's vocabulary. Any lack of vocabulary could indicate a variety of things. One factor might be that the child comes from a background that doesn't supply him with a wide variety of information, that doesn't provide the enrichment that is needed. Typically, such an environmentally deprived child is more likely to show deficits in vocabulary than he will in grammar. The structure of the language has been acquired, but its potential richness remains outside of his experience. We would emphasize "approximate" in this case, because the test was standardized in the Midwest and does not always accurately tap the vocabulary of the inner-city child. However, it does have the advantage of accustoming the child to the test process, and the therapist can then go on to use other tests.

Another comprehensive test that can be given is the Illinois Test of Psycholinguistic Abilities. It is divided into a series of twelve sub-tests, any or all of which may be administered depending on the individual. Since the test in its fullest form may take anywhere from three quarters of an hour to an hour, it is up to the specialist administering it to decide how much of it is practicable to give. Those that we have found most useful in our work are the ones that we will treat at some length.

Auditory Reception, the first of the sub-tests, is designed to give us a measure of comprehension. In it we ask a series of questions to which the child is asked to respond with a "Yes" or "No" answer. Simple questions such as, "Do airplanes fly?" begin the test and increase in difficulty as it progresses. Depending on the age of the child, the questioning would start at different points on the graded scale of vocabulary difficulty. This test, as do most of the others, has a basal and a ceiling level. Five consecutive successes comprise the basal level and three misses out of seven items gives us the ceiling for this sub-test. The test is graded according to age, so that we do not expect all children to answer all of the questions. However, we do want to see how close they come to the level we would anticipate children of that age would reach, based on the norms established from thousands of tests.

The *Visual Reception* sub-test, which is given next, can point up a real difference between visual and auditory skills if the child is having a problem with one and not the other. We show the child a series of pictures of an individual figure or object, at rest or in action, and then flip to a series of four pictures. We ask the child to point to the one which is like the first one he looked at. He must remember what he saw first, pick out what was characteristic about it, and then select from the group of four images the one that most closely resembles the original. For example, we show the child a picture of an electric fan, which he matches to a paper fan on the next page. As with the other sub-tests we first do a couple of demonstration items just so that the child understands the way the test works. In this case, he does not have to name the item among the four images presented to him, just point it out.

Sometimes we work with children who have language difficulties that we find are actually difficulties in the auditory area. In other words, they seem to have a good understanding of what the world is all about. They know what things are for, and how objects function, but when language is incorporated into the mix, they do not seem to do as well. Among those children who have language difficulties but whose visual skills are good, we do observe a real difference in their performance on these two tests. Any child who had difficulties in auditory reception, is, of necessity, going to have trouble in comprehending instructions in school and will not perform up to his potential.

The next test, *Auditory Association*, does not involve any pictures. Instead, the examiner says part of a sentence to the child and asks the child to finish it. As a warmup the youngster would be told "Grass is green. Sugar is . . ." and he should respond with the word "white." We look to see if the child can make the correct analogies, if he can recognize that the quality of grass that is being spoken of is its color, and that we want him to respond with the color of the sugar, not any of its other properties such as sweetness. These sentence completions become more complex as the test progresses and give us an insight into the child's ability to make verbal analogies.

If the child does poorly in this sub-test, it could alert us to the fact that he has difficulty moving away from concrete images to the relationships implied. We also try to measure this ability with a visual-association test. If both these scores are low, we would conclude that while the child does reasonably well at the concrete level, he is on less firm ground the farther he is asked to go from it. The test looks at verbal-abstract ability and also vocabulary. Although, properly speaking, this latter is not part of the scoring for the test, it is revealing to us to hear how children will describe things. For example we might say "Cotton is soft. Stones are . . ." and the child might have the idea of softness versus hardness but doesn't know the word hard, and so he replies, "not soft." Or he might describe it with the statement, "You could hurt yourself with it." Although that does not contribute to the scoring, it does give us information that the child has the concept, but does not have the precise word to express it.

The *Visual-Sequential Memory* sub-test evaluates the child's ability to reproduce from memory a series of figures. The child is shown a sequence of designs on paper. After five seconds the page is removed. The child is given plastic chips, each one having a design on it. The child must then resequence these chips so that they exactly match the sequence in which they were shown. The sequence length varies from two to eight figures. The child is allowed two trials per sequence.

We test *Auditory-Sequential Memory* by asking for immediate recall. It differs from the type of memory we test when we check to see if a child can state the days of the week and the months of the year. We ask the child to listen carefully and to repeat the numbers exactly as the examiner says them. The numbers begin with simple two-digit examples, such as "four, three," and move along to three-digit numbers, as far as the child can progress before losing the thread up to eight digits. As in the visual-sequential memory test, the child has two opportunities to respond with the correct sequence, but receives less credit if he gives the answer after two tries at it. This will pinpoint the fact that a child has a poor short-term auditory memory. Some children just have poor memories in general, and this in itself does not always signal a problem. Many factors affect memory. A child who suffers from chronic anxiety because of emotional difficulties or an environmental problem, will probably not do well on this test, since memory is one of the first functions lost due to that type of stress. There are some children who have poor auditory-memory skills and sometimes, but not always, we see this in children who also have difficulties with grammatical structure.

The two-part test of *Visual Association* again examines an area of abstract thinking. In the first part we show the child a picture and then ask him to pick out, from the multiple choices on a second picture, the object that is most closely related to the first object. If the first were a pillow then we would expect the child to point to the bed among the second set of images.

The second part of the test is slightly more complicated. Demonstration pictures of two related objects are shown side by side, then the test image is shown with four other pictures, only one of which bears the same kind of relationship to it as the demonstration pictures bear to each other. The child is asked to select the correct one. An example is, "A submarine is to water as an airplane is to . . ." Like the auditory-association test, this gives us insight into what the child knows and understands. He has to be able to understand the relationship and then transfer the analogy to different visual stimuli.

Visual Closure is a test in which we present a drawing about as long as a cartoon strip, though not divided up into individual panels. The first line drawing contains three animals and the rest of the drawing shows partial views of them, hidden by various objects, and the child is asked to point out as many of them as he can. Here we are trying to determine whether a child who has seen the whole animal can pick it out from just a partial view. In other words, is he able to "close" the image from the part to the whole. A child should be able to make sense out of part of a thing instead of needing to see or hear all of a thing, and this test offers us evidence of how well that process is taking place. Closure is an integral part of learning.

Verbal Expression gives us very valuable information about a child. We hand a child a simple object, such as a nail, and ask him to give us all of the information that he can about it without offering any clues to direct him. Here we are looking for the richness of the child's responses. That is, exactly how many different aspects of the object he chooses to comment on. When he has finished, we ask the child to state anything about those aspects of the object that he has not mentioned. As with all of the other sub-tests, we go through a demonstration item first.

We want to see whether the child has named the object, given its color, shape, function, what material it is made of, the parts, its length, a comparison with other similar objects, and anything else that the child can think of. It is a general level of verbal expression, and does not evaluate a child's grammar or his ability to put sentences together, but does give us the content of what the child is able to verbalize. Does he use nouns, adjectives, verbs? Does he know a lot about the function of things? Does he know how to describe things? Most children who have language difficulties in any area are going to do poorly on this test. Except for sentence structure, this test makes maximum demands on a wide range of verbal skills. It is a very open test situation and children say the most creative things at times.

We may also present the child with a series of everyday objects and ask him to demonstrate their function by actually using them. During the demonstration portion, the child actually handles the object, but for the rest of the test, he mimes the appropriate actions after seeing a picture of the object or objects. Only certain responses are acceptable according to the guidelines set down on the scoring sheet. The demonstration of understanding without the use of language is the aim of this test. We compare the results of this test of expressiveness with the verbal test to assess the strengths and weaknesses overall, or in one area as opposed to the other. Thus we can compare inner language with verbal language, which can then help us to provide the appropriate remediation.

Auditory Closure examines the ability of a child to pick up the whole word after hearing only a part of it, in the same way that visual closure tells us if a partial visual clue enables the child to identify the whole object. We offer the child words from which various sounds have been omitted such as "da/y" and look for him to supply the two "d's" that would make sense of it as "daddy." The ability to do this is important, because during normal speech the ear is presented with 400–450 units of sounds (phonemes) per minute and we are really only able to process a third, or 150 of these units, in that time. This means that the individual has to have the ability to fill in a lot of this verbal material so as to be able to keep up.

This is a very important part of language acquisition and accounts for the initial difficulties that people have when trying to understand a foreign language in which they have not yet become fluent. Their difficulties stem mainly from the fact that they have a very limited ability to fill in anything. We hypothesize that many aphasic children, who have severe difficulty in that area, have to hear everything in order to make sense out of auditory material.

Frequently, we will give a child an *Articulation Test*, which evaluates his ability to produce sounds in words. We have a booklet full of pictures that we present to the child, flipping over a page at a time. The examiner does not say the name of the object pictured, but merely points to it and asks, "What's that?" The child then responds "knife" or whatever else is pictured, and the test continues. The test evaluates both vowels and consonants, and words are chosen for the variety of sounds they contain not as tests of comprehension. There are norms indicating the average age at which children can be expected to produce certain sounds, and if the child does not measure up to those norms, then some remedial help is needed. Thinking of your own children, you can see the emerging patterns of speech, from babbling to fully inflected speech. Examining thousands and thousands of children, investigators are able to establish reliable guideposts for the formation of correctly articulated speech.

In general, we would expect that by the age of six or seven children are able to produce all sounds correctly. If after this age they are still having difficulty, then they would need some form of remedial help, if they had not already received it. In many cases all that is needed is a little extra help from the parents, but in other cases a specially trained speech therapist would be necessary. Obviously, when we refer to correct production of sounds we are very much aware of the existence of dialects and regional variation in pronunciations.

In the course of our examination we also look at the structure and the functioning of the tongue, the lips, the teeth, the aveolar ridge, the palate and the jaw. This is called a peripheral speech exam. The therapist asks the child to imitate a variety of movements, such as opening and closing the mouth, spreading and puckering the lips, sticking out the tongue, elevating it, moving it from side to side and also moving the jaw from side to side. During the examination we are looking for the quality of movement first of all. That is, we are on the lookout for any tremors, and whether or not the tongue goes immediately to the spot that it was supposed to reach. Also, we want to see if the movements are fully differentiated; for example, if the child can move the tongue without moving his head or jaw. We sometimes encounter a child who will tip the head backward when asked to stick out the tongue and then point the tongue upward. It is obvious that he cannot separate the two movements and this tells us that he has a coordination difficulty. This may or may not be associated with a speech problem, but it is a little warning to us to be on the alert for some speech dysfunction. We look at chewing and swallowing, usually by giving a child a bit of crispy, dry cereal or cookie and observing the movements.

We check diadochokinesis—successive rapid movements—by asking the child to repeat "puh" "puh" "puh" as rapidly as possible for ten seconds and the same with the sounds "tuh" and "kuh." There are established norms by age and sex (girls are generally more skilled), against which the child is evaluated. Significant deviations could indicate a lower (or higher) level of ability to sequence movements and coordination. We find some children who start out well but begin to experience coordination difficulties after about ten seconds. The child might lose the voice aspect and just move the lips without producing the requested sound, or he might run out of breath and have to gasp in the middle of the exercise, producing irregular vocalizations. Ordinarily the average child should be able to perform these tasks easily and smoothly, provided he doesn't get a fit of the giggles.

The ability to sequence the phonemes "puh," "tuh," "kuh" (oroeupraxis) is something that we might look at. We ask the child to put these phonemes together as a nonsense word three times in five seconds. The child doesn't even have to say them too rapidly to meet the norm. This exercise shows us his ability to sequence sounds into words, since the latter are really just sounds when he first hears them. In acquiring vocabulary, the child is constantly dealing with new sounds, and his ability to manipulate them has a direct bearing on the ease with which he will develop his storehouse of words. Most children find the test easy, but there are some children for whom it proves difficult. Some of these children have a tendency to assimilate sounds; that is, they make two dissimilarly produced sounds, sound the same. An example of this would be the tendency of some of us to nasalize a vowel which follows a nasal consonant.

We next look at the sensory aspect of the oral mechanism. We ask the child to imagine that there is an imaginary line drawn down the center of his face dividing it into two halves. We then ask him to close his eyes and to raise his hand on the same side as the side we touch with a finger. There are some children who have adequate mouth movement but are not aware where the tongue and lips are in space, so that the reason they cannot imitate sounds is not that coordination is bad, or that the hearing is deficient, but that the spatial awareness is faulty. Proceeding a little further, we could do the same test touching inside of the mouth. Another test that we do is to ask the child to close his eyes. We then touch spots outside the mouth and ask him to touch them with his tongue. These are all attempts to uncover any difficulty with the sensory aspect of speech.

Aside from specific motor or sensory difficulties, we are particularly interested in evaluating the child's receptive and expressive vocabulary; that is, his ability both to understand words and to produce them spontaneously. Ideally, these abilities should be at about the same level, but often we find that they are not and this, of course, alerts us to the area in which remedial attention is needed. It seems that most children who have a language delay have better receptive skills than expressive ones. A child with a normal IQ and age-appropriate receptive vocabulary could have poor expressive vocabulary because of a lack of coordination. The child might be mentally prepared, but poor motor function could prevent him from playing back the correct answer. Being able to sequence words in a sentence is necessary for expressive language and underlying this ability is the child's grasp of grammar. Children with memory deficits often have difficulty with grammar.

When we are evaluating the child we also observe his ability to deal with things other than the task at hand. The child could be doing well with something right in front of him but might be stumped if asked what he had for lunch. The inability to deal with such a level of abstraction might be an indication of some receptive problem.

The child with adequate grammatical ability but a marked deficiency in vocabulary would make us curious about the child's home environment. Does he, in fact, come from a culturally deprived background? If this were the case, then the remediation would concentrate primarily on enriching that child's environment.

Then there is the anomic or dysnomic child who has inordinate difficulty in learning and retrieving the names of things. We have had some success in improving this condition, but as with any course of remediation, it depends on the severity of the condition. Basically, this type of difficulty is treated with repetition and setting up associations between objects and their functions, such as "letter" and "stamp." These associations can often be very productive in helping to fix the names.

There are some children who have difficulty in naming things but who can nonetheless carry on a conversation without betraying their disability. Instead of using the correct name for a thing the child will employ "these," "them" and "those" excessively. Or alternatively, he might use a descriptive phrase rather than the simple name. For elevator he might say "the thing that goes up." When his vocabulary is tested though, the problem stands out quite clearly.

A deficiency in single-word vocabulary can cause a child a variety of problems in school, the first and most obvious being that he will not understand what the teacher is talking about. Also it is not uncommon for children with language problems on any level—vocabulary, grammar or whatever—to have problems in other areas as well. We see more and more that there aren't all that many children whose problems are isolated in just one area. A child who has an articulation problem due to difficulty with oral movements, for example, may also be clumsy with the fine movements of his hands. Both of these abilities involve a motor function.

Retarded children tend to acquire language skills in a systematic manner, as do average children except that retarded children do it much more slowly. A dysphasic child, however, may acquire such skills out of sequence. He might, for instance, be on the one-word stage but then blurt out the occasional two-word sentence, usually a stereotyped one like "Go home." Ordinarily, we expect the average child to learn about fifty single words before passing along to the two-word stage. And then he acquires a number of two-word phrases before beginning to assemble the short three-word sentence.

We pay attention to the manner in which a child takes the tests that are administered. A child with a learning delay might have an extremely short attention span or will be highly distractible and unable to focus attention on the pictures in front of him. Such a child would have a speech and language problem because he did not attend to anything, such as speech, long enough to master the elements. During a course of remediation we would first concentrate on helping the child maintain attention over progressively longer periods of time. We would want to bring him to the point where he could complete a task, such as assembling a simple puzzle. Hyperactive children often have speech and language deficiencies, not because they are lacking in some ability, but because they do not take the time to acquire the necessary language skills.

In the case of such hyperactive children or very young children we do not attempt to do formal testing. We rely primarily on the language sample that we take from all children. By writing down all of the things that the child says and analyzing them, we can get a very good sense of the child's skills and deficits. The analysis of the child's statements is divided into three main areas. We look at the form (the way in which the child employs the language, which is essentially the grammar) and then content (what it is the child talks about). In evaluating the form we look to see whether the child is dealing in two- or three-word phrases. Does he ask questions? Does he only make direct statements? Can he use a negative? While this is a satisfactory way to evaluate a child we prefer to use formal tests primarily because they are transferable—we can forward them to another therapist or agency and they will make sense. Also, it allows us to measure changes over time to see how well the remediation is succeeding.

While an informal language sample may be the only way to test a hyperactive child, it is important to see how every child interacts conversationally during the evaluation. The emotionally disturbed child might be talking constantly but not be directing language in an interactive way. We also look for good eye contact because a child who will not look at the evaluator may be having some type of emotional turmoil. In any case, the absence of good eye contact is outside the range of normal expectation, and we note this, as we note any inability to focus attention on a particular task, or signs of hyperactivity.

We routinely ask a child to identify items of clothing and body parts to see how well he understands. We take note of how well the child can follow one-step, two-step or three-step commands, as this gives us an insight into his receptive language. At a certain age children are expected to be able to follow a one-step command but not a two-step one. Later they are able to follow the more complex commands. If the child basically has good receptive language skills but does begin to stumble on two- and three-step commands, then we would wonder if there might be a memory problem, and we would pursue that line of investigation. On the other hand, if all the receptive skills are low, then we would think of a more specific language deficit.

In looking at expressive language, we want to determine if a child can speak out and communicate his wishes. We are on the lookout for the child who will only ask for what he wants, but will not initiate a conversation. We also want to see if the child who will not initiate a conversation is able to keep it going after the evaluator has made the opening comment. During this testing we look at the topics that the child picks to speak about and then whether the child mentions attributes of things—"today is cold"—whether he discusses action or location, such as observing that the object is "on the table"—or whether he makes reference to possession—"This is mine."

In listening to the child speak informally we also assess his ability to articulate the language. Just as we do in the formal articulation tests, we divide this ability into three categories: distortion of sounds, substitution of sounds or omission of sounds. We sometimes have to give the child a number of clues to enable him to pronounce the sounds. We might tell him to round his lips, stick out his tongue and then try it, or to watch the evaluator demonstrate it carefully. And we want to see whether he can pronounce single words or words in isolation or just single letters. Testing for pronunciation is called *stimulability testing* and helps determine if a child is a therapy candidate.

The quality of the voice is also classified as to whether it is unusually loud, soft, nasal, breathy, hoarse, high or low. We also note whether the voice has the normal amount of high and low inflections or whether it is flat. Usually, if the voice is flat, the child's whole affect is flat. Though it might be indicative of an emotional problem, a high flat voice might also indicate a hearing problem.

Speech and language are characteristic of man alone in the animal kingdom, and they represent very complex processes. The simple act of requesting a glass of water involves a whole constellation of sensory and motor impulses, and in the speech and language evaluation we attempt to pinpoint the stage at which the process encounters difficulty. When it has been precisely identified, we attempt to implement a course of remedial treatment that will correct the dysfunction and allow the normal flow of receptive and expressive language to take place smoothly. The two following case histories indicate the varying remedial approaches dictated by the specific needs of the children.

❧

When Kenny first came in at age four, he used vowels almost exclusively. There was no early indication in his developmental history that there would be any speech difficulty, since he was able to chew and swallow normally. He did drool when we first saw him and he was found to have fine-motor problems. What Kenny had going for him was good intelligence (in the form of a high-average IQ), but he seemed to have a number of emotional problems and acted nervous and fidgety. He was very withdrawn and would rub his mouth with the back of his hand repeatedly and forcefully. He also used to tug at his pants when he sat in his chair, a habit that disappeared as his speech improved after the first six months of working with him.

Comprehension wasn't his problem, so we started to work first on articulation. We gave him cards with one letter on each and we asked him to pronounce the letters. We started with lip sounds like "p," "b" and "m," then moved to tongue-tip sounds like "t," "d," "n," then teeth and lip, "f" and "p," and finally combinations of sounds, which involve more muscle movement and variations of movement. This was a stimulation exercise to get all of the mouth parts moving and give him the feel of sounds in all contexts.

After several months, Kenny's drooling diminished and he did not have to be told to wipe his chin or swallow. We also had him imitate tongue and mouth movements either in the mirror or looking at the instructor. Exercises such as opening and closing the mouth and moving the tongue up and down or to the side were very difficult for him. He had an oral dyspraxia, meaning that he had difficulty with volitional movements such as the ones used in speech. Automatic movements such as chewing and swallowing presented no problem, though there were times when we were practicing tongue elevation that he cried. He was very upset by his difficulty and though cooperative, would refuse to try certain exercises because he knew how difficult they were going to be for him.

We first worked on the sounds in isolation, beginning with the lip sounds. These sounds were the easiest for him and he picked up on them very quickly in a matter of weeks. Then we worked on syllables, and when he could produce the lip sounds in words we made picture cards. He liked to work with picture cards, so we prepared a deck that he practiced with at home and brought with him to his twice-weekly remedial sessions. Within six to nine months he was generally intelligible to most people, though one still had to know the context that was being referred to. When he started he was only able to say "Mah-ee" for "Mommy," and that was one of his better words.

He was frustrated, but the increasing ability to make himself understood relieved him of much pressure. He was extremely motivated, and since he wasn't in school, this additional source of pressure was not a factor. After a while we brought him into group sessions with another child. Her articulation skills were better than his, but his comprehension skills were superior. It was an effort to help him socialize and see that other children had problems as well.

Once we had established articulation skills at a constant good level through formal drilling, we proceeded to the more informal give and take of conversation to give both children a chance to employ their new skills. In addition to the structured activities, we used unstructured ones such as buying and shopping games, as we concentrated on his articulation. Kenny is now able to carry on a normal conversation at an age-appropriate level.

If we can, we like to have the parents work with the child at home. We ask them to restrict correcting or belittling the child and to encourage him and praise him for successes, rather than harping on failures. The best way to help a child is to give him a good speech model, to speak clearly and slowly and to exaggerate the sound that the child is having difficulty with so that he can hear it correctly. Good parental interest such as Kenny had, aided the remediation very much.

Using his newly developed conversational skills, Kenny demonstrated a great imagination, far beyond that which children at age four ordinarily exhibited. We sometimes gave him pictures with our target sounds and asked him to make up sentences about them, and he not only made up sentences—which is a seven-year-old skill—but whole stories. He attended a head-start program for two years where he received therapy once a week. When he entered kindergarten, he continued to work with speech therapists and began to read.

When Mary Kate first came to us she was about four and a half years old and scored in the mild retardation range with an IQ of 67. She had a history of late development, including both walking and talking. She was found to have moderate to severe delays in both receptive and expressive language together with limitations in articulation. Her father and brother were dyslectic.

The outstanding thing about Mary Kate was that socially she was extremely friendly. She did not seem to experience too much frustration over her lack of communication skills except that at the time of the evaluation her mother said that she had begun to whisper in certain situations and that perhaps she was developing a fear of speaking.

She had immature sentence structure, relying on two- to four-word utterances. She had a very small vocabulary and tended to use stereotyped sentences rather than create her own. She had difficulty with all tongue and lip movements, and she had a great deal of difficulty differentiating her tongue, jaw and lip movements in general. She distorted and substituted sounds and made sound omissions so that it was very difficult to understand her. She was generally below her age level by two years.

There was so much to do that we didn't select any one approach but began to work with a variety of conditions at the same time. Among these were memory, concepts, vocabulary and grammatical structure. To develop her articulation we stressed a large variety of sounds with the lip, tongue and teeth, and she did very well on this program. She progressed from letters to syllables and words, then to phrases, sentences and spontaneous speech. This helped her articulation very much, and we were able to continue to work with her in a less structured manner. Her speech improved to the extent that it was comprehensible to anyone.

She had a host of perceptual problems, though the auditory problems were more outstanding than the visual ones. She had a tendency to acquire utterances and use them in a stereotypic manner. "Poor dear" was a favorite one of hers. She once looked at a picture of the animal and said, "Poor deer." It sounded quite funny but she was dead serious about it.

Visually she was stimulus bound and would pick out the most outstanding element of a picture rather than absorb the context. For instance, we showed her a picture of a person sweeping the floor in black and white with a darkened Teddy bear on the counter. When we asked her to describe the action she picked out the Teddy bear and did not "see" or perceive the rest of the picture.

We did a great deal of work on spatial-relation skills. We showed her pictures of a cat *on* a chair and a cat *under* a chair and drilled her until she grasped these spatial relations correctly. Then we moved on to expressive language, asking her to describe what the therapist was doing with objects and then later to tell the therapist to perform some action with them.

We presented her with concepts of objects "going together" or associated by function, such as soap and water and the like. These exercises were designed to help her remember the names of things and partially to give her an understanding of such associations. Another memory-improving device we used was to give her a sequence of pictures and ask her to tell the simple sequenced story they contained. Then we would remove one of the pictures and ask her to remember the missing picture.

Her mother was very much involved in helping Mary Kate at home during the week between sessions. As a result of the remediation she improved tremendously in her ability to carry on a conversation. We stopped her therapy a year later, and though she still had problems retrieving words, this would not be obvious in normal conversation. She blossomed a great deal since she was able to express the creative and funny thoughts that she had not been able to manage previously.

She did not completely abandon her use of stereotypic phrases, partially because they were amusing and would cause people to laugh and give her some measure of approval. Except for the most complex sounds, she was able to pronounce her words correctly. She had raised her vocabulary level fifteen months during the remediation and had pulled her IQ up to 81, which is low normal. This was certainly a strong improvement from the initial level that had indicated mild retardation.

X. SOCIAL SERVICE EVALUATION AND COUNSELING

At the Lamm Institute the social worker is indeed the man or woman for all seasons. The worker's roles include acting as medical interpreter, parental advocate, primary liaison with schools and other agencies, child advocate and provider of specific concrete services to families in need. The social worker helps to establish the links necessary to insure that specific recommendations for school placement, special classes or supplemental resource-room services are carried out.

The social worker, along with the pediatric neurologist, plays an essential role in communicating the findings of the diagnostic conference to the parents. We help them to understand what has been diagnosed and then what they are to do about it. We try to help them find the necessary resources whether those are internal, an appropriate school or financial aid. We function as mediators explaining the work of the institute to the parents and then act for the parents as advocates in dealing with other agencies. Sometimes parents may be overwhelmed when told for the first time that their child has a learning disability or some other specific problem. Sensitivity to the parents' responses, both verbal and non-verbal, is crucial to developing the kind of relationship necessary between parent, child and treatment agency.

The social worker tries to find out what the parents really think and feel they are confronted with, and similarly, what the child's reaction to his problem is. Ordinarily, people may not be freely forthcoming with that type of information. It must be developed through understanding and frank discussions and the skilled interview is our chief evaluative tool.

We develop information regarding the extent to which the child's disability is causing problems in the family—either emotional, social or financial—and also whether problems in the family may be causing or affecting the child's disability. We deal with children who have been referred because they have learning problems or behavior problems or both. These are often influenced by some interaction difficulties within the family.

We have a very specific mandate; that is, to make sure that the parents understand what is happening and what is being proposed. The evaluation team puts a child through a wide variety of tests and it can be most confusing to someone unacquainted with our operation. Each of the evaluators interprets his own diagnostic findings, but the social worker has to facilitate the process. If there is no problem of comprehension so much the better, but if uncertainty seems present, clarification is the task of the social worker.

Whenever a child is scheduled for the diagnostic conference the social worker on the case is present. And after the diagnosis has been made and a course of treatment is recommended, the social worker along with the examining physician and any other specialist involved, confer immediately with the parent to review the findings and the reasons for the specific course of treatment. Even before the conference, during the course of the work-up, parents will visit the social workers to ask questions about the various tests. Parents are curious to know why their child is asked to assemble blocks in various patterns or why they were asked to copy certain symbols and match them up with numbers.

Usually when parents first bring their child for an evaluation they are very anxious. They have a suspicion that there is something wrong or someone has caused them to suspect that there is something wrong with their child, by referring them to us. Naturally they wonder about what information will be uncovered and what the future holds for their child. With that type of anxiety they are not in the most receptive frame of mind. They may listen attentively to the specialists' explanations, but they are not taking them in because their concerns are elsewhere. The first time they hear an answer to one of the questions, it may not register, and it is only after someone works through the material with them a second time that they begin to get a firm grasp of it.

One woman brought her child in for a psychological examination and didn't understand why she couldn't be present in the room while the testing was being done. She felt that she had to be there because she didn't want anything done to her child that she couldn't observe.

This is common and understandable. The psychologist explained the reason for asking her to remain outside, but she couldn't accept it and was referred to the social worker. He went over the reasons for testing children without their parents' presence and was able to reschedule the psychological examination for another time. These tests are all given under controlled conditions, and it is vital to keep them as standardized as is humanly possible so that the results will be valid. Distractions can cause the child to pay less attention to the test than he should, and this can, in turn, affect his score adversely. The presence of the parent can alter his approach and deprive the specialist of the opportunity to observe the quality of the child's responses in the presence of new material. When this information was imparted to the mother by the social worker (after the psychologist had tried to explain), she was able to accept it.

We have the additional complication of dealing with things that are not so easy to pinpoint; specific learning disabilities, dyslexia and hyperkinesis are some examples. If the physician or psychologist cannot truly say why a child isn't learning to read but is learning arithmetic, then the social worker will have to approximate an explanation by pointing to precise brain pathways that are slightly impaired. We have to be accurate in our communication, so we cannot say that there is brain damage when the neurological examination does not specifically and definitely reveal any. The state of the art at this point just does not permit us to make such an assertion. Yet other tests have confirmed that the child is indeed having difficulty with reading. So while we cannot point to the exact origin of the difficulty, we can explain to them why some of the remedial procedures can be expected to help.

Another source of anxiety arises from feelings of guilt. The parents feel that in some way they have contributed to the condition —whether knowingly or unknowingly. All parents who have learning-disabled children, at some point or another, and to one degree or another, wonder what they may have done to contribute to the problem.

We have seen severely depressed parents whose anger was directed at themselves because they felt that they had done something wrong. Sometimes they have. Perhaps a small percentage of them have contributed to the child's difficulty by smoking too many cigarettes during pregnancy or drinking too much alcohol or taking drugs.

However, the vast majority of parents cannot think of anything that might have contributed to the difficulty. Nonetheless, they may feel guilty, and we try to counsel them, get them to the point where they can understand that they are punishing themselves over something in the past that may or may not be real and that the future lies ahead.

In some cases we provide in-depth clinical counseling for children and parents. In others we can ready parents for the need for psychotherapy and then put them in contact with other staff members or agencies who can provide the necessary services. A large part of the work of the social worker is to help bring people to the point where they will accept counseling or therapy.

As we mentioned earlier, the chief tool of the social worker is the systematic interview, designed to develop as clear and detailed a history of the child and the family as is possible. The main task of the social worker is to derive a comprehensible picture of the world in which the child is living. Frequently, such pertinent information feeds into the formation of a diagnosis when the child's case is being discussed in the diagnostic conference. Neurological diagnosis depends a great deal on the history of social and emotional data. Very often a diagnosis cannot be made without some idea of what the patient's behavior has been like over a period of time. This is precisely the type of information that the social worker is charged with eliciting—family history, patient's behavioral history and the school history. With this the physician can often tightly pin down a diagnosis that would otherwise have to remain tentative.

As a part of the evaluative team a slightly different emphasis is placed on the social worker's contribution. As an individual he would concentrate on the social aspects and use the medical information as adjunctive. As a member of a diagnostic team he concentrates on the medical aspect primarily and the social elements are adjunctive. We are not treating a family that happens to have a handicapped member, we are treating a handicapped child and doing what needs to be done for the family to insure that the handicapped child is cared for properly.

In his initial contact with the parents and child, the social worker follows an outline for the interview. It is an orderly way to proceed, but need not in any way hinder the ability of the experienced social worker to elicit additional information. The better trained the interviewer, the better will be the interview, both in the quantity and the quality of the information recorded. A sensitivity to the parents' feelings and fears is essential.

The interview begins with basic information such as the name and date of birth. The date of the interview is noted as well as the name of the interviewer. We also want to know the names of the people present in the interview and their relationship to the child. Basically, this would give us a sense of just how reliable the history is going to be. If we are interviewing a foster mother who has only had the child for a few months, there is little information that she can give us about the child's early history, except what she has heard second or third hand from the foster-care agency.

In the case of foster care of adopted children, the child may be under duress knowing that someone other than his biological parents is raising him. What effect has it had on him? And if it has had any effect on him at all, is that part of the reason he is referred to us? If he doesn't know, how is he going to be told? How will he find out? Does he have a behavior problem or a learning-disability problem because his mental energy is tied up in worry? We go into this and the other items during the interview with great care because the evaluation is a diagnostic tool and what one fears most in medical care, and especially in the area of learning disabilities, is misdiagnosis. We are all too familiar with the case of the child who is institutionalized as retarded when in fact he is deaf.

The examining physician also takes a history, and in some ways it overlaps with that taken by the social worker and in other ways it is complementary. Usually, each time one asks a parent how old the child was when he uttered the first recognizable word one receives a slightly different answer. So at the conference the two times can be quoted back to the parent and he or she would be asked which one it was. In this way the two histories can serve as a check on one another. It is complementary in the sense that the social worker will try to get much more detailed information relative to the family constellation.

For example, if the grandmother is the informant, the social worker wants to find out why she has this responsibility. Why is the parent not present with the child? There could be a very valid reason; both parents could be working and there is nothing suspicious about their absence. Here again, though, it must be emphasized that the mother is our most reliable informant. Mothers, in our society and probably most others, are trained to take note of all the events that transpire in the child's development. If the mother is not the most reliable informant, then there probably won't be one. Occasionally the father is able to supply the information, but we are never as sure about the reliability of his information.

If a school should refer a child to us for a very specific reason, such as the demonstrated fact that he is three years below grade level in reading but is doing advanced work in math, then we have the impression that the information is reliable. The recommendation seems to indicate a form of specific learning disability with which we are familiar as opposed to a referral that simply cites lack of concentration. As a general practice we investigate any reported behavior that is passed along to us, but we want to be able to place an evaluation on the reliability of the source. If a school has decided to send a child to us for a learning disability or cerebral palsy, it becomes important for us to go to the classroom and find out exactly what is occurring. When possible we always like to visit schools to glean whatever we can from the teachers about the actual classroom situation.

When we ask the parent about their perception of the reason for the social service assessment we are after several different things. First of all, someone has decided that this parent ought to see a social worker, and it may be that they just want to develop the detailed family history that we are speaking of or it may be that they have noticed something that bears looking into. It may be that when the child came for a physical therapy evaluation, the physical therapist saw the mother hit the child with a belt and is concerned about this and wants to know whether excessive force is being routinely used. If that is a concern and the worker doing the interviewing does not happen to observe the same behavior, the worker wants to know the reason for the referral.

We want to see whether there is any difference between the reason that they were sent to us and the reason that they think they were sent to us. Many people have many different ideas about social workers. Most people would rather not deal with a social worker unless they have to. Very few people go by choice to see a social worker. The associations are most often welfare and public assistance.

This is a terribly misleading and inaccurate implication. The fact is that specific learning disabilities, as opposed to environmental impoverishment, are quite independent of socioeconomic status or education level. Some studies suggest that the learning problems we have been discussing are more frequent among children of middle-class and affluent parents. Many people feel that the social worker is someone who is going to pry into their business, and they feel their privacy is on the verge of being violated. It is important for us to learn the parents' idea of why they are being sent to the social worker so that they can be disabused of any notions that are not accurate.

A father who came to the Institute once said that his definition of social worker was 50 percent private investigator and 50 percent amateur psychologist. This is an idea that is probably widespread, and it is part of our job to reassure parents that we are not prying without reason but are simply trying to understand their problem so that we may be able to offer some assistance. We very much want them to understand why we are asking so many questions.

Another area of great concern to us is to learn exactly who lives at home. Is it mother and child or is it mother, grandmother, great-grandfather, and child and three siblings? Or is it the nuclear family, biological parents and offspring? The composition of the home in the latter case tells us that if there are emotional problems in the child then we have to look at how the nuclear family is operating. On the other hand, if there are emotional problems in the child living with the mother alone, we might look for other causes. What is the child's relationship to the mother? How does that distort the way that the child sees the world? If the child is living with grandparents, then we would want to know why the child was not living with the natural parents and how the child feels about this.

Children always think of families as mother, father, brother and sister. They think of the family the way that it is presented to them in books. What the social worker has to do when the actual family situation does not mirror that conception is to find out what effect it is having on the child in his own imagination. If it is just he and his mother living somewhere, he may imagine that he did something awful which sent the father away, whether the father died or whatever other reason. Children are very conventionally minded. No matter what kind of a family they come from, no matter what their circumstances, if they are asked for their idea of a family, nine times out of ten they will respond with the mother, father, brother, sister formulation and perhaps add the dog "Spot." Years ago black children would draw the picture of a white family when asked to picture a "family." That is how conventionally minded children can be—and how much they are influenced by television, school books, movies, etc.

After determining just what the composition of the immediate family is we attempt to find out where the missing members are. A very important piece of information is to discover that an older brother has been institutionalized for an emotional disorder of some description. Is there a sister who is in a group home because she had such a behavior problem that the parents sent her away? What exactly was the problem and what is this youngster's reaction to having his sister sent away? Is there a recent or not-so-recent divorce? What was the cause of the divorce and what does the child imagine was the cause of the divorce? What did the child think was his role in the divorce and is this causing him to have a learning or behavior problem? We always try to first determine exactly what the situation is in fact, then what the perception of it is in the minds of the participants.

We inquire systematically into the brothers' and sisters' medical, emotional and behavioral histories to see whether there are any similarities in behavior or disabilities. Beyond the immediate family, we are interested in close relatives on both sides of the family, again to determine whether there are any other family members who have displayed similar behavior or who have had similar learning disabilities. We do this because a number of the conditions that we see are genetically connected. A doctor would be more likely to make such a diagnosis if the condition were shown to have been present somewhere else in the family lineage.

It really does become a bit of detective work when we are attempting to track down this information in half-brothers and sisters. Imagine the situation in which one brother and sister share one father and another brother and sister share another father but all have the same mother. If the first pair have mild retardation what does that say about their father's family, and what does it say to the mother if she wishes to have more children? These are simply pieces of information to be put together and referred to a genetic counselor. Continuing on with this aspect of the interview we ask about the child's prenatal and neonatal history. The examining physician will have done much the same thing, and this is just a double check on what the parent has told him. We review the developmental milestones for speech, walking and so forth, and at times are able to develop some information that the physician had not noted in his own examination. We also try to ascertain as accurately as possible the exact age of the child when his problem became apparent. The date of the interview is noted so that we can say with certainty what was being displayed when the child came to us, and then we hope that the history will give us a clue as to when it first manifested itself. If, for example, a child became a behavior problem in school when the family moved to a new neighborhood or city, or in the first month that his parents were divorced, or at the time that his grandmother died, then we may be able to make a connection. Behavior problems are not usually so neatly linked to events, and consequently it is difficult to pinpoint the time that the problem began. This is simply because they are ordinarily not so dramatic to begin with—they just grow. Parents will often deny them or not notice them for reasons of their own. However, developmental problems and physical problems are usually spotted quite quickly. As a matter of fact, this keen observation is so respected that young physicians who are training with us are given the following advice: If a mother brings in her child and she has had at least one child already and tells you that there is something wrong with her child and you are not able to pinpoint anything, ask for consultation and repeat visits. This is one case where mother probably knows best!

After we have examined the child and the family history, as well as any possible contributing factors from the outside, we address ourselves to the parent or guardian. One of the things that we look for is "affect," or an appropriateness of response to stimuli. An example of inappropriate affect would be laughter when recounting an essentially unhappy incident. In the extreme, this could represent a hysterical reaction to overwhelming grief. Or the parent could be overly cheerful for no apparent reason. She is not giving the outside world appropriate cues as to what is going on inside herself. This could either be a deliberate pose or it could be evidence of a psychotic process not under the individual's control.

The appearance of the parent may be in striking contrast to that of the child. The parent may be neat, almost compulsively neat, and the child may be slovenly in appearance. We ask ourselves why the parent is allowing the child or causing the child to be so radically different. We also take a look at the ethnic background of the parent because there are some medical conditions that are more prevalent among specific groups. Ethnicity might also offer some clue as to the problems facing a child who has recently arrived in the country and has to adjust to a whole new culture. A child might be referred to us by a school because he is having difficulty keeping up in school and it turns out that a language other than English is the only one spoken at home. In some areas there is also the question of whether the parents are in the country legally or illegally. What effect is that having on the child? The child himself may not even be aware of the specifics of that problem, but the stresses and strains in the family can make themselves felt.

The age of the parent offers a variety of medical clues. The teenage mother may not have the requisite skills to take care of the child's needs. On the other hand, first-time mothers over thirty-five run a greater risk of birth defects. In much older parents we have a situation in which the parents are overwhelmed with the presence of a young child and just can't cope with the fast pace.

It is important to determine the quality of the marital relationship. Here again we need to see whether there is a stressful situation that might throw some light on the development of the child. As with many of the other components in the interview, the assessment made here is subjective. However, the well-trained professional social worker is capable of making these judgments with a substantial degree of accuracy.

The socioeconomic status and income level of the family frequently is a source of stress and anxiety. When we encounter a family living within its income and not incurring any unmanageable debt, we are able to rule money factors out as a source of tension. If, on the other hand, the family is living over its head economically, this could be a source of difficulty. If the family is living just over the poverty level so that they do not qualify for assistance with the medical bills they incur, this would certainly pose a problem for them. We try to assist them in finding a way so that it does not become a choice of food and lodging against medical assistance.

Another source of useful information is a report from the child's school guidance counselor. We are looking for an assessment of both his academic performance and his behavior. We want to see whether the child is living up to or above or below what we have established his intellectual capacity to be. It is important to determine whether behavior is interfering with learning or vice versa.

Overall we try to look at the child as he comes in to us before we have begun any remedial treatment. It is an estimate of the sort of adjustment the child has made on his own without any specialist assistance. The judgment he has made about himself and his world will give us some insight into his resources. The worker puts all of this information together and produces a testable hypothesis about the family and then establishes short-term and long-term goals.

The complex role of the social worker, as is evident in the preceding pages, is essential in eliciting the fullest involvement of parents or parent surrogates in developing a program plan for the learning-disabled child. The more meaningful and constructive that involvement, the higher is the probability of successful intervention. Much of our work consists of matching the child to the proper institution—which is sometimes impossible, as one of the following two cases will demonstrate—or in bringing about changes in attitude—which can be managed.

Deborah was an impressively attractive, articulate and sociable young lady of sixteen in her junior year in a high school that had recently received funds to hire a guidance counselor. Her mother, a widow, also was sociable and attractive, and was pursuing her masters degree. When Deborah came to our attention through the guidance counselor's referral, we found that she could hardly read; she was perhaps at a second- or third-grade grammar school level, and here she was a junior in high school. It seemed that on the basis of her social skills she had somehow been able to advance to that level. Her IQ of 86 placed her in the low-normal group, but she was very popular, the vice-president of her class and involved with a variety of extracurricular activities.

In her sophomore year the school authorities first realized that she had been promoted without ever acquiring the basic skills and that there was no way in which they would be able to graduate her. At this late point they decided that she should no longer stay at the school. They couldn't understand why she couldn't read, but we uncovered a serious dyslexia. She was able to do well verbally but written tests were beyond her.

One small puzzling incident occurred earlier in high school that later became comprehensible in the light of her dyslexia. A girl with whom she was friendly had transferred to another school and sent back a letter describing her new surroundings. The letter was being passed around but when it came to Deborah, she refused to look at it saying that she wasn't interested, which was not at all characteristic, considering her sociability. The other students thought it was odd but nothing further came out of the incident.

Her mother had never spotted this problem because the child was so socially adept that she managed to keep it hidden. The mother said that perhaps she didn't read all that well, but everything else was all right and the schools kept promoting her and never complained. As is often the case, the child had devised an elaborate strategy to disguise her reading problem. Where other children might have become behavior problems and drawn attention to themselves, she went in the opposite direction and did everything right. While we were evaluating her, she was extremely upset that the guidance counselor said that she had been caught cheating on a test. For her to breech her own strong code of behavior showed the depth of her desperation.

The only alternative that we could see for her was to leave her academic school to get some kind of vocational training. She had gone through school with her eyes set on college, but there was no way that we could help her achieve this goal at this particular time. It was just too late. We ended up recommending a special vocational high school for children with disabilities such as dyslexia, in which reading remediation was available. We were able to get her own school to agree to keep her to the end of the junior year and to test her orally and then she would transfer. Since we couldn't produce the desired solution to the problem—to keep her in school and bring her reading up to grade level—the mother and Deborah withdrew from contact with us. If some teacher along the line had spotted the problem, the story might have had a different ending.

❦

When he was eight years old and in the third grade, Michael was referred to us from a local grade school because of a behavior problem. His teacher reported that he wasn't learning because of his behavior. He seemed to be lazy and would rather talk to his classmates than listen to the teacher. Some of this behavior was noticed in the earlier grades, but it seemed to be getting worse. His academic achievement was not up to grade level and he was falling farther and farther behind.

The teacher called the parents in and discovered that they were having some problems with him as well. He didn't want to do his homework, he became depressed a lot, and he seemed lazy. The disinterest extended from homework to helping around the house. There was a lot of tension between him and an eleven-year-old sister who preceded him in the same school and was an outstanding student.

The presenting problem was his behavior, but when we evaluated him we found that he had a classical learning disability. He could not learn to read or write using normal methods because he had graphomotor problems, and he couldn't process material presented visually. Verbally he did well.

The parents felt that the school was picking on Michael due to the fact that the sister had done so well. It was our assessment that the parents also were comparing the child unfavorably to his sister. She had done well both in school and was helpful around the house.

During our work-up, conversations with Michael revealed that he had been working hard in the first two grades and was not having any success and so in the third grade he began to act up. We had to explain to the parents that the real process was exactly the opposite of what they thought it was. It was not that Michael was lazy and therefore didn't learn, it was that he didn't learn after trying so hard, and because of his discouragement his behavior became a problem.

He was frustrated, bored, frightened and very unhappy—and so he acted it all out. The parents had difficulty in accepting that explanation. Michael had average intelligence, and if he could have been instructed and tested verbally he would not have had a problem, but that is not the way society is set up.

The school went on record to say that if his behavior did not improve he would be expelled. The parents very much wanted Michael to remain in the school and fought hard to keep him there. We suggested that perhaps this particular school was not the correct one for Michael and that a public school program with lesser demands academically and access to a resource room might be more beneficial. The parents were at first reluctant to consider a transfer but eventually agreed to go along with it.

The following year Michael began to improve with the aid of the resource room and the imposition of less stringent academic demands. Without any conscious intent a number of family issues also had emerged during family counseling. One of the issues was that the father had adopted the daughter as his favorite, she was "Daddy's little girl." Michael's mother had similarly adopted him and the parents were not aware that this would make a difference to the children. Of course it did.

The little boy felt very strongly that the father did not care for him. Eventually he was able to tell that to the parents during one of the discussion sessions we were having about his behavior problem in school. Michael was finally able to see that his father did love him. Outward manifestations may not have made it look that way, but he finally accepted it as the truth. Bringing such feelings out into the open proved to be beneficial since it opened up a dialogue between the various members of the family.

We brought in the entire family for the diagnostic conference and then we had two more sessions to discuss the course of remediation that we were going to outline for Michael. During the post-conference interview the occupational therapist had Michael write words on the board so the parents could see that he reversed some letters and rotated some, and it became clear what the nature of his problem was.

The attending neurologist said to Michael, "You try very hard, don't you?" and he very solemnly nodded his head. And she continued, "It hurts you very much when people don't believe that!" And he began to cry. It was a revelation to the parents that he felt so strongly about it and that they and the school were wrong and were hurting him even though they had the best of intentions. Reports from the fourth grade indicate that he is catching up to grade level. And, incidentally, he is now going fishing with his father.

EPILOGUE

Throughout this book we have stressed the need for complete and comprehensive diagnosis and evaluation. As important as we believe these areas to be, the primary question remains, "What are we going to do about any identified deficits or weaknesses?"

We have attempted, in the illustrative case material included in the various chapters, to demonstrate specific modes of treatment, special educational techniques, and constructive family and other interpersonal relationship skills that have been of significant help in assisting the learning-disabled child and his family to cope more effectively with this puzzling, upsetting, and difficult-to-define condition. The integration of the evaluations and recommendations of each discipline is a key element. It is through this process that the comprehensive treatment plan is developed and fully communicated to the parents and, if appropriate, to the child as well.

Our experiences provide us with the basis for considerable optimism regarding the long-term outlook for these children.

It is our hope that the reader will have had some questions answered and some issues clarified. We have attempted to direct parents and others concerned with the diagnosis, care and management of children with learning disabilities, to specific sources of help and to explain exactly what can and should be done.

To the extent that these objectives have been achieved, so will the primary purpose of this book and the aspirations of all those involved in its writing be realized.

GLOSSARY

GLOSSARY OF FREQUENTLY USED TERMS

Abstract Reasoning The ability to comprehend relationships, and to react appropriately not only to concrete objects but to complex concepts and symbols.

Academic Ability Competence in the basic school subjects (e.g., reading comprehension and arithmetical computation).

Academic Achievement Level of performance in one or more of the basic school subjects as measured by standardized tests of competence.

Acting Out Behavior inappropriate to a given situation, usually characterized by a higher intensity of aggressive activity and lack of control.

Activities of Daily Living See ADL

Adiadochokinesia The inability to perform rapidly successive movements. May refer to the hands, as in alternating palms up and palms down movements, or to coordinated lip and tongue movements. May suggest cerebellar pathology, involving complex coordinating functions.

ADL The adaptive skills necessary to achieve age-appropriate responses necessary for increasingly independent functioning in the areas of eating, dressing, grooming, etc.

Advocacy A program in the interest of persons who are in some way disabled, in which agencies or individuals act on their behalf. These interests may pertain to legal rights, appropriate educational opportunity, or the availability of required medical or remedial services.

Affect An immediately expressed and observable emotion. A feeling state becomes an affect when it becomes observable as overall demeanor or tone and modulation of voice.

Agnosia A complete or partial inability to recognize and attach meaning to the impressions received by any of the sense organs. This may involve visual, tactile, or auditory agnosia. An individual with agnosia is unable to perceive correctly and identify familiar objects.

Alexia The term used to indicate a serious reading difficulty. The condition is usually characterized by an inability to read more than a few lines at a time with understanding. May be described as a form of aphasia in which there is an absence of the ability to grasp meaning from or to read the written language.

Amentia An obsolete term formerly used to describe severe mental retardation. (IQ scores below 25.)

Amniocentesis The technique of withdrawing amniotic fluid in order to identify possible genetic abnormalities by cytogenetic or biochemical study.

Anomia An inability to name objects or recall and recognize names.

Anoxemia Lack of or diminished oxygen content in the blood.

Anoxia Reduced oxygen content of bodily tissues to a level insufficient to maintain adequate function, particularly as applied to brain function.

Apgar Score A numerical score, ranging from 0–10, that attempts to quantify the condition of the newborn infant with respect to five vital life factors. A score below 6 alerts the pediatrician to possible difficulty.

Aphasia Loss or impairment of the ability to use words and to understand language symbols in reading, writing, or speaking. Usually results from organic defects of the brain.

Apraxia The impairment or loss of ability to perform purposeful movements. A disorder in which sensory pathways are intact, but relatively uncomplicated movements become clumsy.

Aptitude The interest in and capacity to profit from training in some particular area.

Arithmetic Mean See Average.

Articulation The integrated coordination of lips, tongue and jaw muscles involved in the production of intelligible speech.

Asphyxia Suffocation resulting in anoxia and increased carbon dioxide tension in the blood and tissues of the body.

Aspiration Level The goal set by an individual for his own performance. May be influenced by parental and peer pressure, or other significant role models.

Associative Learning The cognitive state in which a previously learned item tends to be recalled when a specific cue or stimulus is experienced.

Astereognosis Loss of the ability to perceive objects, forms or other material according to shape, size and quality of the materials, utilizing the sense of touch.

Ataxia Poor coordination of voluntary muscle action. May involve loss of proprioceptive feedback from muscles leading to incoordination of walking movements.

Athetoid Movements Involuntary, uncontrollable, bizarre movements of the extremities, trunk muscles, facial muscles, and the tongue. These movements lack fixed amplitude, frequency and rhythm.

Athetosis A form of cerebral palsy involving the basal ganglia and the extrapyramidal system. Characterized by athetoid movements.

Atrophy A deterioration or wasting of muscles, tissues, organs, or the entire body.

Attention-Deficit Disorder The essential features are signs of developmentally inappropriate attention and impulsivity. In the past, a variety of names have been attached to this disorder including: hyperkinetic reaction of childhood, hyperkinetic syndrome, minimal brain damage, minimal brain dysfunction, and minimal cerebral dysfunction. There are two subtypes: (1) attention-deficit disorder with hyperactivity, and (2) attention-deficit disorder without hyperactivity.

Auditory Motor Function Expression of motor behaviors guided or elicited by associated auditory stimuli or cues.

Autism A syndrome consisting of withdrawal, totally inadequate social relationships, exceptional object relationships, language disturbances and monotonously repetitive motor behavior. Language may either have never developed, or may disappear after age one-and-a-half or two following normal earlier development.

Average A statistical term used to describe a measure of central tendency—i.e., average size, average weight or average score. There are several types of averages. The most common is the arithmetic mean, in which all of the values on a given measurement are simply divided by the number of measurements to produce the "average."

Avoidance Disorder of Childhood or Adolescence A behavioral term describing activity designed to postpone an unpleasant event or stimulus. It is a form of escape behavior.

Babinski Sign A reflex action in which the great toe is extended upward when the sole of the foot is pressed or stroked with light pressure from the heel to the ball of the foot (usually with a wooden applicator or similar object). When present after two or three years of age it may be indicative of pyramidal tract pathology.

Backward Child A child with social and academic behavior less than that which should be expected on the basis of age-level standards. See borderline intelligence.

Basal Ganglia An area of the brain comprising the interior of the hemispheres and composed of both white matter and gray matter. A complex structure that has connections with all sensory pathways and receives nerve fibers from the cerebral cortex. Various motor pathways also leave the basal ganglia. Many of the extrapyramidal functions of the cerebral cortex are mediated through the basal ganglia, i.e., tone, movement, and posture.

Base Line The usual level of functioning proficiency or the state of an individual with respect to a particular characteristic.

Behavioral Disturbance The breaking up of usual and successful patterns of coping with natural and social demands of the environment.

Behavior Disorder Impaired or abnormal development of internalized controls or mechanisms with which the individual attempts to cope effectively with the demands of his environment.

Behaviorism A doctrine stating that the data of psychology consist of the observable evidence of activity to the exclusion of introspective data or references to consciousness and the mind.

Behavior Modification Precisely planned systematic application of methods and experimental findings of behavioral science with the intent of altering observable behaviors, including increasing, decreasing, extending, restricting, teaching, and maintaining specific behaviors.

Behavior Rating Scales Scales that contain specific descriptions of behavior in a variety of situations. Measurement techniques or instruments providing classification of the level of the individual's adaptive behaviors, such as the Vineland Social Maturity Scale or the American Association on Mental Deficiency Adaptive Behavior Scales.

Biofeedback The use of knowledge gained from awareness of autonomic nervous system functions, in the control of such functions. Thus pulse rate, blood pressure, etc., may be modified by behavior learned to have an effect upon such functions. Electronic devices are frequently employed that provide visual and/or auditory signals which immediately reflect increases or decreases in pulse rate, for example, upon attempts at voluntary control.

Birth Injury Primarily refers to temporary or permanent damage to the brain sustained by the newborn infant during the birth process.

Birth Trauma Literally means an injury received during birth. It is, however, commonly used to denote the effect upon the psyche from the stress of the birth process.

Borderline Intelligence Intellectual functioning in the range of 1–2 standard deviations below the test mean (68–83 on the Stanford Binet, or 70–84 on the Wechsler). Sometimes referred to as slow learner.

Brain Damage Organic damage to any portion of the brain that can be demonstrated by clinical, neurological, radiographic or other diagnostic tests.

Brain Dysfunction Disturbed mental or intellectual processes, which may or may not be associated with demonstrable brain damage.

Brain Injury Known or inferred trauma to the brain resulting in brain damage.

CAT Scan A noninvasive, computerized, radiographic study of selected areas of the brain or other parts of the body.

Central Nervous System The brain and its various subdivisions, together with the spinal cord.

Cerebral Cortex The gray matter composing the external layer of the brain, which contains billions of brain cell bodies in addition to nerve fibers and supporting structures.

Cerebral Dominance Refers to that side of the cerebral cortex which exercises primary control of motor behavior. Thus, right-handed individuals are said to be left-brain dominant, while left-handed or left-sided individuals are said to be right-brain dominant. The left side of the brain controls language function in approximately 90 percent of the population.

Cerebral Palsy A descriptive term used to characterize a neuromotor disorder dating from birth or early infancy. The syndrome may also include sensory disorders, seizures, mental retardation, learning difficulty, and behavioral disorders. The neuromotor disturbance may manifest in paralysis, weakness, and/or incoordination.

Cerebrum The portion of the brain comprising the cerebral hemispheres and some other brain structures but excluding the cerebellum and the brain stem.

Chemotherapy Treatment of mental, physical, and social malfunctioning by means of chemical substances or drugs to arrest or lessen the symptomatology.

Choreiform Movements Involuntary movements that are rapid, jerky, of small amplitude, and involve muscles all over the body.

Chromosome Abnormality Any body in the cell nucleus that carries genetic material which differs in any way from the usual state or structure.

Clonus On stimulus, the rapid, repetitive, uncontrolled contractions and relaxations of a muscle.

Clumsy Child A child who demonstrates below average skills in dressing, feeding, and walking and has difficulty in writing, drawing and copying. All of this in the absence of any evidence of neuropathology.

Cognition A general term for any process by which an organism becomes aware. It includes perceiving, reasoning, conceiving and judging.

Cognitive Of or related to thoughts and ideas.

Cognitive Deficit An inadequate or subaverage perceptual or intellectual level of performance or functioning.

C.O.H. See Committee on the Handicapped.

Committee on the Handicapped A group consisting of school personnel, including specialists in the areas of neurology, psychiatry, psychology and learning disabilities along with parent representatives. The Committee is designed to review recommendations for special educational programming, and is responsible for the placement of children requiring such specialized programs in the least restrictive, most appropriate educational setting.

Computerized Axial Tomography See CAT Scan.

Concept A general idea of the characteristics of a class or group of objects.

Conduct Disorder See Behavior Disorder.

Convulsive Disorder See Epilepsy.

Counseling Professional guidance on the basis of knowledge of human behavior and the use of special interviewing skills to achieve specified goals that are beneficial to the individual and mutually accepted by both counselor and client.

Craniostenosis Premature closure of one or more of the sutures of the skull (the normal openings between the bones of the skull in the young infant) with resultant deformity of the head. May cause damage to the developing brain as a result of reduced space in the cranial vault, but in many cases follows failure of normal brain development.

Cultural Deprivation The condition in which the infant or young child receives insufficient, inconsistent, or inappropriate stimulation or care.

Cytogenetics Examination of the structure and formation of cells concerned with heredity (i.e., chromosomes and genes).

Developmental Aphasia This form of aphasia usually results from brain injury or delayed development of the central nervous system. See Aphasia.

Developmental Articulation Disorder The essential failure to develop consistently correct articulation of the later acquired speech sounds, such as r, sh, th, f, z, l or ch.

Developmental Disability A disability, as defined in the Federal statutes, attributable to mental retardation, cerebral palsy, epilepsy, or any other neurological condition which is closely related to or which may produce mental retardation. The condition originates in childhood, is likely to continue throughout adulthood, and constitutes a substantial handicap to the individual.

Developmental Language Disorder This is the most common type of language disorder and may involve difficulty in either comprehending oral language (receptive type) or in expressing verbal language (expressive type). See Developmental Aphasia.

Developmental Reading Disorder See Dyslexia.

Diagnosis In general usage this term refers to the process of identifying specific mental, educational or physical disorders.

Differential Diagnosis The process of refining a diagnosis to differentiate between diseases or conditions with similar, but significantly different, characteristics.

Distractibility One of the aspects of the attention deficit disorder (*q.v.*), characterized by a markedly decreased span of attention. Difficulty in concentrating on a task long enough to complete it.

Dominance See Cerebral Dominance.

Dominant Hemisphere Most frequently used to refer to that cerebral hemisphere, either left or right, which controls movement on the opposite side. See Cerebral Dominance.

Down's Syndrome A syndrome in which the majority of affected individuals are trisomic (having three pairs of chromosomes instead of the normal two) for chromosome #21. A less frequent cause is the translocation of a portion of a chromosome to some other chromosome. Among the characteristics are hypotonia, a moderate degree of mental retardation, and congenital heart disease.

Dull Normal Intelligence That level of intellectual ability at or near the lower limits of the average range (IQ between 85 and 90).

Dysgraphia The inability to express thoughts in writing or written symbols, usually caused by a brain lesion.

Dyskinesia A distortion or derangement of, or the inability to control, involuntary movements such as tics, spasms or clonus. These manifestations usually disappear during sleep.

Dyslexia A term used to indicate severe reading difficulty. The condition, characterized by an inability to read more than a few lines or words with understanding, is most often associated with problems in visual decoding and word or symbol recognition. Sometimes used synonymously with alexia.

Dysnomia An impaired ability to name objects or recall or recognize names.

Dysphasia An impaired ability to recognize spoken or written language or the inability to interpret gestures and integrate symbolic formulations and to express them.

Dystonia An alteration of normal muscle tone usually associated with hypertonicity. Slow turning movements, especially of the trunk muscles, with rotation of the extremities, producing distorted postural attitudes.

Early Childhood Education See Preschool Education.

Echolalia The noncognitive repetition of a word or group of words or sentence just spoken by oneself or by another person. The senseless repetition of a word, a group of words, or a sentence. Sometimes found among severely retarded children, those with speech and language disorders, and in a variety of psychogenic disorders.

EEG See Electroencephalogram.

Elective Mutism The voluntary or involuntary lack of speech, due to emotional conflict.

Electroencephalogram (EEG) A measurement of the electrical activity of the brain. It is of value in establishing the presence of a central nervous system abnormality, and of assistance in the diagnosis of epilepsy.

Electronystagmography A procedure for the precise measurement of nystagmic eye movements using electronic instrumentation.

Encephalitis Inflammation of the brain resulting from the response of the cerebral tissue to a variety of infections and occasionally toxic substances.

Encopresis Involuntary defecation generally not caused by illness or any organic malfunction. Frequently associated with emotional problems when it occurs in children.

Enuresis The involuntary passage of urine, not caused by illness or any organic malfunction. Frequently used synonymously with bed-wetting, but not necessarily limited thereto.

Environmental Deprivation See Cultural Deprivation.

Epilepsy A disorder characterized by single or recurring attacks of loss of consciousness, convulsive movements, or disturbances of feeling or behavior. These episodes are associated with excessive neuronal discharges occurring diffusely or focally within the brain. See EEG.

Etiology The cause of an abnormal or pathological condition.

Evaluation The application of techniques for the systematic appraisal of physical, mental, social, economic and intellectual resources of an individual and his family, for the purpose of devising an individual program of corrective action or remediation.

Evoked Potential The technique for the assessment of auditory, visual or other responses to stimuli, taking the measurements directly from the nervous system, thus obviating the need for a verbal or conscious motor response.

Exceptional Child The term for a child who deviates significantly from the average in intelligence, social behavior, emotional development, or learning.

The term is correctly used to describe both superior and inferior performance, but it is more often used to refer to individuals with a deficit.

Expressive Language Language directed toward someone else. Ordinarily refers to spoken or written language, but may include gestures or signs. The ability to communicate with others through language.

Extrapyramidal System Includes all descending neural pathways, exclusive of the pyramidal tract, that act on primary motor cells. It is integrated with the motor system in the control of muscular activity. Disturbances in the extrapyramidal tract is thought to cause athetosis, tremor, ataxia, and rigidity.

Feedback The process of providing a person (or other organism) with information related to the success, failure or effectiveness of any response to a given stimulus or task. Immediate feedback is believed to facilitate learning.

Figure-Ground Refers to the relationship between a specific pattern (figure) and its background. Frequently disturbed in patients with minimal brain dysfunction or attention-deficit disorder.

German Measles See Rubella.

Grand Mal Epilepsy Seizures characterized by generalized tonic and/or clonic movements of the extremities, face or body, associated with loss of consciousness.

Graphomotor Skills Those skills involving fine motor coordination necessary for writing and drawing activities.

Gray Matter Portions of the central nervous system made up primarily of cell bodies and fibers lacking a myelin sheath.

Group Therapy Treatment of psychosocial problems using the interacting forces within a small unit of individuals who may have similar or differing characteristics or problems. Groups are led by a qualified psychotherapist.

Habilitation Similar to rehabilitation except that no prior skill is assumed.

Hallucination A sensory perception without external stimulation of the relevant sensory organ.

Handicapped Person One who, because of physical, intellectual or emotional impairment, is significantly hindered from learning, working, playing, or adapting to the expectations or demands of society or doing things that other individuals of equivalent age are able to do.

Hard Signs A term used by neurologists to indicate that a child performs in an observably different way from the average child in certain central nervous system functions. These differences may be qualitative or quantitative. When present, a hard sign suggests organic pathology.

Hemiparesis Similar to hemiplegia but suggestive of a weakness rather than paralysis. May describe a residual weakness following partial recovery from a hemiplegia.

Hyperactivity Persistent excessive or above average expression of physical energy. The inability to sit quietly for more than a few moments at a time, or evidence of misdirected activity. May be caused by organic or emotional factors.

Hyperkinesis Similar to hyperactivity but more frequently used to describe the "fidgety" child. One who may be in constant motion even while seated.

Hypertrophy Excessive growth of an organ or tissue due to the multiplication of its constituent cells, or increased size of the cells. General increase in the bulk of a muscle or group of muscles.

Hypochondriasis Unrealistic interpretation of physical signs or sensations as abnormal, leading to a preoccupation with disease or the fear of having a disease.

Hypotrophy Diminished growth or wasting of an organ or tissue, resulting from the failure of the cells to develop properly or the deterioration of such cells after normal development. A general decrease in the bulk of a muscle or group of muscles.

Hypoxemia A condition in which there is insufficient oxygen present in the blood.

Hypoxia A state in which there is an insufficient amount of oxygen available in the tissues.

Identity The sense of self, providing a unity of personality over time.

I.E.P. See Individual Educational Plan.

Impulsivity The tendency to react to a stimulus immediately, without adequate reflection or deliberation. Frequently associated with hyperactivity and attention-deficit disorder.

Inborn Errors of Metabolism Deviations from normal metabolic processes usually expressed at birth or during the first days of life, caused by genetic abnormalities.

Individual Educational Plan A specific individualized educational prescription designed to meet the special educational needs of an individual with a learning disability or a developmental disability.

Infantile Autism A condition characterized by a lack of responsiveness to other people, gross impairment in communicative skills, and bizzare responses to various aspects of the environment, all developing within the first thirty months of age.

Intelligence Quotient A numerical value used to describe the relative level of intelligence. Formerly determined by mental age, as measured by intelligence tests, multiplied by 100 and divided by the chronological age. Currently all major standardized individual intelligence tests present the IQ in terms of standard scores which provide comparisons with chronological age peers. Frequently referred to as IQ.

IQ See Intelligence Quotient.

Karyotyping The analysis of the chromosomal makeup of an individual usually presented as a series of microphotographs of chromosomes of a single cell nucleus, arranged in pairs in descending order of size.

Labile Behavior characterized by unstable feelings, emotions, and moods. The highly labile individual demonstrates rapid shifts from one extreme to the other.

Laterality The internal awareness of the two sides (right and left) of the body and their differences. A sensory motor awareness of right versus left. The consistent expression of a preference for either right or left.

Lead Poisoning Toxicity resulting from the ingestion of lead. May come from lead-based paint, old lead plumbing or gasoline exhaust fumes. Affects the central nervous system, resulting in progressive or permanent damage.

Learning The process of organizing sensory input and integrating the perceived material with past experiences related to similar situations or objects.

Learning Disability See Specific Learning Disability.

Lesion Any wound or morbid change in the structure or functioning of the living tissues of the body.

Maelstrom A state of mental turbulence or chaotic mental confusion. The allegory is to the turbulence of a giant whirlpool in the ocean.

Mainstream Used primarily in describing an educational setting in which the majority of students are able to learn without the necessity of using techniques required for the teaching of handicapped or learning-disabled children.

Mainstreaming The effort, in special education, to provide handicapped or learning-disabled children with the special remedial attention that will allow them to move to the least restrictive appropriate educational setting.

Maturation The process of changing from an immature (small, undifferentiated) to a mature or adult state.

Maturational Lag The delayed development or appearance of certain age-related skills. These may involve motor function, speech, and other behaviors that we expect to see by a given chronological age.

Mean See Arithmetic Mean.

Measured Intelligence The capacity to perceive and understand relationships as measured by standardized general intelligence test, such as the Stanford-Binet Intelligence Test, the Wechsler Intelligence Scale for Children (WISC), the Wechsler Adult Intelligence Scale (WAIS) and the Wechsler Preschool and Primary Scale (WPPS).

Median An average score that denotes the point in a series of measurements at which 50 percent of the measurements are above it and 50 percent are below. See Average.

Mental Age The level of measured mental ability or capacity as determined by an intelligence test. It is distinguished from the chronological age of the individual.

Mental Disorder A disorder in which the individual manifests significantly aberrant behavior or impairment in one or more important areas of mental functioning.

Mental Retardation Significantly subaverage general intellectual functioning of various degrees, existing concurrently with deficits in adaptive behavior and manifested during the developmental period.

Microcephaly Hypoplasia of the cerebrum resulting in a small head. May result from neonatal asphyxia, prenatal injections, genetic abnormality or birth injury. Usually associated with mental retardation of severe degree.

Milestones Key states in the development of an infant, which are expected to appear by a certain chronological age. For example, the age at which the infant holds his head up, sits alone, babbles, stands alone, walks independently, speaks in words and sentences, etc.

Minimal Brain Damage A term which is currently out of favor, describing a condition in which there is little or no evidence of neurological abnormality, but some clear disorder of cognition, thought, or affect, such as is commonly associated with manifest neurological abnormalities. The term is probably derived from the concept of brain injury and the brain-injured child as put forth by Strauss and Lehtinen in 1947. The syndrome has been described as consisting of hyperkinetic behavior, short attention span, lability of mood, antisocial behavior, varying intellectual deficits including perseveration, and attacks of anxiety and ritualistic behavior. The authors believe that this term should be reserved for individuals with evidence of organic neuropathology. See Attention-Deficit Disorder.

Minimal Brain Dysfunction Essentially similar to the concept of minimal brain damage, stressing the absence of any specific evidence of neurological damage or pathology in the central nervous system. Involves learning difficulty, hyperkinetic behavior and emotional lability. The existence of underlying brain dysfunction is implied rather than proven. See Attention-Deficit Disorder.

Mongolism See Down's Syndrome.

Mood A pervasive and sustained state of mind, which in the extreme markedly colors an individual's perception of the world.

Morbid A diseased or unhealthy condition of the body or mind.

Morpheme The smallest meaningful unit of language, which occurs either as a word or within a word. For example, troubleshooting contains three morphemes, trouble-, -shoot- and -ing.

Muscle Tone The condition of muscle fibers both at rest and during use. A flabby quality, as compared with a firmness and appropriate degree of tension during flexion or extension, may suggest neuromotor difficulty.

Neurosis A functional disorder, psychogenic in origin. Manifestations may include hysteria, phobic responses, anxiety and obsessive compulsive behavior.

Neurotic Disorder A mental disorder in which the predominant disturbance is a symptom or group of symptoms reflecting emotional turmoil that is distressing to the individual and is recognized by him or her as unacceptable. Reality testing is grossly intact.

Nonverbal Ability The power or special skills necessary to perform an act or task, physical or mental, not involving the use of words.

Nystagmus An involuntary oscillation of the eyeball, usually characterized by lateral movements but they may also be vertical, rotary or mixed.

Obsessions Recurrent persistent ideas, thoughts, images or impulses that involuntarily invade consciousness.

Occupational Therapy Occupational therapy involves the assessment of goal-oriented, purposeful activity in the evaluation and treatment of individuals with psychological, physical, or developmental disabilities. The primary concern of the occupational therapist is to help the patient develop optimal levels of adaptive skills and performance capacities for independent living.

Oppositional Disorder A pattern of disobedient, negativistic, and provocative opposition. The oppositional attitude is usually manifested toward family members, particularly the parents, and toward teachers.

Organic Generally used to describe a malfunction of mental processes or physical behavior that has a demonstrable physiological basis.

Organicity See Organic.

Percept A mental impression derived from an immediate sensory experience and the mental reaction thereto.

Perception Awareness and meaningful interpretation of stimuli transmitted by the visual, auditory, olfactory, taste, tactile or kinesthetic sensory systems. Also used to indicate the awareness of sensory stimulation or the reactions thereto.

Perceptual Disorder A high-level impairment of the awareness and/or interpretation of visual, auditory, cutaneous, olfactory or other sensory input.

Perseveration The persistent repetition or continuation of a word or sentence or action after it has been once begun, or recently completed. An inability to discontinue a response to a previous stimulus.

Personality Deeply ingrained patterns of behavior, which include the way one relates to, perceives and thinks about the environment and other people.

Personality Disorder An inflexible and maladaptive pattern of relating to others that causes significant impairment in adaptive functioning or feelings of subjective distress.

Phobia A persistent, irrational fear of a specific object, activity, or situation that results in a compelling desire to avoid the dreaded object, activity or situation.

Phoneme A distinct sound unit recognized by speakers of a language. There are 46 phonemes in English: 9 vowels and 37 consonants.

Physical Therapy The treatment of neuromotor or trauma-associated disturbances of motor function. May involve the use of therapeutic exercises, gait training, balance training or the application of various therapeutic modalities.

Pica The eating of non-nutritional substances, such as paint or hair. Also the craving for unusual foods.

Plumbism See Lead Poisoning.

Pneumoencephologram X-ray study of the brain where added contrast is obtained by replacing some of the cerebrospinal fluid with air or oxygen.

Preschool Education A training program or nursery school experience in which emphasis is placed on developing self-help, motor, communication and social skills.

Premature Infant One usually born after the twenty-seventh week of pregnancy and before the thirty-seventh, and weighing between 1,000 and 2,499 grams (2.2 to 5.5 pounds). Infants born prior to the twenty-eighth week or weighing less than 1,000 grams are termed immature.

Prognosis A statement expressing the probable outcome of a physical illness or a mental or social dysfunction or deficit.

Proprioceptive Stimuli Stimuli arising from receptor neurons within the muscle, organ or associated structures, which provide additional sensory input related to position and postural orientation. They permit continuous monitoring of these factors and fine motor adjustments which enable one to "zero in" on picking up a pin or to bring a spoon unerringly to the mouth.

Psychological Testing A general term to describe a process of assessment that measures or evaluates abilities or personality traits, either general or specific.

Psychometric Testing A series of various psychological tests administered to test one or several of the factors in mental ability, such as intelligence, special abilities, manual skills, vocational aptitudes and interests, and personality characteristics that are capable of being measured in an objective manner.

Psychomotor Agitation Excessive motor activity associated with a feeling of inner tension. The activity is usually unproductive and repetitious. See Hyperactivity and Hyperkinesis.

Psychomotor Delay The failure to develop appropriate physical reactions, speech, and appropriately adaptive environmental responses within the normal developmental time frame, as a result of central nervous system or severe psychogenic disturbance. See Maturational Lag.

Psychomotor Retardation Delay in development of or generalized slowing down of physical reactions, movements and/or speech, related to activities of the cerebral cortex.

Psychomotor Seizures A form of epilepsy characterized by short attacks of extreme motor activity of which the individual has no subsequent recollection. They usually originate in the temporal lobe of the brain. See Epilepsy.

Psychopharmacology The use of drugs to influence affective, emotional, and behavioral states. Drugs used to modify behavior are generally classified as stimulants, tranquilizers and/or anti-depressants.

Psychotic Disorder Behavioral manifestations indicating gross impairment of reality testing. Delusions or hallucinations without insight into their pathological nature is diagnostic of this condition.

Pyramidal System The pyramidal system is primarily comprised of motor fibers arising in the area immediately anterior to the central sulcus (Rolandic fissure), joined by pathways from other areas of the brain. Dysfunction in the pyramidal tract is thought to cause spasticity.

Receptive Language Understanding language messages from others. Generally related to spoken or written language, but may include the comprehension of gestures.

Recessive Trait A genetically determined trait that remains latent or subordinate to a dominant trait except in those cases in which both members of the gene pair are recessive.

Reflex A simple stimulus-response connection believed to be unlearned and characteristic of a specific species. Inborn, permanent, and unchangeable reactions of an organism to a specific stimulus that take place through the activity of the nervous system.

Rehabilitation The process of improving an individual's skill or level of adjustment to maintain a satisfactory level of functioning in a variety of areas.

Remedial Education Teaching techniques specifically designed for use with children with learning difficulties. Remedial instruction may be specific to the difficulty, such as remedial reading.

Resource Room An educational setting in which a child is given the opportunity for concentrated remedial instruction in an area of learning difficulty while continuing in the mainstream of the educational setting. See Mainstream.

Reversal One of the perceptual problems associated with reading disability and dyslexia. The mirror-image perception of letters, symbols or words.

Rh Incompatibility A hyperimmune state in which the expectant mother has Rh-negative blood and the fetus has Rh-positive blood, causing the formation of antibodies in the mother with the resultant destruction of fetal blood cells. May produce kernicterus, cerebral palsy, or possibly mental retardation.

Rotation One of the perceptual disturbances frequently associated with reading disabilities and dyslexia. The perception of letters, symbols, numbers, or words, as rotated in space. The rotation is frequently 180 or 360 degrees but may be of any magnitude.

Rubella German measles. When occurring in the mother during the first trimester of pregnancy, the infection may cause congenital abnormalities in the fetus, including deafness, cataracts, cardiac malformation, cerebral palsy and/or mental retardation.

School Phobia A neurotic manifestation of fear of attending school that exceeds age-appropriate, normally expected parameters.

Seizures See Epilepsy.

Semantics The meanings in words and phrases. For example, in English it would be unacceptable to say "bachelor's wife" since the two words are contradictory in meaning. Further, the sentence "The baseball bat bit the girl" is unacceptable since a baseball bat is not an animate object.

Sensory Deprivation A condition in which one or more of the major senses such as vision or hearing is so impaired as markedly to reduce or restrict the use of sensory stimuli. Intellectual retardation may occur if compensatory methods for sensory input are not provided.

Sensory Integration The ability to organize sensory information for use in facilitating an appropriate response. Deficits in the sensory integrative process impair the ability to learn and to interact effectively with the environment.

Sensory Motor Difficulty A disturbance in the neural pathways that interferes with the effective transmission of sensory input or stimuli through the synapses and with the appropriate motor response.

Separation Anxiety Disorder A clinical picture in which the major disturbance is excessive anxiety on separation from parents or major attachment figures or from home or other familiar surroundings. The child may experience anxiety to the point of panic.

Sequellae Specific areas of deficit or dysfunction, either transient or permanent, which follow an illness or injury.

Sequencing The process of planning motor responses in a sequential manner. Difficulty in this area is evident when the child is unable to plan a series of motor responses necessary to complete a given task.

Sex-Linked Inheritance Inheritance of genetic characteristics carried by specific sex-linked genes.

Sign An objective manifestation of a pathological condition. Signs are observed by the examiner rather than reported by the individual.

Sign Language Communication using gestures, usually manual. A substitute for spoken words, phrases, or letters.

Slow Learner A child with social behavior and/or academic achievement less than that expected on the basis of chronological age. In the range of one to two standard deviations below the mean (69–83 on the Stanford-Binet, or 70–84 on the Wechsler).

Social and Emotional Development The process of self-identification. The exploration and mastery of interpersonal relationships, including the building of internal controls.

Soft Signs A term used by neurologists to indicate that a child performs in a slightly different way from the average child in certain nervous system functions. These differences may be qualitative or quantitative. Relating soft signs to learning disabilities involves the concept of minimal brain dysfunction or attention-deficit disorder. The validity of this relationship has not been confirmed.

Somatic Pertaining to the body.

Spasticity Increased tonus or tension in a muscle on movement, which may be associated with exaggerated deep tendon reflexes and impairment of voluntary control of the muscle action or movement.

Spatial Relationships Refers to the perceived position of two or more objects or subjects in relation to the observer and in relation to each other.

Special Class A group of children assigned to a particular class on the basis of some disability, such as educable mental retardation or emotional disturbance, and given instruction by teachers with specific training in the areas of the disability. Classes are generally small—that is, under twelve.

May also, although less frequently, be used to describe classes for intellectually gifted children.

Specific Learning Disability As defined in Public Law 94-142 Amended (Education of all Handicapped Children Act), SLD means a disorder in one or more of the basic psychological processes involved in understanding or in using language, spoken or written, that may manifest itself in an imperfect ability to listen, think, speak, read, write, spell or do mathematical calculations. The term does not include learning problems that are primarily the result of visual, auditory, or motor handicaps, of mental retardation or severe emotional disturbance, or of environmental, cultural, or economic disadvantage.

Speech Therapy A specialized area of evaluation and treatment involving disorders of speech, language, voice and fluency. Utilizes a variety of techniques to correct or improve language function and verbal communication.

Standard Deviation A statistical measurement that describes the extent of the dispersion of individual scores or values around the arithmetic mean of those values. In a normal (Gaussian) distribution, 68 percent of all values in the group data will be contained within plus or minus one standard deviation from the mean. Approximately 95 percent fall between plus or minus two standard deviations, and 99.73 percent of all such scores fall between plus and minus three standard deviations from the average.

Stanford-Binet Intelligence Scale See Measured Intelligence.

Stereognosis The ability to perceive objects, forms, or other material according to shape, size and quality of the materials, utilizing the sense of touch. See Astereognosis.

Strabismus An eye condition in which there is a lack of coordination of the eye muscles, characterized by a persistent squint or cross-eye.

Stretch Reflex Clonic movements in a given muscle when the antagonist muscle is placed in extension. This is demonstrated by an increased resistance to the passive extension of a muscle. Normal stretch reflexes are required to maintain muscle tone and balance. Abnormal reflexes are one of the diagnostic signs in spasticity. See **Clonus.**

Structured Setting A term used to describe an educational or child-rearing environment in which the various stimuli or the elements of the material to be learned are presented in a very highly organized and directive manner. An attempt to present the material to be learned in a clear, unambiguous and objective manner.

Stuttering A non-fluency of speech in which the even and regular flow of words is disrupted by rapid repetition of certain speech elements.

Symptom Any recognizable sign or manifestation of a pathological condition.

Syndrome The aggregate of clinical manifestations associated with any morbid process and constituting together the picture of the disease or clinical condition or entity.

Syntactic Structure The structural relationships between words in a sentence representing the grammatical pattern. For example, "The man is going to the store" consists of noun phrase + auxiliary verb + verb-ing + preposition + noun phrase.

Tactile Refers to the perception of cutaneous stimuli through the sense of touch.

Tactile Agnosia A condition characterized by difficulty in the tactile recognition of objects. Often due to lesions in the post-central cortical areas of the brain.

Temperament The predisposition of an individual to characteristic emotional reactions to a given stimulus or stimuli. Sometimes used synonymously with personality.

Testing and Evaluation Tests, examinations, evaluations or diagnostic statements made by a psychiatrist, physician, psychologist, social worker, rehabilitation specialist, educational specialist, occupational therapist, speech pathologist or other professional person in a related discipline that assess an individual's capacity to acquire specific skills.

Tic See Transient Tic Disorder.

Toxemia of Pregnancy A condition characterized by elevated blood pressure, edema, and kidney malfunction in the expectant mother, which may cause intracranial hemorrhage or other serious difficulties in the fetus.

Toxemic See Toxemia of Pregnancy.

Tranquillizer A drug designed to bring about tranquillity by calming, soothing, quieting, or pacifying an individual without producing marked depression.

Transient Tic Disorder An uncontrolled nervous twitch, which may be of organic (neural) or psychological origin. Recurring, involuntary, repetitive rapid movements. Onset is during childhood or adolescence and the duration is at least one month, but not more than one year. An eye blink or other facial tic would be a primary example.

Treatment Provision of specific educational, mental, physical, or social interventions and therapies to halt, control or reverse processes that cause, aggravate or otherwise affect malfunctions or dysfunctions. Also, a term used in research to mean any experimental manipulation applied to one or more subjects.

Tremor Trembling or repetitive rapid spastic motions. These movements are not subject to voluntary motor control and are usually rhythmical, showing regularity of amplitude and frequency. They may be present either at rest (extrapyramidal) or upon purposeful movement.

Trisomy 21 See Down's Syndrome.

Underachiever An individual who does not perform in the academic setting as might be expected from certain known characteristics, such as intellectual level, or on the basis of previous performance.

Ungraded Class An obsolete term used to describe a class that is not organized on the basis of grade and has no standard grade designation. Primarily used to describe special classes for mentally retarded pupils.

Verbal Test An intelligence test or sub-test that requires the use of language to understand the problem and produce the required response. See Measured Intelligence.

Vestibular System The labyrinth of the inner ear together with the eighth nerve and parts of the brain. Involved in balance and body orientation.

Vineland Social Maturity Scale A rating scale of adaptive behavior based upon the presence or absence of certain everyday behaviors found to be characteristic at given age levels. Intended to measure how well the individual routinely performs, rather than the maximal performance of which he is capable. The information upon which the rating is based is obtained from the mother or other primary care giver.

Visual-Motor Behavior Activities dependent upon the expression and integration of motor responses appropriate to the visual cues, such as reaching accurately for a visually perceived object or copying a design.

Visual Perception See Perception.

Visual-Motor Skills Skills normally accomplished through visual perception and an integrated motor response. Often involving spatial relationships and tactile perception.

Wechsler Adult Intelligence Scale See Measured Intelligence.

Wechsler Intelligence Scale for Children See Measured Intelligence.

Wechsler Preschool and Primary Scale of Intelligence See Measured Intelligence.

White Matter Portions of the central nervous system made up primarily of myelinated fibers of nerve cells.

Word Blindness See Alexia.

SOURCES OF HELP

STATE ASSOCIATIONS AND INFORMATION SOURCES

Alabama Association for Children with Learning Disabilities
P.O. Box 11588
Montgomery, AL 36111
(205) 821-7810

Alabama Director of Special Education for Exceptional Children and Youth
State Department of Education
Montgomery, AL 36104
(205) 832-3230

Alabama Psychological Association
109 Crosslin Ave.
Florence, AL 35630

Alabama Speech and Hearing Association
University of Montevallo
Montevallo, AL 35115
(205) 655-2521, X 536

Alaska Association for Children with Learning Disabilities
7420 Old Harbor Ave.
Anchorage, AK 99504
(907) 333-6372

Alaska Director of Special Education
Division of Instructional Services
State Department of Education
Pouch F
Juneau, AK 99801
(907) 465-2970

Alaska Psychological Association
SRA Box 32F
Anchorage, AK 99507
(907) 277-6551, X 332

Alaska Speech and Hearing Association
2023 Jacks St.
Fairbanks, AK 99701
(907) 452-5659

Arizona Association for Children with Learning Disabilities
P.O. Box 15525
Phoenix, AZ 85060
(602) 263-8981

Arizona Director of Special Education
State Department of Education
1535 W. Jefferson
Phoenix, AZ 85007
(602) 255-3183

Arizona Federal Information Center
230 N. First Ave.
Phoenix, AZ 85025
(602) 261-3313

Arizona Psychological Association Student Counseling Center
Arizona State University
Tempe, AZ 85281
(602) 965-6146

Arizona Speech and Hearing Association
7115 N. Skyway Dr.
Tucson, AZ 85718
(602) 622-5833

Arkansas Association for Children with Learning Disabilities
P.O. Box 7316
Little Rock, AR 72217
(501) 666-6112

Arkansas Director of Special Education
Division of Instructional Services
State Department of Education
Arch Ford Education Bldg.
Little Rock, AR 72201
(501) 371-2161

Arkansas Psychological Association
115 N. Beverly
N. Little Rock, AR 72116
(501) 374-3361, X 208

Arkansas Speech and Hearing Association
Speech and Hearing Center
University of Arkansas at Fayetteville
Fayetteville, AR 72701
(501) 575-4509

California Association for Children with Learning Disabilities
P.O. Box 61067
Sacramento, CA 95860
(213) 831-8644

California Director of Special Education
721 Capitol Hall, Room 614
Sacramento, CA 95814
(916) 445-4036

California Psychological Association
1025 Fifth St.
Novato, CA 94947
(415) 897-7181

California Speech and Hearing Association
1545 Thirty-fifth Ave.
San Francisco, CA 94122
(415) 566-8894

Los Angeles Federal Information Center
Federal Bldg.
300 North Los Angeles St.
Los Angeles, CA 90012
(213) 688-3800

Sacramento Federal Information Center
Federal Bldg., U.S. Courthouse
650 Capitol Mall
Sacramento, CA 95814
(916) 440-3344

San Diego Federal Information Center
Federal Bldg.
880 Front St.
San Diego, CA 92188
(714) 293-6030

San Francisco Federal Information Center
Federal Bldg., U.S. Courthouse
450 Golden Gate Ave.
San Francisco, CA 94102
(415) 556-6600

Colorado Association for Children with Learning Disabilities
P.O. Box 10535
University Park Station
Denver, CO 80210
(303) 457-3064

Colorado Director of Special Education
State Department of Education
State Office Bldg.
Denver, CO 80203
(303) 839-2727

Colorado Federal Information Center
Federal Bldg.
1961 Stout St.
Denver, CO 80294
(303) 837-3602

Colorado Psychological Association
3206 S. Emporia Court
Denver, CO 80218
(303) 388-3627

Colorado Speech and Language Association
University of Colorado
Boulder, CO 80302
(303) 447-9612

Connecticut Association for Children with Learning Disabilities
20 Raymond Rd.
W. Hartford, CT 06107
(203) 236-3953

Connecticut Director of Special Education
Bureau of Pupil Personnel & Special Educational Services
State Department of Education
Hartford, CT 06115
(203) 566-4383

Connecticut Psychological Association
7 Orangewood Dr.
Derby, CT 06418
(203) 734-8552

Connecticut Speech and Hearing Association
400 N. Quaker Lane
West Hartford, CT 06119
(203) 827-7558

Delaware Association for Children with Learning Disabilities
15 Barnard St.
Newark, DE 19711
(302) 737-3295

Delaware Director of Special Education
State Department of Public Education
Townsend Bldg.
Dover, DE 19901
(302) 678-5471

Delaware Psychological Association
Pennsylvania Ave.
Claymont, DE 19703

Delaware Speech and Hearing Association
Division of Public Health
Sussex City Health Unit
Georgetown, DE 19947
(302) 856-5214

Florida Association for Children with Learning Disabilities
2766 Banchory Rd.
Winter Park, FL 32792
(305) 671-8021

Florida Director of Special Education
Bureau of Education for Exceptional Students
Florida Department of Education
319 Knott Bldg.
Tallahassee, FL 32304
(904) 488-1570

Florida Psychological Association
P.O. Box 1117
Eaton Park, FL 33840

Florida Speech and Hearing Association
2118 Lake Bently Court
Lakeland, FL 33803
(813) 534-1511

Miami Federal Information Center
Federal Bldg.
51 Southwest First Ave.
Miami, FL 33130
(305) 350-4155

St. Petersburg Federal Information Center
William C. Cramer Federal Bldg.
144 First Ave. South
St. Petersburg, FL 33701
(813) 893-3495

Georgia Association for Children with Learning Disabilities
P.O. Box 29492
Atlanta, GA 30329
(404) 633-1236

Georgia Director of Special Education
State Office Bldg.
State Department of Education
Atlanta, GA 30334
(404) 656-2678

Georgia Federal Information Center
Federal Bldg.
275 Peachtree St., N.E.
Atlanta, GA 30303
(404) 221-6891

Georgia Psychological Association
3224 Peachtree Rd., N.E.
Atlanta, GA 30305
(404) 237-0950

Georgia Speech and Hearing Association
VA Hospital
1670 Clairmont
Decatur, GA 30033
(404) 321-6111, X 270

Hawaii Association for Children with Learning Disabilities
200 N. Vineyard Blvd., #402
Honolulu, HI 96817
(808) 988-4962

Hawaii Director of Special Education
State Department of Education
Box 2360
Honolulu, HI 96804
(808) 548-6923

Hawaii Federal Information Center
P.O. Box 300
300 Ala Moana Blvd.
Honolulu, HI 96850
(808) 546-8620

Hawaii Psychological Association
94–553 Alapoai St.
Mililani, HI 96789
(808) 521-6266

Hawaii Speech and Hearing Association
163 Kuuala St.
Kailua, HI 96734
(808) 261-0792

Idaho Association for Children with Learning Disabilities
5217 Wylie Lane
Boise, ID 83703
(208) 343-8620

Idaho Director of Special Education
Department of Education
Special Education Division
Len Jordan Bldg.
Boise, ID 83720
(208) 384-2203

Idaho Psychological Association
8345 Cory Court
Boise, ID 83704

Idaho Speech and Hearing Association
647 Mountain View Dr.
Twin Falls, ID 83301
(208) 734-2074

Illinois Association for Children with Learning Disabilities
P.O. Box A-3239
Chicago, IL 60690
(312) 939-3513

Illinois Director of Special Education
Department of Special Educational Services
100 North First St.
Springfield, IL 62777
(217) 782-6601

Illinois Federal Information Center
Everett McKinley Dirksen Bldg., Room 252
219 South Dearborn St.
Chicago, IL 60604
(312) 353-4242

Illinois Psychological Association
161 East Erie
Chicago, IL 60611
(312) 787-9612

Illinois Speech and Hearing Association
1310 B. Kingsbridge Court
Normal, IL 61761
(309) 438-2654

Indiana Association for Children with Learning Disabilities
51416 Orange Rd.
South Bend, IN 46628
(219) 272-9018

Indiana Director of Special Education
Division of Special Education
Department of Public Instruction
229 State House
Indianapolis, IN 46204
(317) 927-0216

Indiana Federal Information Center
Federal Bldg., 1st Floor
575 N. Pennsylvania
Indianapolis, IN 46204
(317) 269-7373

Indiana Psychological Association
2421 Willowbrook Pkwy., S-514
Indianapolis, IN 46205
(317) 251-8252

Indiana Speech and Hearing Association
2100 N. Maddox Dr.
Muncie, IN 47304
(317) 285-4230

Iowa Association for Children with Learning Disabilities
2819 Forty-eighth St.
Des Moines, IA 50310
(515) 277-4266

Iowa Director of Special Education
Grimes State Office Bldg.
Des Moines, IA 50319
(515) 281-3176

Iowa Psychological Association
2035 Blake Blvd.
Cedar Rapids, IA 52403

Iowa Speech and Hearing Association
1921 Ordinance Rd.
Ankeny, IA 50021
(515) 964-2550

Kansas Association for Children with Learning Disabilities
114 W. Eighth St., Suite 4
Topeka, KS 66604
(913) 235-5078

Kansas Director of Special Education
State Department of Education
120 E. Tenth St.
Topeka, KS 66612
(913) 296-3866

Kansas Psychological Association
506 Lake Forest
Bonner Springs, KS 66012

Kansas Speech and Hearing Association
Box 1456
Hutchinson, KS 67501
(316) 662-4458

Kentucky Association for Children with Learning Disabilities
4501 S. Sixth St., #94
Louisville, KY 40214
(502) 368-5779

Kentucky Director of Special Education
Bureau of Education for Exceptional Children
W. Frankfort Complex
8th Floor Capital Plaza Tower
Frankfort, KY 40601
(502) 564-4970

Kentucky Federal Information Center
Federal Bldg.
600 Federal Place
Louisville, KY 40202
(317) 269-7373

Kentucky Psychological Association
251 Dickey Hall
University of Kentucky
Lexington, KY 40506
(606) 257-9000

Kentucky Speech and Hearing Association
Box 3525
Lexington, KY 40201
(606) 258-2666

Louisiana Association for Children with Learning Disabilities
P.O. Box 205
Tioga, LA 71477
(318) 640-2499

Louisiana Director of Special Education
State Department of Education
Capitol Station
P.O. Box 44064
Baton Rouge, LA 70804
(504) 342-3641

Louisiana Federal Information Center
Federal Bldg., U.S. Post Office
701 Loyola Ave.
New Orleans, LA 70113
(504) 589-6696

Louisiana Psychological Association
4608 Prytania St.
New Orleans, LA 70115

Louisiana Speech and Hearing Association
14641 Stoneberg Ave.
Baton Rouge, LA 70816
(504) 272-6242

Maine Association for Children with Learning Disabilities
Box 93
West Southport, ME 04576

Maine Director of Special Education
Division of Special Education
State Department of Educational and Cultural Services
Augusta, ME 04330
(207) 289-3451

Maine Psychological Association
Shaving Hill Rd.
Box 5024
Limington, ME 04049

Maine Speech and Hearing Association
Northeast Speech and Hearing Center
43 Baxter Blvd.
Portland, ME 04101
(207) 775-3491

Maryland Association for Children with Learning Disabilities
RR 2, Box 2362-B
La Plata, MD 20646
(301) 870-3323

Maryland Director of Special Education
Division of Special Education
Maryland State Department of Education
P.O. Box 8717, BWI Airport
Baltimore, MD 21240
(301) 796-8300, X 256

Maryland Federal Information Center
Federal Bldg., 31 Hopkins Plaza
Baltimore, MD 21201
(301) 962-4980

Maryland Psychological Association
Joseph Square Village Center, #248
Columbia, MD 21044
(301) 992-4258

Maryland Speech and Hearing Association
16303 Gales Court
Laurel, MD 20810
(301) 776-3014

Massachusetts Association for Children with Learning Disabilities
154 West St.
Randolph, MA 02368
(617) 963-5407

Massachusetts Director of Special Education
State Department of Education
31 St. James Ave.
Boston, MA 02116
(617) 727-6217

Massachusetts Federal Information Center
John F. Kennedy Federal Bldg.
Lobby, 1st Floor Cambridge St.
Boston, MA 02203
(617) 223-7121

Massachusetts Psychological Association
14 Beacon Street, #704
Boston, MA 02108
(617) 523-6320

Massachusetts Speech and Hearing Association
14 Fayette St.
Cambridge, MA 02138
(617) 956-5300

Michigan Association for Children with Learning Disabilities
20777 Randall
Farmington Hills, MI 48024
(313) 471-0790

Michigan Director of Special Education
Special Education Services
State Department of Education
P.O. Box 420
Lansing, MI 48902
(517) 373-1695

Michigan Federal Information Center
McNamara Federal Bldg.
477 Michigan Ave.
Detroit, MI 48226
(313) 226-7016

Michigan Psychological Association
29446 Ravine Dr.
Livonia, MI 48152
(313) 525-0460

Michigan Speech and Hearing Association
34128 Northwick
Farmington Hills, MI 48018
(313) 577-3337

Minnesota Association for Children with Learning Disabilities
1821 University Ave.
St. Paul, MN 55104
(612) 646-6136

Minnesota Director of Special Education
State Department of Education
Capitol Square, 550 Cedar St.
St. Paul, MN 55101
(612) 296-4163

Minnesota Federal Information Center
Federal Bldg., U.S. Courthouse
110 S. Fourth St.
Minneapolis, MN 55401
(612) 725-2073

Minnesota Psychological Association
1569 E. River Terrace
Minneapolis, MN 55414
(612) 870-9708

Minnesota Speech and Hearing Association
Box 222-D, Route 3
Bemidji, MN 56601
(218) 751-6622

Mississippi Association for Children with Learning Disabilities
P.O. Box 12083
Jackson, MS 39211
(601) 982-2812

Mississippi Director of Special Education
State Department of Education
P.O. Box 771
Jackson, MS 39205
(601) 354-6950

Mississippi Psychological Association
University of Mississippi
University, MS 38677
(601) 232-7383

Mississippi Speech and Hearing Association
University of South Mississippi
Dept. of Speech Pathology and Audiology
Hattiesburg, MS 39401
(601) 544-5265

Missouri Association for Children with Learning Disabilities
P.O. Box 3303
Glenstone Station
Springfield, MO 65804
(417) 831-6291

Missouri Director of Special Education
Department of Elementary and Secondary Education
P.O. Box 480
Jefferson City, MO 65101
(314) 751-2965

Missouri Federal Information Center
Federal Bldg.
601 E. Twelfth St.
Kansas City, MO 64106
(816) 374-2466

Missouri Federal Information Center
1520 Market St.
St. Louis, MO 63103
(314) 425-4106

Missouri Psychological Association
1515 N. Warson Rd.
St. Louis, MO 63132
(314) 423-8033

Missouri Speech and Hearing Association
1308 Christine Dr.
Des Peres, MO 63131
(314) 968-4710

Montana Association for Children with Learning Disabilities
511 Burlington
Billings, MT 59101
(406) 259-9321

Montana Director of Special Education
State Dept. of Education
Office of the Superintendent of Public Instruction
State Capitol
Helena, MT 59601
(406) 449-5660

Montana Psychological Association
507 S. Fifth St.
Hamilton, MT 59840

Montana Speech and Hearing Association
2211 Cherry Dr.
Great Falls, MT 59404
(406) 453-7830

Nebraska Association for Children with Learning Disabilities
P.O. Box 6464
Omaha, NE 68106
(402) 391-8622

Nebraska Director of Special Education
Special Education Section
State Dept. of Education
223 S. Tenth St.
Lincoln, NE 68508
(402) 471-2471

Nebraska Federal Information Center
Federal Bldg., U.S. Post Office and Courthouse
215 N. Seventeenth St.
Omaha, NE 68102
(402) 221-3353

Nebraska Psychological Association
Creighton University
2500 California St.
Omaha, NE 68178
(402) 280-4325

Nebraska Speech and Hearing Association
3501 S. Thirty-fifth St.
Lincoln, NE 68506
(402) 475-1081, X 360

Nevada Association for Children with Learning Disabilities
6208 S. El Camino Road
Las Vegas, NV 89121
(702) 876-7280

Nevada Director of Special Education
State Dept. of Education
400 W. King St., Capitol Complex
Carson City, NV 89701
(702) 885-5700, X 214

Nevada Psychological Association
6161 W. Charleston Blvd.
Las Vegas, NV 89102

Nevada Speech and Hearing Association
3340 Elaine Way
Sparks, NV 89431
(702) 358-2313

New Hampshire Association for Children with Learning Disabilities
Clement Ave.
Kingston, NH 03848
(603) 642-8394

New Hampshire Director of Special Education
State Dept. of Education
105 Loudon Road, Building #3
Concord, NH 03301
(603) 271-3741

New Hampshire Psychological Association
7 Trinity St.
Concord, NH 03301

New Hampshire Speech and Hearing Association
R.F.D. #5
Derry, NH 03038
(603) 668-5423

New Jersey Association for Children with Learning Disabilities
P.O. Box 249
Convent Station, NJ 07961
(201) 539-4644

New Jersey Director of Special Education
State Department of Education
225 W. State St.
Trenton, NJ 08625
(609) 292-7602

New Jersey Federal Information Center
Federal Bldg.
970 Broad St.
Newark, NJ 07102
(201) 645-3600

New Jersey Psychological Association
50 Northfield Ave.
West Orange, NJ 07052
(201) 736-8480

New Jersey Speech and Hearing Association
188 Stirling Rd.
Warren, NJ 07060
(201) 232-0280

New Mexico Association for Children with Learning Disabilities
7021 Prospect Place, N.E.
Albuquerque, NM 87110
(505) 522-0009

New Mexico Director of Special Education
State Educational Bldg.
300 Don Gaspar Ave.
Santa Fe, NM 87503
(505) 827-2793

New Mexico Federal Information Center
Federal Bldg., U.S. Courthouse
500 Gold Ave., S.W.
Albuquerque, NM 87102
(505) 766-3091

New Mexico Psychological Association
P.O. Box 4068
Albuquerque, NM 87296
(505) 247-1914

New Mexico Speech and Hearing Association
2100 Ridgecrest, S.E.
Albuquerque, NM 87108
(505) 265-1711, X 2295

New York Association for Children with Learning Disabilities
217 Lark St.
Albany, NY 12210
(518) 436-4633

New York Director of Special Education
State Education Dept.
55 Elk St.
Albany, NY 12234
(518) 474-5548

New York Federal Information Center
Lobby Federal Bldg.
26 Federal Plaza
New York, NY 10007
(212) 264-4464

New York Federal Information Center
Federal Bldg.
111 W. Huron St.
Buffalo, NY 14202
(716) 846-4010

New York State Psychological Association
250 W. Fifty-seventh St.
New York, NY 10107
(212) 541-6600

New York Speech and Hearing Association
P.O. Box 790
Wantagh, NY 11793
(516) 298-8084

New York State Society for Autistic Children
275 State St.
Albany, NY 12210
(518) 436-0611

North Carolina Association for Children with Learning Disabilities
Route 5, Box 269, Lamb Rd.
Lexington, NC 27292
(704) 956-6769

North Carolina Director of Special Education
Division for Exceptional Children
State Dept. of Public Instruction
Raleigh, NC 27611
(919) 733-3921

North Carolina Psychological Association
P.O. Box 33731
Raleigh, NC 27606

North Carolina Speech and Hearing Association
Winston-Salem State University
Winston-Salem, NC 27102
(919) 761-2017

North Dakota Association for Children with Learning Disabilities
2025 Ida Mae Ct.
Minot, ND 58701
(701) 839-6877

North Dakota Director of Special Education
Special Education
Dept. of Public Instruction
Bismarck, ND 58501
(701) 224-2277

North Dakota Psychological Association
623 N. Twenty-fourth St.
Grand Forks, ND 58201

North Dakota Speech and Hearing Association
1424 Eighth Ave. South
Fargo, ND 58103
(701) 237-4523

Ohio Association for Children with Learning Disabilities
4601 N. High St.
Columbus, OH 43214
(614) 267-7040

Ohio Director of Special Education
Division of Special Education
State Dept. of Education
933 High St.
Worthington, OH 43085
(614) 466-2650

Ohio Federal Information Center
Federal Bldg.
550 Main St.
Cincinnati, OH 45202
(513) 684-2801

Ohio Federal Information Center
Federal Bldg.
1240 E. Ninth St.
Cleveland, OH 44199
(216) 522-4040

Ohio Psychological Association
5 E. Long St., #610
Columbus, OH 43215
(614) 262-2444

Ohio Speech and Hearing Association
300 Village Square Rd.
Centerville, OH 45459
(513) 225-4610

Oklahoma Association for Children with Learning Disabilities
3701 N.W. Sixty-second St.
Oklahoma City, OK 73112
(405) 943-9434

Oklahoma Director of Special Education
State Dept. of Education
2500 N. Lincoln, Suite 263
Oklahoma City, OK 73105
(405) 521-3351

Oklahoma Federal Information Center
U.S. Post Office and Courthouse
201 N.W. Third St.
Oklahoma City, OK 73102
(405) 231-4868

Oklahoma Psychological Association
6565 S. Yale, #602
Kelly Professional Bldg.
Tulsa, OK 74177
(918) 742-1992

Oklahoma Speech and Hearing Association
120 Hanner Hall
Oklahoma State University
Stillwater, OK 74074
(405) 624-6020

Oregon Association for Children with Learning Disabilities
Portland State University
P.O. Box 751
Portland, OR 97207
(503) 229-4439

Oregon Director of Special Education
Oregon Department of Education
942 Lancaster Dr., N.E.
Salem, OR 97310
(503) 378-3598

Oregon Federal Information Center
Federal Bldg.
1220 S.W. Third Ave., Room 109
Portland, OR 97204
(503) 221-2222

Oregon Psychological Association
1584 High St., S.E.
Salem, OR 97302
(503) 225-8320

Oregon Speech and Hearing Association
7405 S.W. Beveland Rd.
Tigard, OR 97223
(503) 225-8356

Pennsylvania Association for Children with Learning Disabilities
1383 Arcadia Rd.
Lancaster, PA 17601
(717) 393-8284

Pennsylvania Director of Special Education
Bureau of Special and Compensatory Education
Dept. of Education
P.O. Box 911
Harrisburg, PA 17126
(717) 783-1264

Pennsylvania Federal Information Center
William J. Green Jr. Federal Bldg.
600 Arch St.
Philadelphia, PA 19106
(215) 597-7042

Pennsylvania Federal Information Center
Federal Bldg.
1000 Liberty Ave.
Pittsburgh, PA 15222
(412) 644-3456

Pennsylvania Psychological Association
209 N. Craig St.
Pittsburgh, PA 15213
(412) 682-8220

Pennsylvania Speech and Hearing Association
Schuylkill I.U., #29
410 N. Centre St.
Pottsville, PA 17901
(717) 628-5687

Rhode Island Association for Children with Learning Disabilities
P.O. Box 6685
Providence, RI 02904
(401) 884-0877

Rhode Island Director of Special Education
Rhode Island Dept. of Education
Division of Special Education
235 Promenade St.
Providence, RI 02908
(401) 227-3505

Rhode Island Psychological Association
VA Medical Center
Davis Park
Providence, RI 02908
(401) 273-7100

Rhode Island Speech and Hearing Association
109 Pleasant St.
N. Kingston, RI 02852
(401) 277-5485

South Carolina Association for Children with Learning Disabilities
608 Hatrick Rd.
Columbia, SC 29209
(803) 776-0608

South Carolina Director of Special Education
Office of Programs for the Handicapped
State Dept. of Education
Room 309, Rutledge Bldg.
Columbia, SC 29201
(803) 758-7432

South Carolina Psychological Association
Clemson University
Clemson, SC 29631
(803) 656-3210

South Carolina Speech and Hearing Association
310 Rutledge Bldg.
Columbia, SC 29201
(803) 758-7432

South Dakota Association for Children with Learning Disabilities
1605 S. Tenth Ave.
Sioux Falls, SD 57105
(605) 339-9640

South Dakota Director of Special Education
Division of Elementary & Secondary Education
New State Office Bldg.
Pierre, SD 57501
(605) 773-3678

South Dakota Psychological Association
2 Linda Lane
Aberdeen, SD 57401
(605) 622-2621

Tennessee Association for Children with Learning Disabilities
101 Stanton Lane
Oak Ridge, TN 37830
(615) 574-3179

Tennessee Director of Special Education
Education for the Handicapped
103 Cordell Hull Bldg.
Nashville, TN 37219
(615) 741-2851

Tennessee Federal Information Center
Clifford Davis Federal Bldg.
167 N. Main St.
Memphis, TN 38103
(901) 521-3285

Tennessee Psychological Association
798 Charles Place
Memphis, TN 38112
(901) 529-7011

Tennessee Speech and Hearing Association
2606 Barton Ave.
Nashville, TN 37212
(615) 320-5353

Texas Association for Children with Learning Disabilities
1011 W. Thirty-first St.
Austin, TX 78705
(512) 458-9234

Texas Director of Special Education
Texas Education Agency
201 E. Eleventh St.
Austin, TX 78701
(512) 475-3501, X 3507

Texas Federal Information Center
Federal Bldg., U.S. Courthouse
515 Rusk Ave.
Houston, TX 77208
(713) 266-5711

Texas Federal Information Center
Fritz Garland Lanham Federal Bldg.
819 Taylor St.
Fort Worth, TX 76102
(817) 344-3624

Texas Psychological Association
P.O. Box 9404
Austin, TX 78766
(512) 258-5351

Texas Speech and Hearing Association
Southwestern Medical School
5323 Harry Hines Blvd.
Dallas, TX 75235
(214) 688-3571

Utah Association for Children with Learning Disabilities
4180 Mackay
Taylorsville, UT 84119
(801) 969-5459

Utah Director of Special Education
250 E. Fifth South
Salt Lake City, UT 84111
(801) 533-5982

Utah Federal Information Center
Federal Bldg.
125 S. State St.
Salt Lake City, UT 84138
(801) 524-5353

Utah Psychological Association
482 Third Ave.
Salt Lake City, UT 84203
(801) 531-6185

Utah Speech and Hearing Association
University of Utah
1201 Behavioral Sciences Building
Salt Lake City, UT 84113
(801) 581-6725

Vermont Association for Children with Learning Disabilities
9 Heaton St.
Montpelier, VT 05602
(802) 223-5480

Vermont Director of Special Education
State Dept. of Education
Montpelier, VT 05602
(802) 828-3141

Vermont Psychological Association
9 Heaton St.
Montpelier, VT 05602

Vermont Speech and Hearing Association
R.F.D. 2, Box 15
Orleans, VT 05860
(802) 748-4569

Virginia Association for Children with Learning Disabilities
3851 N. Upland St.
Arlington, VA 22207
(703) 532-6497

Virginia Director of Special Education
State Dept. of Education
322 E. Grade
Richmond, VA 23216
(804) 786-2673

Virginia Federal Information Center
Room 106, Stanwick Bldg.
3661 E. Virginia Beach Blvd.
Norfolk, VA 23502
(804) 441-3101

Virginia Psychological Association
109 Amherst St.
Winchester, VA 22601

Virginia Speech and Hearing Association
James Madison University
Harrisonburg, VA 22801
(703) 433-6630

Washington Association for Children with Learning Disabilities
444 N.E. Ravenna Blvd., Rm. 206
Seattle, WA 98115
(206) 523-9768

Washington Director of Special Education
Special & Institutional Education
Department of Public Instruction
Old Capitol Bldg.
Olympia, WA 98504
(206) 753-2563

Washington Federal Information Center
Federal Bldg.
915 Second Ave.
Seattle, WA 98174
(206) 442-0570

Washington Psychological Association
13500 Lake City Way, N.E., #208
Seattle, WA 98125
(206) 362-4905

Washington Speech and Hearing Association
Western Washington University
Bellingham, WA 98225
(206) 676-3881

West Virginia Association for Children with Learning Disabilities
1931 Seventh Ave.
St. Albans, WV 25177
(304) 722-2254

West Virginia Director of Special Education
Dept. of Education
Capitol Complex, Room B-057
Charleston, WV 23505
(304) 348-2034

West Virginia Psychological Association
301 Scott Ave.
Morgantown, WV 26506

West Virginia Speech and Hearing Association
501 W. Main St.
Clarksburg, WV 26301
(304) 623-6533

Wisconsin Association for Children with Learning Disabilities
922 E. Fillmore
Eau Claire, WI 54701
(715) 834-3078

Wisconsin Director of Special Education
126 Langdon St.
Madison, WI 53702
(608) 266-1649

Wisconsin Psychological Association
625 W. Washington
Madison, WI 53703
(608) 251-1450

Wyoming Association for Children with Learning Disabilities
710 Gerald Place
Laramie, WY 82070
(307) 742-7603

Wyoming Director of Special Education
State Dept. of Education
Cheyenne, WY 82002
(307) 777-7416

Wyoming Psychological Association
1221 W. Fifth St.
Sheridan, WY 82801

Wyoming Speech and Hearing Association
Wyoming State Training School
Lander, WY 82520
(307) 332-5302

District of Columbia Association for Children with Learning Disabilities
3611 Joselyn St., N.W.
Washington, DC 20015
(202) 244-3649

District of Columbia Director of Special Education
Division of Special Education
Educational Programs
415 Twelfth St., N.W.
Washington, DC 20004
(202) 724-4018

District of Columbia Federal Information Center
Room 5716
Seventh and D Sts., S.W.
Washington, DC 20407
(202) 755-8660

District of Columbia Psychological Association
2811 Cortland Place, N.W.
Washington, DC 20008
(202) 332-8945

District of Columbia Speech and Hearing Association
651 E St., S.E.
Washington, DC 20003
(202) 483-6030

REGIONAL ASSOCIATIONS AND INFORMATION SOURCES

Guam Speech and Hearing Association
Dept. of Public Health and Social Services
P.O. Box 2866
Agana, Guam

Puerto Rico Association for Children with Learning Disabilities
11–19 Salamanca, Torrimar
Guaynabo, PR 00657
(809) 782-3635

Special Education Program for Handicapped Children
Dept. of Education
P.O. Box 759
Hato Rey, PR 00919
(809) 764-1255

Virgin Islands Director of Special Education
Division of Special Education
Department of Education
P.O. Box 630, Charlotte Amalie
St. Thomas, VI 00801
(809) 774-0100, X 213

NATIONAL ASSOCIATIONS AND INFORMATION SOURCES

American Academy of Pediatrics
1801 Himma Ave.
Evanston, IL 60204
(312) 869-4255

American Association of Higher Education
Health Resource Center
1 Dupont Circle
Washington, DC 20036
(202) 293-6447
Resources for People Interested in Learning Disabilities on the Post-Secondary Level

American Association of University Professors
1 Dupont Circle
Washington, DC 20036
(202) 466-8050
Project to Make Faculty Members Aware of Responsibilities Under Laws Relating to Education for the Handicapped

American Association on Mental Deficiency
5201 Connecticut Ave., N.W.
Washington, DC 20015
(202) 686-5400

American Occupational Therapy Association
1383 Piccard Dr.
Rockville, MD 20850
(301) 948-9626

American Orthopsychiatric Association
1775 Broadway
New York, NY 10019
(212) 586-5690

American Physical Therapy Association
1156 Fifteenth St., N.W.
Washington, DC 20005
(202) 466-2070

American Psychiatric Association
1700 Eighteenth St., N.W.
Washington, DC 20009
(202) 797-4900

American Psychological Association
1200 Seventeenth St., N.W.
Washington, DC 20036
(202) 833-7600

American Speech, Language and Hearing Association
10801 Rockville Pike
Rockville, MD 20852
(301) 897-5700

Association for Children and Adults with Learning Disabilities
4156 Library Rd.
Pittsburgh, PA 15234
(412) 341-1515

Association for Learning-Disabled Adults
P.O. Box 9722, Friendship Station
Washington, DC 20016

Association of Junior Leagues, Inc.
Child Advocacy Project
825 Third Ave.
New York, NY 10022
(212) 355-4380

Child Neurology Society
Box 486
420 Delaware St., S.E.
Minneapolis, MN 55455

Children
130 E. Orange Ave.
Lake Wales, FL 33853

Child Welfare League of America
67 Irving Place
New York, NY 10003
(212) 254-7410

Clearing House on the Handicapped
Office of Special Education
U.S. Dept. of Education
330 C St., S.W.
Washington, DC 20202
(202) 245-0080

Closer Look
Parents' Campaign for Handicapped Children and Youth
Box 1492
Washington, DC 20013
(202) 833-4160

Educational Resources Information Center
National Institute of Education
U.S. Dept. of Education
Washington, DC 20208
(202) 254-5500

Epilepsy Foundation of America
1828 L St., N.W.
Washington, DC 20036
(202) 293-2930

Foundation for Children with Learning Disabilities
99 Park Ave.
New York, NY 10016
(212) 687-7211

National Association of Private Schools for Exceptional Children
130 E. Orange Ave.
Lake Wales, FL 33853

National Autism Hotline
101 Richmond St.
Huntington, VA
(304) 523-8269

National Clearing House for Mental Health Information
National Institutes of Mental Health
5600 Fishers Lane
Rockville, MD 20852
(301) 443-4513

National Easter Seal Society
2023 W. Ogden Ave.
Chicago, IL 60612
(312) 243-8400

National Institute of Child Health and Human Development
National Institutes of Health
U.S. Dept. of Mental Health and Human Services
Building 31
Bethesda, MD 20205
(301) 496-5133

National Network of Learning-Disabled Adults
P.O. Box 3130
Richardson, TX 75080

National Society for Autistic Children
1234 Massachusetts Ave., N.W.
Washington, DC 20005
(202) 783-0125

Office of Special Education
U.S. Dept. of Education
400 Sixth St., S.W.
Washington, DC 20202
(202) 245-0661

Office of Special Education and Rehabilitative Services
U.S. Dept. of Education
330 C St., S.W.
Washington, DC 20202
(202) 245-0565

Council for Exceptional Children
Information Service
1920 Association Dr.
Reston, VA 22091
(800) 336-3728

National Association for Mental Health, Inc.
1800 N. Kent St.
Rosslyn, VA 22209

National Center, Educational Media and Materials for the Handicapped
Ohio State University
Columbus, OH 43210
(614) 422-7596

The Orton Society
8415 Bellona Lane
Towson, MD 21204
(301) 296-0232

United Cerebral Palsy Associations, Inc.
66 E. Thirty-fourth St.
New York, NY 10016
(212) 889-6655

UNIVERSITY-AFFILIATED PROGRAMS

Educational Diagnostic Clinic
Learning Center
De Anza College
Cupertina, CA 95014
(408) 966-4838

Launch, Inc.
Dept. of Special Education
East State Texas University
Commerce, TX 75429

Learning Disability Center
Ventura College
Ventura, CA 93001
(805) 642-3211

Learning Disability Coordinator
Social Work Service Center
Adelphi University
Garden City, NY 11530
(516) 560-8060

Learning Opportunities Center
Kingsborough Community College
Brooklyn, NY 11235
(212) 934-5000

Program for Learning-Disabled College Students
Adelphi University
Garden City, NY 11530
(516) 294-8700

Programs and Services for Handicapped Students
Montgomery Community College
51 Mannakee St.
Rockville, MD 20850
(301) 279-5058

Special Learning Center
The College of the Ozarks
Clarksville, AR 72830
(501) 754-3034

Time Out to Enjoy, Inc.
113 Garfield St.
Oakpark, IL 60304
(312) 383-9017

University of Kansas
Institute for Research in Learning Disabilities
Lawrence, KS 66103
(913) 864-4780

SPECIALIZED CAMPS

Camp Consulting Services, Ltd.
14 Wesley Court
Huntington, NY 11743
(516) 549-3902

Camp Finders, Inc.
9 Brad Lane
White Plains, NY 10605
(914) 761-1252

Ramapo Anchorage Camp, Inc.
Rhinebeck, NY 12572
(914) 876-4273

Shadybrook Language and Learning Center
Route 151
Moodus, CT 06469
(203) 873-8800

The Summerbrook Camp
Box 110
Solebury
Bucks County, PA 18963
(215) 862-5505

DIRECTORIES OF RESOURCES FOR THE LEARNING-DISABLED

Directory for Exceptional Children
Porter Sargent Publishers, Inc.
11 Beacon St.
Boston, MA 02108
(617) 523-1689

Directory of Educational Facilities for the Learning-Disabled
Academic Therapy Publications
20 Commercial Blvd.
Novato, CA 94947
(415) 883-3314

Directory of Special Education Personnel in State Education Agencies
U.S. Office of Education
Bureau of Education for the Handicapped
Seventh and D Sts., S.W.
Washington, DC 20202
(202) 724-4018

Directory of Special Education Facilities for the Learning-Disabled
Association for Children & Adults with Learning Disabilities
4156 Library Rd.
Pittsburgh, PA 15234
(412) 341-1515

Listing of Services for the Postsecondary Learning-Disabled Adult
20 Commercial Blvd.
Novato, CA 94947

Mental Health Directory
DHEW Publication No. (HSM) 73-9028
Superintendent of Documents
Washington, DC 20402
(202) 727-1000

National Directory of Children & Youth Services
CPR Directory Services Co.
1301 Twentieth St.
Washington, DC 20036
(202) 785-4061

PERIODICALS OF INTEREST

The Directive Teacher
Ohio State University
Columbus, OH 43210

Educators Publishing Services, Inc.
75 Moulton St.
Cambridge, MA 02238
(Catalog)
(617) 547-6706

The Exceptional Parent
296 Boylston St.
Boston, MA 02116
(617) 536-8961

Exceptional People Quarterly
5288B North Colonial Ave.
Fresno, CA 93704

Journal of Learning Disabilities
Professional Press, Inc.
101 E. Ontario St.
Chicago, IL 60611
(312) 337-7800

The LD Observer
P.O. Box 237
Wellesley Hills, MA 02181

Learning: The Magazine for Creative Teaching
530 University Ave.
Palo Alto, CA 94301
(415) 312-1770

Partners in Publication
Box 50347
Tulsa, OK 74150
College "Helps" Newsletter
(918) 584-5906

Perceptions, Inc.
P.O. Box 142
Millburn, NJ 07041
(Newsletter)

Project Head Start—Mainstreaming Preschoolers: Children with Learning Disabilities
DHEW Publication No. (OHDS) 79-31117
Superintendent of Documents
Washington, DC 20402
(202) 783-3238

Taking the First Step to Solving Learning Problems
Association for Children and Adults with Learning Disabilities
4156 Library Rd.
Pittsburgh, PA 15234
(412) 341-1515

Topics in Learning and Learning Disabilities
Aspen Systems Corp.
1600 Research Blvd.
Rockville, MD 20850
(301) 251-5000

SELECTED BOOKS AND ARTICLES FOR FURTHER READING

Birch, H. and **Belmont, L.** "Auditory-Visual Integration in Retarded Readers," *American Journal of Orthopsychiatry,* 34:852, 1964.

Chess, S., Thomas, A., and **Birch, H. G.** *Your Child Is a Person: A Psychological Approach to Parenthood Without Guilt.* New York: Viking Press, 1965.

Critchley, M. *Developmental Dyslexia.* London: Heinemann, 1964.

———. *The Dyslexic Child.* Springfield: Charles C. Thomas, 1970.

Duffy, F. H., Denckla, M. B., et al. "Dyslexia: Automated Diagnosis by Computerized Classification of Brain Electrical Activity." *Annals of Neurology,* 7:421, 1980.

Gaddes, W. H. *Learning Disabilities and Brain Function.* New York: Springer Verlag, 1980.

Geschwind, N. "Selected Papers on Language and the Brain." Boston Studies in the Philosophy of Science, XVI. Boston: D. Reidel, 1974.

———. "Disconnection Syndromes in Animals and Man." *Brain,* 88:237, 1966.

——— and **Levitsky, W.** "Human Brain: Left-Right Asymmetries in Temporal Speech Region." *Science,* 161:186, 1968.

Gillingham, A., and **Stillman, B.** *Remedial Work for Reading, Spelling and Penmanship.* New York: Hackett and Williams, 1936.

Masland, R. "Advantages of Being Dyslexic." *Bulletin of the Orton Society,* XXVI:10–18, 1976.

Orton, S. T. *Reading, Writing and Speech Problems in Children.* New York: W. W. Norton, 1937.

Rudel, R. G. and **Denckla, M. B.** "Relationship of IQ and Reading Score to Visual-Spatial and Temporal Matching Tasks," *Journal of Learning Disorders,* 9:169, 1976.

Sapir, S. G., and **Wilson, B.** *A Professional's Guide to Working with the Learning-Disabled Child.* New York: Bruner/Mazel, 1978.

Strauss, A. A., and **Lehtinen, L.** *Psychopathology and Education of the Brain-Injured Child.* New York: Grune and Stratton, 1947.

Swaiman, K. and **Wright, F.** *The Practice of Pediatric Neurology (2nd edition).* St. Louis: Mosby, 1982.

Vaughan, V. C.; McKay, R. J.; and **Behrman, R. E.** *Nelson Textbook of Pediatrics* (11th edition). Philadelphia: W. B. Saunders, 1979.

Wilsher, C.; Atkins, G; and **Manfield, P.** "Piracetam as an Aid to Learning in Dyslexia." *Psychopharmacology,* 65:107, 1979.

INDEX